BRADEN T. LEAP

Gone Goose

The Remaking of an American Town
in the Age of Climate Change

TEMPLE UNIVERSITY PRESS
Philadelphia • *Rome* • *Tokyo*

TEMPLE UNIVERSITY PRESS
Philadelphia, Pennsylvania 19122
tupress.temple.edu

Library of Congress Cataloging-in-Publication Data

Names: Leap, Braden T., 1987– author.
Title: Gone goose : the remaking of an American town in the age of climate change /
   Braden T. Leap.
Description: Philadelphia : Temple University Press, 2019. | Includes bibliographical
   references and index. |
Identifiers: LCCN 2018021211 (print) | LCCN 2018032730 (ebook) |
   ISBN 9781439917350 (E-book) | ISBN 9781439917336 (cloth : alk. paper) |
   ISBN 9781439917343 (pbk. : alk. paper)
Subjects: LCSH: Community development—Environmental aspects—Missouri—Sumner. |
   Climatic changes—Social aspects—Missouri—Sumner. | Geese—Migration—Climatic
   factors—Missouri—Sumner. | Sumner (Mo.)—Environmental conditions. | Sumner
   (Mo.)—Social conditions.
Classification: LCC HN80.S86 (ebook) | LCC HN80.S86 L43 2019 (print) |
   DDC 307.1/40977825—dc23
LC record available at https://lccn.loc.gov/2018021211

♾ The paper used in this publication meets the requirements of the American National
Standard for Information Sciences—Permanence of Paper for Printed Library Materials,
ANSI Z39.48-1992

Printed in the United States of America

9 8 7 6 5 4 3 2 1

For my dad, who took me everywhere.

Love and miss you.

Contents

Acknowledgments

I thank everyone in Sumner who granted their time, company, and advice. I never would have been able to write this book if they hadn't been willing to invite me into their community. Many of them described Sumner as small and simple, but I'll never forget how vibrant their community was. I've tried to draw attention to the complexities of Sumner in this book, and I hope that they will appreciate my attempts to do so. Some may find that the details included in this account are incomplete or too critical. By writing about the intricacies of the community, including the inequalities underpinning it, I hope others who are living in communities that are no less complicated will be able to respond more effectively to socioenvironmental disruptions. I greatly admired how much many of the residents of Sumner cared about their community and the lengths to which they went to sustain it, and I believe there's a tremendous amount that can be learned from their efforts.

I've been fortunate to be mentored by a wonderful group of scholars. Tola Pearce, Mary Grigsby, Clarence Lo, Jason Rodriquez, and Rebecca R. Scott were a fantastic dissertation committee whose insightful, supportive guidance throughout all stages of this project was indispensable. Others at Mizzou, such as Eileen Bjornstrom, Wayne Brekhus, Jay Gubrium, Joan Hermsen, Mary Jo Neitz, Daniel Petrin, Amit Prasad, Srirupa Prasad, Sandy Rikoon, Mike Sickels, and Jesse Van Gerven, also provided me with invaluable assistance—sometimes in class but more often as unofficial mentors. Funds received from the Robert W. Habenstein and Raymond White dissertation fellowships from the University of Missouri Department of Sociology and the University of Missouri, respectively, also supported this research.

My colleagues and students at Mississippi State have also been especially important to the development of this book. I'm greatly appreciative of how welcoming and supportive they have all been, and I'm thankful that I can now count them among my mentors, colleagues, and friends. A special thanks goes to the graduate students in my rural sociology seminar, as well as Margaret Hagerman, David. M. Hoffman, and Kimberly Kelly, for reading an earlier draft of this book. Their advice was centrally important to the substance and style of the book.

Thanks also go to Marybeth Stalp and James M. Thomas. We work at different institutions, but they still generously provided guidance for this project. I was also especially lucky to receive assistance from Peter M. Hall, who will be greatly missed. Finally, thanks go to those who provided feedback when I presented parts of this book at the annual Chicago Ethnography Conference and the annual meetings of the American Sociological Association, the Midwest Sociological Society, and the Society for the Study of Symbolic Interaction. Feedback from members of the Environmental Sociology and Animals and Society sections of the American Sociological Association were particularly helpful.

I also thank my editor at Temple University Press, Ryan Mulligan. His enthusiasm and advice were both appreciated and irreplaceable. I offer thanks also to the two anonymous reviewers who supported this book while still providing me with key ways to improve it. Additional thanks go to Nikki Miller at Temple University Press for a tremendous amount of behind-the-scenes work. Finally, thanks go to Rebecca Logan at Newgen North America for very skillfully managing the production of this book.

My friends and family have also supported me every step of the way, and I could have never written this book without them. I extend a special thank-you to my parents, Tom and Diane, whose love for me has always been unconditional and infinite. Finally, I thank Ashley for being an amazing partner whose intelligence, support, and love I couldn't do without.

Gone Goose

Introduction

Sumner sits just east of the Grand River in an agricultural region of northwest Missouri. Like those of so many other rural towns throughout the central United States, Sumner's population has receded dramatically over the last one hundred years. Sumner started the 1900s as a railroad boomtown with nearly 500 inhabitants, but a century of outmigration induced by factory closures and farm consolidation throughout the region has reduced its population to just 102. The nearby towns are not much bigger. Hale, a fifteen-minute drive to the west, has a population of 419. Mendon, a fifteen-minute drive to the east, has a population of 171.[1] Kansas City and Columbia, both two-hour drives away, are the closest metropolitan areas.

With just over ten people per square mile in the county,[2] the predominantly flat landscape around town is dominated by sprawling fields of corn and soybeans that are interrupted by gravel roads and the occasional patch of timber. During the spring and summer this sparsely populated countryside is a vibrant mix of greens, but it gradually turns to faded yellows, browns, and grays as the crops are harvested and the trees drop their leaves throughout the fall. Tractors and combines still provide pops of color to the increasingly muted landscape during this transition to winter. The green John Deeres and silver Gleaners stand out against the faded fields, but the Case IH combines really catch your eye. Hulking, fire-engine red masses of machinery, their boxy frames move methodically back and forth across the fields spewing swirling clouds of corn or soybean debris in their wake.

Sumner proper is a mix of mobile homes and dated houses arranged in a four-by-five-block grid with a main street of redbrick storefronts at its heart. Residents of small towns will joke about their communities having only one stoplight at the center of town, but Sumner has managed without so much as a four-way stop. Those going north or south on Elm Street find a stop sign once they get to Centre Street, but those going east or west on Centre can roll right on through Sumner central.

Besides the mud-caked vehicles and four-wheelers that pass through, Labrador retrievers frequent the intersection. Sometimes they lope by on their way to somewhere else, but they usually loiter outside the front door of the bar that occupies one of the corner lots at the center of town. Clyde, the bar owner's yellow Lab, is the most frequent offender. A laundry list of regulars at Foster's Sportsman Inn occasionally slip him a scrap if he acts pitiful enough. Even if he does not find anyone willing to part with their food, he knows he can get a sip of beer from the tap overflow behind the bar.

There is also a mechanic garage, general store, post office, hair salon, and grain elevator in town, but most residents commute to jobs in other towns. The median household income is below the statewide average, but the area is not typified by widespread poverty or unemployment.[3] Most households have two incomes, with women working service jobs in fields such as retail or education and men working in construction trades or agriculture. Some men even make the two-hour trip to Kansas City or Columbia, daily, for construction work. They would prefer to work closer to home, but compared to the hustle and bustle of cities, which many portray as being overrun with greed and crime,[4] the friendships, hunting opportunities, and sense of security offered by Sumner justify the time and money committed to the long commute.

Residents tend to vote Republican in state and national elections, and everyone is white. The region of Missouri in which Sumner is located is only slightly more diverse. Similar to the racial demographics in neighboring counties, people of color make up less than 5 percent of the population of Sumner's county.[5]

For all its similarities with other rural communities in the midwestern United States, Sumner is also unique. If not for the steel grain elevator reaching toward the sky on the west side of town, Maxie might be the tallest manmade structure in Sumner. Perched on a dark green pedestal on the side of Missouri Route 139, she is hard to miss. Towering forty feet high and with a wingspan stretching greater than sixty feet, Maxie is the largest Canada goose in the world. Meant to be a timeless "reminder that Canada geese and Sumner are synonymous,"[6] community members scheduled the installation of this fiberglass goose to coincide with Bicentennial celebrations across the United States in 1976.

At the time, nearly two hundred thousand Canada geese spent every fall and winter just a mile south of town at Swan Lake National Wildlife Refuge (NWR), and they were centrally important to how the residents of Sumner arranged their lives and community.[7] A goose-hunting-based tourist economy annually generated $4 million,[8] and the town proudly claimed the title of Wild Goose Capital of the World. In addition, the U.S. Fish and Wildlife Service (USFWS), the Missouri Department of Conservation, and the University of Missouri carried out an extensive goose research program in the area.[9] In more mundane respects, the geese infused how residents thought of themselves and organized their relationships with each other and the surrounding landscape. Al Manke, who managed Swan Lake NWR during the 1970s, described the scene:

> By late October geese are everywhere. On the water, in the fields, in the air no matter which direction one looks. Small wonder Sumner calls itself the "Wild Goose Capital of the World." . . . Already thousands of visitors have come to view the geese, and now the "Sumner Fall [Wild] Goose Festival" and hunting season are at hand. The population of Sumner swells to twenty times its normal 300 inhabitants. Parades, bands, queens, games, contests and dances hold sway. It is homecoming. It is a time for renewing acquaintances and making new. It is a gala time. It is a festival celebrating the return of the wild geese. Geese touch the lives of everyone in the community. They permeate the thoughts, talks, plans, actions, and economics of its people.[10]

Sumner revolved around geese and goose hunting. From the title of the town to its yearly Wild Goose Festival, to how individuals arranged their work calendars and social lives, the geese transformed the community. Unfortunately for the residents of this rural Missouri town, Canada geese no longer spend their falls and winters at Swan Lake. Geese at the refuge hit their historic peak in 1977, at over 181,000 birds. Then the geese increasingly began to winter in Iowa, Minnesota, the Dakotas, and southern Canada as climate change, shifts in agricultural production, and (sub)urban

development made these more northern latitudes suitable wintering locations.[11] Peak numbers on the refuge fluctuated some through the 1980s,
1990s, and early 2000s, but there was an unmistakable downward trend as
the geese stopped migrating as far south from their nesting grounds along
the western Hudson Bay. By 1995 Canada geese numbers had dipped to
34,000, and by 2013, peak numbers reached just 1,500 birds. For all intents
and purposes, the Wild Goose Capital of the World is now gooseless.

This has been a traumatic transformation for a community that revolved
around geese and goose hunting. In addition to bemoaning the dissolution
of the goose-based tourist economy, residents felt that the social ties that
depended on the geese and the activities associated with them had slipped
away. Some even mourned the loss of the geese themselves. "It hurts me
down in my soul," Darla told me, patting her heart as she looked at me sol-
emnly from across the bar in Foster's. In her fifties, she had grown up in
Sumner during the goose hunting heyday and then returned after retiring.
She tended the bar during the afternoons and was usually infectiously
cheery, but not when talking about the geese. "I used to see and hear the
geese, and the whole sky would be filled with them," she recalled, spreading
her arms wide. "Now I hear them and run outside to look, and all I see is
just those little groups."

As much as community members like Darla wished the geese would
return, the birds' disappearance did not stop the residents of Sumner from
going about their lives. Kids kept going to school and moving away, older
men kept gathering at the bar to spin tall tales, and crops continued to be
planted each spring and harvested in the fall. Flocks of geese no longer
blackened the sky, and droves of shotgun-wielding hunters no longer
streamed into town, but the Goose Festival continued to be held each October. As one might suspect, though, it was all unmistakably different compared to when large numbers of geese still migrated to Swan Lake. The geese
were centrally important to Sumner's organization, so community members
responded to their absence. With an eye toward maintaining their roots,
they dreamed and worried about the future as they worked to reorganize
and sustain their ways of life and community.

How were they doing this? Academics, politicians, and journalists routinely lament that rural towns are dying throughout the central United
States,[12] and a number of authors emphasize that the social complexities of
communities allow them to be reorganized in response to social and ecological disruptions such as shifting goose migration patterns.[13] How were
the members of this racially homogeneous, rural community with a popula-

tion of just 102 able to reorganize their senses of self, their ways of life, and their relationships with each other in the face of a transformation that upended the foundation of their community? How were they able to rework their connections with the people and places that were important to them? How were they able to respond effectively to a dramatic shift in transnational goose migration patterns? And what role did the geese ultimately play in the community such that their loss confronted Sumner with these questions in the first place?

These are especially significant questions because we live in a time when people and communities around the world are responding to the localized consequences of global climate change. As part of a $1 billion effort to facilitate adaptations to climate change in the United States, the Rockefeller Foundation and the U.S. Department of Housing and Urban Development earmarked $48 million in 2016 to resettle the entire community of Isle de Jean Charles, Louisiana.[14] Located on the Mississippi River Delta southwest of New Orleans, erosion and rising sea level have caused saltwater to inundate 98 percent of the coastal community's land, where inhabitants had carried out their lives. It will be the first community in the lower forty-eight states to be officially relocated because of climate change,[15] but it was just one more reminder that many of the most pressing challenges of our time stem from shifting climatological conditions.[16] Whether it is the rising sea level, shifting goose migrations, strengthening storms, droughts, floods, or a wildfire season that never seems to end, climate change means spiraling, profound consequences for communities across the globe.[17] Given the inadequate efforts by global leaders to mitigate the effects of climate change, it is increasingly apparent that cultures and communities will have to be rearranged over the coming decades and centuries if they are to be sustained.[18]

Unfortunately, policy makers and researchers have granted limited attention to how cultures and communities are reorganized in response to environmental features rendered temporary by climate change, and we have a limited understanding of how individuals and groups work to rearrange their senses of who they are, their ways of life, and their relationships with each other as all three are disrupted.[19] This oversight must be addressed. If we hope to sustain communities, we need to know much more about how they respond.

Identities, cultures, and communities will have to be remade in response to climate change, and Sumner offers a unique opportunity to explore how. Consequently, while others have often focused on the potentially catastrophic social and ecological consequences of climate change, that is not this book's subject.[20] I acknowledge the immense challenges presented by climate change, but this book makes the case for paying far more attention to how lives and communities are rearranged in response to these challenges. This is a story about the members of a rural community in the central United States who creatively made do with what they had so that they could rearrange and sustain their senses of worth and their connections with the people and places they valued. This is a story about a community that can provide us with clues about the intricate ways climate change will disrupt our lives and communities and how to more effectively respond to these challenges. This is a story about resilience.[21]

Entangled Adaptations

I spent twenty months in Sumner exploring how individuals and groups were working to sustain their culture and community. From October 2013 to May 2015 I conducted over 1,800 hours of participant observation, interviewed twenty-one people, and gathered textual materials from within the community and nearby. As I worked as a volunteer at the refuge, spent time on the barstools in Foster's, and attended meetings of civic groups, I came to realize that while Sumner was small, it was anything but simple. There was far more to the town of just 102 people than one might expect.

Residents liked to tell me they lived in a "one-horse town" where there "wasn't much going on," but this could not have been further from the truth. Individuals negotiated friendships and reputations they had built over years and decades of living, working, and hunting in the community. Intricate understandings of right and wrong that were held with incredible emotional conviction informed how residents thought of their community and their place in it. Intersecting differences and inequalities related to race, class, and gender transformed how individuals related to each other as well as the surrounding landscape. Institutions such as the U.S. legal system, the U.S. Department of Agriculture, and the USFWS also influenced the community. And nonhumans beyond geese such as ducks and floods constantly complicated residents' lives.

In becoming aware of these complexities, I realized that the social and ecological particularities of Sumner intersected with social and ecological processes that played out on national and even global scales to inform how culture and community were rearranged in response to a lack of geese. Friendships. Inequalities. Plants and animals. Dreams for and fears about the future. Regional, national, and global political-economic institutions.

Shifting climatological conditions. They all converged to transform how culture and community were being reorganized in Sumner. In short, adaptations to a lack of geese emerged through constant convergences of social and ecological things, beings, and processes.

Acknowledging the significance of social and ecological interconnections corresponds with a recent shift across the social sciences called the posthuman turn. Instead of assuming that understanding people allows us to understand communities, since the 1980s social scientists have increasingly stressed the significance of interactions between humans and material objects, plants, and nonhuman animals.[22] Whether analyzing mundane interactions[23] between (non)humans[24] or their effect on the evolution of communities and societies,[25] scholars have found that material objects, plants, and nonhuman animals constantly transform how people go about their lives and organize their communities. From the relationships between individuals and their pets to the relations between societies and global climatological conditions, humans and nonhumans constantly affect each other.

The concept of entanglements clarifies the significance of interconnections between what are often considered distinctly social or ecological things, beings, and processes.[26] Invoking an image of a bird's nest of different materials intricately woven together, this concept highlights the sprawling webs of entangled humans, material objects, plants, and nonhuman animals that are constantly making the world through their interactions. Who we are, how we go about our lives, and even the communities in which we live emerge from entangled knots of social and ecological things, beings, and processes that are intricately wound into each other.

Research on entanglements has found that historically contingent perceptions, meanings, and institutions influence the social and ecological interactions that create our communities, but scholars also note the significant role materiality plays in entanglements.[27] The material landscape around Sumner was especially important for adaptations to the shifting presence of geese, for example. Inequalities also inform and are informed by (non)human interactions.[28] While our lives are constantly made and remade through interactive webs of (non)humans, often particular (non)humans neither meet on equal terms nor benefit equally from their interactions. As community members worked to reorganize Sumner, for example, they navigated complex systems of inequality while using different skills and degrees of status in the community to influence processes of adaptation. And as they rearranged their community, there were different benefits and drawbacks for particular (non)humans because of how Sumner was reorganized.

My argument is that adaptations to changing goose migrations emerged from an entangled dance of social and ecological things, beings, and processes. If particular (non)human entanglements had not been present, and if (non)humans had not been able to navigate and use them, Sumner would not have been reorganized and sustained. Ways of life and community were being sustained only because individuals and groups creatively leveraged and rearranged the entangled interconnections among the social and ecological things, beings, and processes that composed Sumner.

That adaptations emerged through entanglements corresponds with research from across the social sciences finding that the complexities of communities create opportunities for transformation and change.[29] Communities are informed by the mundane details of particular places as well as regional, national, and global social and ecological processes. As a result, our lives and communities are often distorted by inequalities and disrupted by social and ecological processes that seem largely beyond our control. This can make it seem as though we are trapped and unable to have any meaningful effect on our own lives, much less our communities. Nevertheless, these churning entanglements actually make it possible to transform cultures and communities. Like an impossibly jumbled interchange with numerous roads branching off, intersecting, and looping back in on themselves, the intricacies of entanglements provide opportunities to veer[30]—to change direction, take different routes, and adapt.[31]

By emphasizing the transformative potential of social and ecological entanglements, I do not mean to suggest that climate change does not present serious challenges. Entanglements do not mean that adaptations to climate change will inevitably happen in manners that sustain ways of life and communities. Opportunities for transformation are often overlooked or purposefully avoided. In places such as Isle de Jean Charles, arrangements of social and ecological things, beings, and processes can also undermine individuals' and groups' abilities to sustain their ways of life and communities no matter what they try. Still, only by acknowledging the significance of entanglements and considering them in greater detail can we ever hope to tap into these complexities to promote resilience in those circumstances when entanglements *do* present opportunities for transformation.

Changing Landscapes, Climate, and Migrations

Swan Lake NWR was established in 1937 with the primary intent of providing migrating ducks with a place to safely rest and refuel.[32] Canada geese were rarely seen in the area at the time, and they were mentioned only in passing in early refuge reports.[33] By 1948 goose numbers had climbed to eighteen thousand birds during a time when Canada geese were not common nuisances in communities across the country. Drawn to Swan Lake NWR by the extensive fields of wheat, soybeans, and corn in the region and the relative safety of the newly constructed lakes and marshes on the refuge itself, the Eastern Prairie Population (EPP) of Canada geese began using Swan Lake as their primary wintering location instead of migrating to Arkansas and Louisiana as they had done in the past.

Large numbers of people had also started coming to the area by the late 1940s to hunt the birds that were prized more for their symbolic value than their meat.[34] So many hunters were coming to town that land values near the refuge skyrocketed as they jostled to secure the rights to the best hunting spots.[35] According to the refuge manager at the time, the "Lord must have been on the community's side," because nobody was hurt even though drunk drivers "indiscriminately shooting from the highways" created a "safety hazard of large proportions."[36]

Goose numbers surpassed 100,000 for the first time in 1954,[37] and a portion of the refuge was opened for public hunting the following year. Twenty thousand geese were killed in the area, and more would have been if conservation officials had not closed the season two weeks early because they were concerned that EPP numbers might not recover.[38] By 1977 goose numbers on the refuge had climbed to just over 181,000, which is even more impressive when the additional 88,700 geese in the surrounding area are included for a grand total of roughly 270,000.[39] Aside from the hunters, Swan Lake NWR was a veritable goose paradise. In addition to availing themselves of the lakes and marshes on the refuge, the geese had plenty to eat. They feasted on corn, soybeans, and wheat in the agricultural fields surrounding the refuge, and the USFWS had even entered into cooperative agreements with local farmers to grow thousands of acres of crops on the refuge so that the geese had ample food for the winter.

Then why did the geese start spending falls and winters at more northern latitudes? In short, because they no longer needed to migrate as far south from their nesting grounds to survive the winter. By the early 1980s, Iowa, Minnesota, the Dakotas, and southern Canada had become suitable wintering locations for EPP geese.[40] Climate change, in combination with other socioecological processes, had encouraged the northward shift in their migration patterns.

Rising corn production in Iowa, Minnesota, and the Dakotas was centrally important to why the geese began to winter north of Missouri. Corn production skyrocketed in these states in the 1970s (Figure I.1). Roughly 1.5 billion bushels of corn were produced in Iowa, Minnesota, and the Dakotas at the start of the 1970s, but by the end of the decade their annual yields had doubled. Yields have shown no signs of slowing down, either. By 2013, 5 billion bushels of corn were produced in Iowa, Minnesota, and the Dakotas, an increase of nearly 250 percent compared to production at the start of the 1970s.

Dramatically expanded corn production in these states north of Missouri is especially important because Canada geese prefer to eat waste corn when temperatures turn cold. With its high-energy, easily accessible kernels spread across the ground after fields have been harvested, waste corn is the perfect food source for wintering geese. Corn yields remained relatively stagnant in Missouri, so the gap in the amount of food available to geese in these more northern landscapes compared to what was available farther south only continued to grow. It is no coincidence that EPP migrations shifted to Iowa, Minnesota, and the Dakotas right when corn production expanded exponentially in these states.[41] There was more food there, and the geese took advantage.

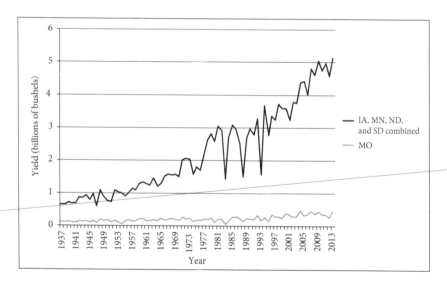

Figure I.1 Yearly corn yields in billions of bushels from 1937 to 2013 (U.S. Department of Agriculture 2014).

Another piece to the puzzle of shifting migration patterns is the availability of suitable roost sites. Roosts are bodies of water such as ponds, lakes, and rivers where geese can spend the night while safely drinking and resting. Landscape changes have contributed to the propagation of roosts north of Missouri. New conservation areas such as Big Stone NWR in Minnesota have been important, but the growth of (sub)urban landscapes has been equally significant. As any suburbanite annoyed with the presence of geese and goose poop will readily attest, geese have taken advantage of (sub)urban landscapes in which there seems to be a pond in every park, neighborhood, golf course, and office complex. In Winnipeg, Manitoba, for example, over a hundred thousand EPP geese now stop over in the city each fall. The proliferation of power and sewage treatment plants because of (sub)urban sprawl has also contributed to the growth in roosts. Big Stone power plant in South Dakota, for example, became a roost for EPP geese when it came online in 1975 because its warm-water discharge helped keep water open during the cold South Dakotan winters. Taken together, the increase in conservation areas, (sub)urban landscapes, and utility sites has provided migrating geese with more than enough places to safely rest in Iowa, Minnesota, the Dakotas, and southern Canada.[42]

Expanded corn production and the availability of roosts are linked to climate change. The growth in corn production has been encouraged by subsidies, corn prices, and new farming technologies,[43] but yields have also been enhanced by longer, wetter, and slightly cooler growing seasons in the Midwest since the start of the 1980s.[44] Noting cooler summers while discussing climate change may seem odd because it is often associated with warming temperatures. In contrast to global warming, though, which denotes how the average surface temperature across the globe has been increasing, climate change focuses attention on how the average seasonal temperature and precipitation patterns of particular regions change over time. Global warming and climate change are related because a warmer planet means many regional climates are warming, but the consequences of a warmer planet are experienced unevenly across regions. In outlier cases such as the midwestern United States, increasing global temperatures have been associated with cooler summers there. Corn can be grown farther north than used to be possible in part because of a longer growing season, and wetter and cooler summers have contributed to yield expansions even in places where corn was already cultivated.[45] Because longer, wetter, and cooler growing seasons in the Midwest are all dimensions of climate change, increased corn production north of Missouri is at least partially explained by shifting climatological conditions.[46]

In contrast to summers, falls and winters have, on average, become warmer in the upper Midwest since the 1970s.[47] Over the last forty years, the decade-to-decade average temperature for October to February has warmed more than three degrees across Iowa, Minnesota, and the Dakotas.[48] EPP geese use these landscapes during this period, and warmer temperatures help keep ponds, lakes, and rivers from freezing over. When roosts freeze, geese must find new ones, which can force them to move farther south, where warmer temperatures have kept water open. Because warmer winters in the upper Midwest are a dimension of climate change, the availability of roosts north of Missouri is at least partially explained by shifting climatological conditions. Because of warmer falls and winters across Iowa, Minnesota, and the Dakotas, geese have not had the same pressures pushing them out of these more northern latitudes.

Todd, a highly respected waterfowl biologist who conducted extensive research on EPP geese across the North American continent, provided an apt summary of these interrelated dynamics of corn, roosts, and climate change.[49] During our interview, I asked him why EPP geese stopped using Swan Lake, and he explained:

> I think it's a matter of expansion of the corn belt further north, even into Canada. . . . I think climate change has been a factor as well. . . . As long as there's food available on the ground and there's open water on a reservoir or river, or a power plant, or whatever, I think it's just simply a matter of changing the climate, changing the availability of food, and the adaptability of these birds; they take advantage of it.

Like shifts in the ranges of a staggering array of other species,[50] the northward shift in EPP migration patterns since the 1970s occurred because of entanglements between geese, landscape uses, and shifting temperature and precipitation patterns.

This convoluted interplay of humans and nonhumans over space and time that led to shifting goose migration patterns typifies the variability communities will have to respond to because of climate change.[51] Although the social and ecological particularities of specific communities make processes of adaptation unique, Sumner offers a "window"[52] to see how adaptations to climate change play out during individuals' everyday lives. Like so many other communities around the world, this rural community and its residents in the heartland of the United States were doing what they could to respond to the localized effects of climate change.

Methods

I have been asked how I found out about Sumner, and the answer is simple. Many of my first memories involve hunting Canada geese near Sumner with my dad in the early 1990s. He began hunting geese around Swan Lake in the 1970s, and he started taking me with him in 1989, when I was just two years old. We were part of a hunting club composed of an assortment of old-timers and middle-age men who worked as insulators, carpenters, and linemen in Kansas City. Every Friday evening during goose hunting season, my dad packed us up and drove us to the old three-bedroom house that served as our club's headquarters just south of Sumner. When we arrived, the other men in the club would usually be sitting around the table in the dining room playing poker, talking trash, and drinking beer, as the smoke from their Camels and Marlboros hung thick in the air. With its sea green Formica top and chrome sides, the table was straight out of the 1950s. Adding to the antique feeling of the room were the black rotary dial phone and outdated Norman Rockwell calendar that hung on the yellowing walls. Even as a boy I was right in the middle of it all. Playing cards and taking a sip of Hot Damn! Cinnamon Schnapps whenever my dad would let me. I liked the cinnamon candy taste, and my dad liked seeing the wild-eyed looks from the other men when I took a pull.

We usually managed to get a goose every time we went hunting in the early 1990s, but by the late 1990s Canada geese had become few and far between. There were numerous mornings when we did not hear, much less see, a goose while hunting. I will never forget listening to the men in the club reminisce about how many geese used to come to the area. They related stories of a sky blackened by geese and hunters crowding into the surrounding towns, filling every motel room, bar, and restaurant in the vicinity of the refuge. How the fields around Swan Lake would be filled every morning and evening with hunters shooting at the birds. The blasts from their shotguns rumbling across the river bottoms in the area, making it sound more like a war zone than a sparsely populated countryside. They assured me these were not tall tales, and my imagination ran wild. At the time I had no clue why the geese stopped coming to Swan Lake, but I distinctly remember listening to worried conversations about the lack of geese and its effect on the communities surrounding the refuge.

When I began this project I decided that a combination of participant observation, interviews, and textual analysis was the best methodological design. Participant observation is ideally suited for learning how individuals understand and go about their lives. Interviews can produce invaluable information, but what people say they do and what they actually do in their everyday lives does not always align.[53] Consequently, it would have been inappropriate to rely solely on interviews to try to understand how people were going about remaking their lives and community in response to shifting goose migrations. Interviews can, however, help clarify questions resulting from observations, and both interviews and texts allow analysts to better situate the ongoing interactions they are observing within the histories of communities. Texts also enable researchers to trace how individuals' everyday lives are informed by regional, national, and global social and ecological processes.[54] Combining these data sources allows me to strengthen my insights and claims while situating what I was observing within the history of the community and broader social and ecological processes.[55]

The refuge was the ideal place to begin the project because it was the epicenter of goose migrations. Consequently, when I met someone at a barbeque who knew the refuge manager, I asked for an introduction. Upon receiving approval for the project from the University of Missouri's institutional review board, my contact arranged a meeting with the refuge manager. After the manager and I talked for about an hour in his office, he agreed I could begin participant observations on the refuge on October 1, 2013. Unfortunately, a congressional squabble over health care shut down the federal government from October 1 through 16, and I was not able to start until the federal government and refuge had reopened. Though frustrating at the time, it was also an enlightening introduction to the complexities of the refuge.

Over the next year and a half, my work as a volunteer at the refuge became like a second job and the refuge became like a second home. After a few months, I was given a set of keys to each and every lock across the refuge and an office in the visitor center. When I was in Sumner for several days at a time, which was just about every week, I stayed in the refuge bunkhouse. An older two-story house that used to be occupied by refuge managers and their families, it could not have been a better place to stay. Aside from the mice and the sound of someone rolling marbles across the second-story floor at about 11:15 every night, which had been heard for at least the last fifteen years, it was quiet, extremely convenient, warm in the winter, cool in the summer, and free.

I generally worked at the refuge as a volunteer at least two days a week. Although staff knew about my research project, they often referred to me as the "bio tech," which is a temporary position in the USFWS typically filled by recent college graduates. I welcomed this role because it facilitated a unique degree of behind-the-scenes access. Among other tasks, I wrote internal proposals, grants, and press releases; worked on heavy equipment; went through USFWS training courses; sat in on internal meetings; gave refuge tours; conducted deer and waterfowl surveys; participated in prescribed burns; organized public events; and mowed a lot of grass. Working with staff members taught me far more about the refuge than if I had just observed them. In particular, and as I discuss at length in Part II, I became all too familiar with the frustrations that stemmed from trying to work within increasingly restrictive regulations coming from the regional and federal levels of the USFWS.

I started my project with a gendered skill set that facilitated building rapport with the rural men working at the refuge. Because I had grown up hunting, fishing, and working construction jobs with other rural men, my "country-masculine habitus"[56] enabled me to relate to staff members and participate in their work tasks. I had no trouble riding all-terrain vehicles, grassing hunting blinds,[57] hooking up and backing trailers, operating mowers, and using power tools, for example.

Beyond gaining an in-depth knowledge of the inner workings of the refuge, assisting staff members allowed me to build a tremendous amount of rapport with staff and members of the public because both perceived Swan Lake as being underfunded and understaffed. Members of the public were also particularly interested in the inside information I gained from working at the refuge. I openly, but discreetly, talked about some aspects of the inner workings of the refuge. Men in the community who hunted ducks, for example, were often especially appreciative when I divulged the results of waterfowl surveys before they were officially released to the public.

Over time, I branched out into the community by following leads for my project that developed while working at the refuge. By March 2014, I was regularly talking with locals at the town bar. When I first began fieldwork, community members repeatedly told me the bar was where I could get the real scoop on Sumner, but I did not know how to gain access. Eventually the owner of the bar came into the refuge visitor center to ask about hunting regulations. We set up an interview, and after I got to know him better, he told me to come by the bar whenever I wanted. The bar was one of the only places in town where community members regularly met to talk and proved to be a rich site for observing and learning about residents' everyday lives.

At first, I was uncomfortable in the bar. Everyone seemed to know every other person in the bar, except me. Without the comfort of anonymity provided by bars in larger towns, I felt out of place. I would sit at the bar, staring stiffly forward, unsuccessfully trying to be an invisible fly on a barstool. After Darla and I got to know each other, she made fun of me for this. In her customarily playful manner, she would look at me, start laughing, and then contort her face into a grumpy scowl while slumping her shoulders. "You used to sit here just like that!" she joked. Everyone knowing everyone else eventually worked in my favor, though. After three weeks of my fly-on-a-barstool approach, one of the regulars asked who I was and what I was up to. From that point on, the patrons of the bar were eager to talk about and even help with my project. They gave me historic documents, facilitated contacts with other community members, and suggested titles for a chapter focusing on the bar. "Beer and Bullshit" and "Monkey Business" were my favorites. As is common for researchers conducting fieldwork in spaces like bars,[58] I sat with, watched, listened to, and talked with patrons whenever I was there. Even if I tried to just observe, local residents regularly pulled me into interactions and bought me rounds of beer that I would nurse as best I could.

Once I got to know its patrons, I did not have much trouble fitting in at the bar. I am white, am heterosexual, and had hunted in the area my whole life, but my status as a sociology graduate student presented some complications. The bar was occupied primarily by people employed in or retired from working-class occupations. Not surprisingly, then, some of the men in Foster's liked to give me a hard time by calling me "college boy," "career student," or "the professor." I was used to it from my time working construction jobs during the summers, and I knew they would not make such comments unless we had grown familiar enough to enter into the playful banter that often characterizes male friendships predicated on a veneer of emotional distance.[59] These labels were a way to put me in my place, but they were also an indication I was being integrated into the community. To help navigate these labels and their stigmas, I actively avoided talking about graduate school and anything having to do with sociology because both marked me as out of place. When anyone asked what I had been up to, I talked about whatever had been happening at the refuge.

Using leads from the refuge and the bar, by April 2014 I was attending the monthly meetings of three community groups—the Friends of Swan Lake NWR, the Swan Lake Sportsman's Club, and the Wild Goose Festival Planning Committee. I also began attending monthly city council meetings in January 2015. In contrast to the predominately male setting of daily refuge work, Friends of Swan Lake and city council meetings brought women and men together, and the Wild Goose Festival Planning Committee was composed of only women. These meetings proved invaluable because they allowed me to see how women were participating in processes of adaptation. They also allowed me to develop relationships with women in the community, which sometimes made the women more willing to be interviewed. By the end of May 2015, I had completed over 1,800 hours of participant observation.

In addition to countless informal conversations with local residents, I formally interviewed twenty-one others. These included refuge personnel, community leaders, men who had hunted geese, and waterfowl biologists who had worked at the refuge when goose numbers were high. I chose these people for interviews primarily because they were key players in the processes of adaptation on which my research eventually focused. Ranging in age from thirty-five to over eighty, fourteen interviewees were men and seven were women. Interviews lasted from thirty minutes to over three hours. All were audio recorded and then transcribed.

I also gathered historical and contemporary documents for this analysis. USFWS documents included annual refuge narratives written by refuge managers that dated to 1938, public reports, press releases, event flyers, pamphlets, and Facebook posts. Texts produced by public sources included newsletters and pamphlets from the Friends group, Wild Goose Festival programs, past and contemporary news coverage of the refuge, biological and economic research conducted on and around Swan Lake, and social media posts made by residents. Historic documents were particularly important because they provided me with a better understanding of the history of the community and how this history affected contemporary processes of adaptation.

The real names of places are used in this book because the historical particularities of Sumner that were integrally important to this project made the community easily identifiable.[60] Instead of changing these details or attempting a veneer of anonymity that could be seen through by anyone searching for "Wild Goose Capital of the World" on the Internet, I name Sumner and the refuge. Specific groups and places in the community are also identified because Sumner's size makes it unrealistic to think pseudonyms would provide anonymity. Using a pseudonym for the only bar in town, for example, would do little to obscure its identity. Also, the town and refuge are named because community members were excited about the creation of an identifiable, historical record of their community. As is evident throughout this book, most living in Sumner care deeply about their town and the refuge. Consequently, it was very important to many that I talked with that their community and its past would not be forgotten. Disguising the community would have made it impossible to provide such a record.

Because the community is identified I have gone to special lengths to protect those who participated in this study. In addition to using pseudonyms, I omitted or slightly altered specific details about people and interactions to obscure their identities to outsiders. Because it is especially difficult to make it so that community members do not recognize each other, I omitted observations that could be embarrassing or harmful if other residents of Sumner identified a person. Having to do this is uncommon in a study that covers common knowledge: what is presented in this book will not tell the residents of Sumner anything they do not already know about themselves, each other, and their community.

Anonymity at the refuge was particularly difficult because just four staff members worked at Swan Lake NWR. I have obscured who was who at the refuge, and all confidential conversations that could get someone in trouble with superiors have been omitted. Again, having to do this is uncommon because what is covered in this book is common knowledge for those working within the USFWS. For example, that refuge staff were sometimes frustrated by regulations coming from the regional and federal levels of the organization should not surprise anyone in the USFWS. Such frustrations are common within the USFWS and large organizations more generally,[61] and Swan Lake staff openly and almost daily worked through these issues with each other as well as USFWS staff in the regional office. Presenting data on such topics provides an illustration of what USFWS officials already know about their organization and its staff members. A final note on pseudonyms and refuge staff regards my decision to not use the refuge manager's pseudonym in my transcriptions of public meetings, using only his title instead. These meetings were open to the public, so confidentiality was not possible, but if I had identified him by his pseudonym, he would be identified throughout the rest of the book.

Unless I specifically note that a quotation came from an interview or textual source, quotations throughout this book are from field notes. Except during city council and Friends meetings, when I transcribed meetings directly into a Word document on my computer, I made "jottings"[62] on my smartphone while conducting participant observations. I then used these jottings, which contained key excerpts of conversations, to jog my memory when writing detailed notes each night after participant observations. This is standard practice for ethnographers because it allows the researcher to record details in a less conspicuous and disruptive manner.[63] Especially with the growing ubiquity of smartphones, making notes on a phone was far less disruptive than using a recording device or furiously writing in a notebook the entire time I was in the community. For further details on my data generation and analysis strategies, see the Appendix.

Overview of the Book: Lives Are Changing, but How?

State officials, nongovernmental organizations, researchers, and members of the public urgently need to know far more about how cultures and communities are rearranged in response to the effects of shifting climatological conditions. Research on the environmental consequences of climate change has often obscured its significant social ramifications.[64] Even when analysts have considered the human dimensions of climate change, they often omit the mundane intricacies involved in how people rearrange their ways of life as well as their relationships with each other and the landscapes in which they live. An impressive array of research examines the political-economic drivers and ramifications of climate change,[65] knowledge about and perceptions of climate change,[66] and how both are interconnected.[67] Analysts have also documented what adaptations have taken place[68] or theorized what facilitates and constrains adaptations,[69] but how adaptations actually play out during individuals' everyday lives has remained largely unexplored.[70]

This is a huge oversight. Climate change is disrupting cultures and communities across the globe, and there is no indication that this will change anytime soon. It is far more likely that climate change will cause increasing ecological and social disruptions in the coming decades and centuries.[71] It is absolutely crucial to acknowledge this, but focusing on the potential disarray of climate change tells us nothing about how communities might respond to a world characterized by climatological upheaval.

The primary argument advanced in this book is that individuals and groups draw on the social and ecological entanglements that compose their communities to rearrange and sustain their ways of life. This can be further broken down into three supporting arguments. First, interactions among (non)human beings, things, and institutions influence how cultures and communities are sustained. Second, entangled inequalities inform and are informed by how cultures and communities are reorganized in response to climate change. Third, entanglements of the past, present, and future are centrally important to rearrangements of cultures and communities. In addition to previous interactions among (non)humans, individuals' understandings of the past and anticipations of the future are especially important to how they try to rework and sustain their cultures and communities.

My background as a sociologist will be evident to readers throughout this book. I draw heavily on sociologists who look at how meanings and institutions constructed by people inform how we arrange our lives and communities. I also highlight ways these theorists enable more complete understandings of adaptations. In addition, I incorporate works from across the social sciences to approach adaptations with an interdisciplinary lens. The sociological literature on adaptations is relatively underdeveloped,[72] so it was important to use research from related fields such as anthropology, gender studies, geography, political-ecology, and the posthumanities. By using the strengths of these different traditions of scholarship to supplement the weaknesses of others, I could better investigate the complexities of adaptations in Sumner.[73]

Chapters 1 through 3 explore the links between inequalities, adaptations, and community. These chapters draw on my time in the bar and with community groups to illustrate how entangled inequalities related to gender, race, class, and rurality complicated efforts to rearrange ways of life and community in Sumner. While still drawing attention to the inequalities introduced in the first half of the book, Chapters 4 through 6 focus on how community members worked to repurpose the refuge in response to the lack of geese. These chapters draw from my work at the refuge to explore how the interface between the USFWS and the public complicated reconstructions of the meanings and uses of the refuge in response to shifting goose migration patterns.

Chapter 1 introduces Sumner and the inequalities that infused how individuals thought of themselves and organized their community. Contrary to the perception that rural communities are simple, homogeneous, or harmonious, Sumner was a community built on inequalities that intersected with and transformed one another. In addition to inequalities between men and women and between socioeconomic classes, race was integrally important to how individuals arranged their lives and community even though everyone in Sumner was white. Further, though Sumner did not conform to idyllic representations of rural communities, residents' understandings of what it meant to be a good rural person still informed how they went about their lives and organized their relationships with each other.

Chapter 2 focuses on how the community shifted from being associated with goose hunting to being associated with duck hunting. Men in Sumner framed this shift as an inevitable process, but I argue it was contingent on divergent behaviors between ducks and geese, the surrounding landscape, federal institutions, and inequalities among men. The chapter concludes with an exploration of how this shift undermined the degree to which individuals in Sumner felt they were part of a broader community of people.

Chapter 3 continues to explore the links between inequalities, adaptations, and communities. In response to the decline in geese and goose hunters coming to town, a handful of women were reorganizing the annual Wild Goose Festival in an effort to sustain it and their community. But as they did so, they reproduced some inequalities in Sumner and rearranged others. Modifying the festival into a family friendly affair was advantageous for some men and women, disadvantageous for others, and simultaneously (dis)advantageous for other men and women in the community.

Acknowledging that individuals and groups were simultaneously (dis)-advantaged by this transformation forces us to see that individuals and groups can be simultaneously privileged and oppressed because of how their communities are refashioned in response to climate change. Though researchers have stressed that inequalities inform and are reconstructed through adaptations, they have often focused on a single dimension of inequality or multiple dimensions of inequality separately.[74] This has led some to claim that distinct groups of winners and losers will emerge because of how communities are reorganized in response to climate change.[75] Adaptations and inequalities are not simple enough to be understood in such dichotomous terms. I draw on critical and feminist scholars to conclude that we should expect individuals and groups to be simultaneously (dis)advantaged because of how their communities are reorganized in response to climate change.[76] I also discuss how individuals and groups can rearrange and sustain their communities by creatively working within the complexities and contradictions of the inequalities that inform their lives.[77]

Chapter 4 provides a baseline understanding of the refuge. I first explore how Swan Lake NWR had been constructed through mundane interactions between (non)humans. Then I detail how understandings of progress, conservation, and governance popularized in the United States over the prior centuries influenced how refuge staff and members of the public conceptualized Swan Lake. Chapters 5 and 6 concern how the simultaneous significance of (non)human interactions and understandings of the refuge converged to inform how the uses and meanings of Swan Lake were rearranged in response to the shifting presence of geese.

Chapter 5 explores how the meanings and uses of the refuge were being reconstructed through conflicts among USFWS staff and members of the public that hinged on divergent perceptions of the future and the risks therein. In spite of objections from refuge staff and members of the public, the federal and regional levels of the USFWS implemented policies throughout 2014 and 2015 to reduce the likelihood that litigation would be brought against the organization. As a result, the very thing that members of the public and refuge staff feared most—declining public uses of the refuge—took place. Chapter 6 shows how members of the public and refuge staff worked to connect their community to the refuge amid increasing tensions over regulations. By drawing on interpersonal networks, feelings of belonging and respect, and the structures and norms of interpersonal interactions, they continued working together to try to connect local residents with the refuge in spite of a lack of geese and escalating tensions over regulations.

Combined, Chapters 5 and 6 provide two key takeaways. First, how risks, or perceptions of harms that could arise in the future, are part of adaptations is far more complex than other studies often represent it. Individuals and institutions must juggle multiple risks concerning the relatively immediate and distant futures, and we need to discard the idea that a lack of focus on the distant future is why adaptations to climate change do not happen.[78] Second, we need a more nuanced understanding of the messy interface between state institutions and the public. Previous works have rightly stressed that partnerships between state institutions and the public can facilitate adaptations, but these works often imagine a neat split between members of the public and representatives of state institutions.[79] Things are not so clear-cut, though, because representatives of state institutions can also be members of the communities in which they work. I argue that, to promote adaptations, we must conceptualize representatives of state institutions as ambivalent members of the communities in which they work in order to better comprehend the complex interface between state institutions and the public.

I conclude by synthesizing Chapters 1 through 6 to draw out the three arguments that flow throughout the book: (1) Adaptations occur through swirling entanglements between (non)human beings, things, and institutions. (2) Inequalities inform and are remade through adaptations to climate change. (3) A churning mixture of the past, present, and future influences how ways of life and communities are rearranged in response to shifting climatological conditions. These three points offer a framework for analyzing how cultures and communities can be rearranged in response to climate change. Given the breadth and depth of challenges facing communities because of shifting climatological conditions, researchers and policy makers seeking to understand and promote adaptations urgently need such a framework.

Aside from Chapter 2, in which men compete to adapt more effectively, this book focuses on community members cooperating to do what they could to refashion and sustain their community in response to the localized consequences of climate change. Although residents of Sumner knew they were adapting to shifting goose migration patterns, it was not apparent that they knew they were adapting to climate change. I heard people talk about climate change only when I asked them about it, and there was not a consensus among community members that climate change had affected goose migration patterns. Nevertheless, they were rearranging and sustaining their community effectively in response to disruptions linked to shifting climatological conditions by drawing on the social and ecological entanglements that made up their community.

I believe this is a hopeful story of resilience that is necessarily tempered by the complex realities of communities and climate change. Community members sustained Sumner by reorganizing their lives in manners that, in some respects, were more equitable and ecologically beneficial than during the era of high goose numbers. Nevertheless, the residents of Sumner also reproduced and even intensified some inequalities as they reorganized their community. This hopefulness is further tempered by not all communities having social and ecological entanglements that enable adaptations to climatological upheaval.

Part I

Community, Inequalities,
Adaptations

A Rural Community Permeated by Differences and Inequalities

Foster's Sportsman Inn: The Place to Be

City hall and a singlewide mobile home, Foster's Sportsman Inn, the post office, and a defunct service station occupy the corner lots at the heart of Sumner. With its whitewashed exterior and boarded-up windows, the service station is probably what many people expect to find in a town like Sumner. Built sometime before the 1950s, it indicates a past that was livelier than the present, but focusing solely on such dilapidated buildings belies the vibrancies of rural communities and their inhabitants.[1] The whole of Sumner central provides a better microcosm for imagining the community. The gas station was a reminder of a more populated past, but getting to know those who frequented the bar, post office, and city hall revealed there was far more to the community than decay. Distinct senses of pride in Sumner mingled with an awareness of depopulation. Everyday frustrations and struggles were mashed together with overwhelming senses of joy and a good bit of laughter. Feelings of togetherness merged with an awareness that the community was fractured by and built on inequalities related to gender, race, and class.

All these complexities that characterized Sumner were readily apparent in Foster's. Like many bars in the rural Midwest, it served cheap beer and had a couple of coin-operated pool tables. It was dimly lit no matter the time of day, and smoke from decades of cigarettes infused the yellowed ceiling panels, wood panel walls, and even the bar top itself. The old-style tube televisions scattered around the oblong room displayed occasional forecasts from the Weather Channel, but they mostly remained turned off, their blank screens reminding patrons that they should be at the bar to socialize, not gaze at a TV while keeping to themselves. Every now and then the mayor threw *NSYNC on the jukebox for a laugh, but the whine of steel guitars from country artists such as Alan Jackson and Travis Tritt usually cut through the ambient noise of conversations about the weather, work, and whatever people had been up to lately.

Those who spent time in Sumner often swore Foster's had a special atmosphere that stemmed from the current regulars as well as the generations of characters who had passed their time on the round stools lining the bar. That it was at the center of the rollicking social scene during the goose hunting heyday only added to Foster's mystique. There were stories of hunters being packed like sardines into the premises, fistfights spilling into the street, meetings between conservation officials to hash out Swan Lake National Wildlife Refuge management strategies, and ill-fated encounters between star-crossed lovers. Darla liked to say Sumner was "where the beer flowed like water," and anyone who spent much time in Foster's would have had a hard time arguing with her. The bar did not serve hard liquor, but it served plenty of beer at two dollars a can or draft. Regulars also slipped in and out for sips of whiskey—or "shots of personality" as they were often described—and it was not unusual to see a mason jar full of blueberry- and cinnamon-steeped booze sitting just outside the front door.

References to the past and contemporary friendships that made the bar special to its patrons were scattered throughout it. Collages of prior events hosted by the bar, tributes to deceased friends, and references to the accomplishments and friendly rivalries of current residents adorned the walls between dust-covered Anheuser-Busch neon and mirror signs. Beside the TV in the upper left corner of the room behind the bar was a picture of a black Labrador retriever, John Wayne. Owned by a man who lived in town, John was a bit of a local celebrity because he had placed in some events in the Dock Dogs competition circuit. Even the name of the bar was an homage to its past. Donald Dean Foster was a local man who had owned the establishment for nearly forty years before he passed away in 2012. Throughout my time in Sumner I repeatedly heard stories emphasizing his endless generosity, ability to see the good in others, and efforts to make Sumner a better community.

In addition to being a space considered special because of the friend-ships and memories it evoked, many considered Foster's important because it was a major hub of interpersonal interaction in their community. Roughly an equal number of men and women passed through the front door, and it was not unusual for children to come in with their parents or grandparents. Like bars in other small-town, working-class communities, Foster's was a place where local residents met to swap stories, discuss current goings-on, conduct business, and host events such as the Halloween costume contest.[2] In the process, they also managed to create a sense of community and their place in it. Consequently, when I began fieldwork both men and women in the community said I needed to head to the bar because that was where someone could get the inside scoop on Sumner (though they also warned me to be careful not to let the older men in the bar draw me too far into their tall tales).

Mitch explained the importance of the bar to me with some assistance from Stan while we sat at the bar one afternoon. Both over sixty, they had grown up in the area and could be found bellied up to the bar at least a couple of afternoons each week, Mitch in his overalls, Stan in a camo T-shirt and blue jeans, and both gossiping and giving other patrons a hard time.

"You know, around here you never have to have an empty beer," Mitch informed me after asking Darla to get me a beer. "Once you get to know people, there's always a beer sitting there waiting for you."

I thanked him for the beer and asked, "So how long have you been com-ing in here?"

"Oh, a while now," Mitch noted, understating how many years he had been coming into Foster's. "Used to go over to Bosworth, but that bar burned. Used to have a bar in Hale too, but that one burned too. They rebuilt it, but it isn't worth a shit."

"So what do you like about coming in here, then?" I asked.

"To talk to people. This is the meeting place around here, you know?" Mitch said.

Stan added, "Yeah, this is the place to meet in Sumner."

"It's one of those old town bars," Mitch continued. "It's got history. It's one of the original bars around here, and people come in here to meet. You know, Sumner has, what, 102 people, and there's, what, 40 to 50 people in here every Thursday?" Mitch asked rhetorically, looking around at the crowd in the bar for effect. "I'm retired now, so that's what it's about. Having fun."

"You want to know about Sumner? You just keep coming in here," Stan said, agreeing with Mitch that the bar was the place to be.

Mitch, Stan, and others who told me to go to Foster's were right. It was the place to go to see and be seen in Sumner. Though just 102 people lived in Sumner proper, the bar regularly managed a crowd of 30 or more. Many of those who passed through the front door lived in Sumner or immediately adjacent to it, but others came from nearby towns such as Hale, Mendon, Meadville, Forker, and Tina.

Rural bars are not simply idyllic spaces that encourage social integration and community cohesion, though.[3] They are also spaces involved in the reproduction of differences and inequalities. Foster's was a major hub of interpersonal interaction that was integrally important to social life in Sumner, but it was not different in this respect from other rural bars.

This chapter discusses Foster's in greater detail to explore inequalities in Sumner. While Sumner was exceptionally small, it was neither simple nor homogeneous. Intersecting forms of difference and inequality related to gender, race, and class informed how people thought of themselves, arranged their lives, and tried to sustain their community.[4] Residents' understandings of what it meant to be a proper rural person living in a rural community were also particularly important. These threads of gender, race, class, and rurality intersected to inform residents' understandings of what it meant to be an upstanding citizen of Sumner. While gender, race, and class are addressed separately at the outset of the chapter to more clearly introduce Sumner and its residents, this should not be taken as an indication that any one of these was more important than the others or that these dimensions of difference and inequality should ultimately be considered separately.

A Traditional Gender Dichotomy: The (Heterosexual) Ideology of Separate Spheres

"You know, it's a privilege for you to sit here today," Rachel teased Carl while they and their friends, all Foster's regulars in their fifties and sixties, sat at the round table next to the front door of the bar. Seated by his wife, Stacy, Carl was outnumbered by women at the table seven to one. Never one to cut anyone much slack, Rachel continued, "When Jill and I walked in and she saw you sitting here, she just looked at me and gave me this look, like [*gives a look of bewildered shock*]!"

"Oh, I know!" Carl admitted sheepishly.

"Coed is fun sometimes!" Stacy said, covering for her husband.

Raising her voice so that the men sitting at the bar with their backs to the round table could hear her, Rachel asked Carl, "It's a lot more fun than those guys just sitting at the bar, isn't it? Look at them over there; they aren't even laughing!"

Being one of those guys at the bar, I began to laugh as I swiveled in my seat to face the table. "Oh, I'm laughing, because I'm listening to you-all," I wisecracked.

As the members of the table burst out laughing, Rachel responded, "You've got better hearing than they do, though! They're old. Like Mitch—I bet he can't even hear us right now!"

Still laughing, I turned back to the bar in time to hear Stan whispering to Mitch. With both of them staring straight ahead as though they could not hear what was going on just behind them, Stan whispered, "You know, they're talking about you."

"Oh, I know. I hear them. I'm just ignoring them," Mitch grumbled just loud enough for Stan and me to hear.

Interactions like this between the women who sat at the round table and the men who sat at the bar every Thursday afternoon were common. The women teased the men for being boring, and the men complained the women were lushes who became rowdy whenever they drank beer.

"Those women are getting wild over there," Paul told Sam as they sat next to each other at the bar one afternoon. Both in their sixties, they regularly came into Foster's throughout the week.

"Wild?" Sam asked.

"They're getting loud!" Paul clarified.

"Oh, yeah, they are," Sam agreed, nodding his head vigorously.

"Every beer they have, their hearing goes down, and their voices go up. That never happens when we drink," Paul concluded sarcastically as the two started laughing.

On another occasion, Gary used an outburst of laughter from the women at the round table as an opportunity to start a conversation with me while we sat quietly facing the jackolope hanging on the wall behind the bar.[5]

Gary, who was in his fifties, lived near Sumner and came into the bar occasionally. Nudging me on the shoulder, he said, "I tell you what, you'd have to be dumber than shit to go over to that table right now. All those women over there." I began to laugh because I was not sure how to respond. Gary continued, "You say the wrong thing, and they'll whip your ass. All of 'em would get in on it too. Not just one of 'em. I was in the army for over twenty years, and I'll tell you what, I won't go over there."

Still not sure how to respond to Gary's prophecy, I kept laughing and just shrugged my shoulders.

Then he tried to goad me into approaching the table: "I'll tell you what, I'll get you a beer if you just go over there."

Wanting to avoid a scene but also playing along, I said, "Yeah, I don't think so. Beers aren't that expensive here."

Laughing, Gary exclaimed, "But it'd sure be entertaining!"

Having listened to our conversation, Darla interjected, "Yeah! That'd sure be entertaining!"

As often happened, the volume of the voices of the women at the round table facilitated an interaction between men at the bar who used a brief increase in volume as an opportunity to draw distinctions between men and women. Of course, the women at the round table were not always louder than the ambient noise of conversations in Foster's. And they certainly were not always louder than the men in the bar.[6] Nevertheless, both men and women actively played into the idea that the women at the round table really were having more fun than the men in the room. Even when the women were being particularly reserved, men drew attention to this and explained it away in order to portray men and women as two distinct kinds of people.

"That round table will get stirred up here real quick. You watch, they'll be like a bunch of old hens carrying on over there," Greg explained to me as we sat at the bar one afternoon while the women at the round table talked quietly among themselves. Greg had grown up in the area and regularly came into the bar. Tall, wiry, in his fifties, and with calloused hands the size of bear paws, he had a playfully antagonistic relationship with the women at the table that suited his sociable, somewhat rebellious personality.

This playful banter between the men who sat at the bar and the women who sat at the round table helps illuminate the significance of gender and gendered inequalities in Foster's and Sumner. Since the 1980s, scholars have conceptualized gender as something that people do. In other words, by perceiving and (inter)acting in particular ways we do masculinities and femininities. What we wear. How we interact with others. What we eat and drink. The jobs we work. Even what we do for fun. These are all influenced by historically contingent, culturally approved ways of being men and women. Further, feminist scholars have repeatedly stressed that men and women perceive and act, and are expected to perceive and act, in manners that facilitate and undermine the continued reproduction of inequalities between and among men and women.[7] How we do gender, in other words, is political because it is informed by and involved in the reproduction of inequalities between and among men and women.

How women at the round table and men at the bar were portrayed by their fellow patrons is especially significant then. Associating women with emotion and men with reason supports what feminist scholars refer to as "the ideology of separate spheres."[8] According to this ideology, women are assumed to belong in the domestic sphere of the home, where they can act as emotional caregivers. In contrast, men are assumed to belong in the public sphere, where they can be rational workers, businessmen, and politicians. Consequently, men are not expected to be good domestic caretakers because they are supposedly emotionally inept, and women are not expected to be qualified for the public sphere because they are supposedly irrational.

Feminist scholars argue that these divergent understandings of where men and women belong enables women's continued marginalization from political and economic power because framing women as irrational caretakers makes it easier to marginalize them in the public sphere or exclude them from it altogether.[9] Representing the women at the round table as out of control, or even dangerous, and the men at the bar as cool, calm, and collected was not just plain, simple joking around, then. It split women and men into camps that rested on the dichotomy between emotional women and rational men that encourages inequalities between men and women in the United States and beyond.

This division of men and women extended far beyond the front door of Foster's. From the most mundane interpersonal interactions to the very organization of the community itself, polarized understandings of men and women transformed how individuals arranged their lives and relationships with each other. The spatial organization of patrons at the bar, individuals' occupations and hobbies, arrangements of households, expectations of how individuals should participate in the reproduction of their community—it was all influenced by the understanding that women and men were two distinct kinds of beings. It was all informed by the understanding that men and women belonged in particular spaces associated with skills and roles that suited their gendered natures—men in the public sphere and women in the private sphere.

An exchange during a city council meeting is illustrative. The members of the council covered far more at their monthly meetings than just official city business. Seated around a small rectangular table in faded office chairs from the 1970s and 1980s, they gossiped and joked with each other in the cramped, wood-panel-lined room that served as city hall.

"Are we going to need a replacement for you once you have your baby?" Richard asked Elizabeth. A local businessman in his fifties, Richard was generally quiet during council meetings except when he wanted to stir the pot a little.

"No," Elizabeth responded curtly. Elizabeth was a college graduate in her thirties who took her council work seriously.

"Okay," Richard replied, as a mischievous grin spread across his face. "So this is how you're going to get your husband to look after the kid once a month then?"

As the members of the council laughed with Richard, Jan gestured to the women in the room: "There's plenty of babysitters here!" Jan, in her sixties, had lived in Sumner for thirty-plus years. Of average height and usually wearing a pair of jeans and cowboy boots, she was a fierce, savvy proponent for the community who undertook an extensive amount of unpaid civic work to sustain and improve Sumner.

As everyone in the room continued to laugh, Elizabeth said, in a tone of disbelief and with a look of shock, "He thinks—honest to God this is what he said—he said a guy at work told him that if the baby cries at night after a month that you just need to stop getting up to feed it!"

Over the outburst of laughter, Jan joked, "Yeah, I guess it wouldn't cry if you starved it and it became too weak to cry!"

"Yeah, and I'm supposed to leave a kid with him? Alone?" Elizabeth said, feigning incredulity to emphasize how incompetent of a caretaker her husband would be.

The men and women in the room were drawing direct attention to the significance of the ideology of separate spheres. Richard suggested that council meetings could be the one time that Elizabeth could get her husband to take care of their baby, but Elizabeth explicitly rejected this suggestion. Not because her husband would regularly be taking care of their baby anyway but because men were so incompetent at domestic duties that they could not be trusted, even for a brief period, to be left alone with a baby. And it was not just her husband who was likely to be a poor caretaker. This was a problem that characterized men more generally, because another man had provided him with bad advice on childcare. Jan's gesture toward the women in the room when she noted that there were "plenty of babysitters" only emphasized the significance of the ideology of separate spheres. Men and women were different, and it was best if they kept to their particular skill sets.

The ideology of separate spheres is closely linked with heterosexuality in this example and in the United States more generally.[10] According to the ideology of separate spheres, men and women are like salt and pepper—different but also complementary if they are in heterosexual families together.

Given the prevalence of the ideology of separate spheres in Sumner and in view of research finding that heterosexuality is integrally important to rural people and communities,[11] heterosexuality informed how individuals thought about themselves and arranged their lives. I saw people identify only as heterosexual, and it was generally accepted that people ought to be heterosexual. In addition to interactions that framed heterosexuality as normal, such as the city council exchange or when men indicated particular women were attractive, men regularly expressed homophobic beliefs that framed homosexuality as deviant and disgusting.

After Michael Sam, a former football player at the University of Missouri, came out as gay before the 2014 National Football League draft, several men were upset that their home state was now associated with a gay man. Some even implied I ought to be worried about my well-being because I worked at a university where there was a confirmed gay man. Then, when Sam kissed his boyfriend on national television after getting drafted, men said seeing the two men kiss made their "stomach turn" and their "skin crawl." With the close links between heterosexuality and masculinity in Sumner—and the United States—men constructed masculinities through these homophobic statements,[12] but they also insisted that heterosexuality was the norm in Sumner.

I do not suggest that no one in Sumner ever transgressed this gender dichotomy. Individuals, such as the women who were prominent members of the city council, undoubtedly violated the ideology of separate spheres. Nevertheless, men and women were still invested in its significance and carried out their lives according to the conception that men and women really were two distinct kinds of people who belonged in two distinct kinds of spaces characterized by particular, complementary roles and responsibilities. As when Rachel chided Carl and then his wife, Stacy, covered for him, when men and women transgressed the gender dichotomy underpinning their community, they often needed to implement strategies that allowed them to more effectively navigate the tensions that emerged from such transgressions. The ideology of separate spheres was more of an ideal than something that was actually achieved, but it was still exceptionally important to Sumner and its residents.

Contested Whiteness in a White Landscape

"Your dog is so cute!" Darla exclaimed from across the bar.

"Thank you," Clayton responded, beaming down at the dog sitting in his lap. An outgoing man in his fifties, Clayton often came into the bar to grab a beer and catch up with his friends.

"What kind of dog is she?" Mark asked across me, his voice gravelly from years of smoking Winstons. A retired heavy-equipment operator in his sixties, he regularly came into Foster's.

"A Westie," Clayton noted, using the shorthand for the small white terriers.

"She's pretty well behaved. How old is she?" I asked.

"She's fifteen. She's been in a lot of beer joints, that's for sure," Clayton explained. "Here, watch this." Turning his attention to his dog, he began to whisper, "Alice. Alice. Would you rather be dead or a n——?"[13]

Alice immediately lay down on her side, and Clayton began to cackle as he looked at me for approval.

Caught off guard, I managed a surprised "Uh" that must have conveyed that I did not find the racist joke funny, because Clayton promptly enrolled Alice in another joke.

"Okay, or this one," he said, turning to the dog and beginning to whisper again. "Alice. Alice. Get the money. Get the money."

This time Alice put her front paws on the bar and snatched the ones and fives sitting in front of him.

"Like I said, she's been in a lot of beer joints," Clayton concluded, clearly proud of Alice.

Clayton seemed to assume that Darla, Mark, and I would find his racist joke humorous. When I did not laugh, he was taken aback and told another joke to distract from the tension. Though Clayton's joke fell flat, it helps illuminate the racial dynamics of the bar.

Foster's was a white space.[14] I never saw a person of color in the bar, and whiteness informed how individuals thought of themselves, each other, and their community. Instead of comments on Foster's being a white space, or what whiteness was or its desirability, however, the importance of being white was conveyed through jokes and stories like Clayton's that displayed the stigmas associated with people of color. The importance and desirability of whiteness, in other words, was articulated through references to other races that portrayed them as deviant and inferior.[15]

The men at the bar commonly exhibited the desirability and importance of whiteness while talking about their trips to cities in the surrounding region such as Columbia and Kansas City.[16] Drawing on broader American cultural representations of cities as dark, exotic, dangerous places where crime is perpetrated by a black underclass,[17] the men regularly told stories about how they had escaped dangerous black men while in cities. By consistently associating people of color with urban places that were portrayed as violent dystopias, these narratives also implied rural contexts like Sumner were idyllic at least partially because they were white. They were ideal spaces, in other words, because people of color were absent.

While we sat at the bar one afternoon, Paul told Stan and me that he was trying to avoid going on vacation with his wife to a nearby city because he did not like how crowded and dangerous cities were. After I asked what he meant, Paul explained:

> Well, you'll be walking along, and you'll see somebody, and it's just like, whoa, what a fucking weirdo. Now, I don't have a problem with blacks. I grew up where there were some black people, you know? I learned you just have to talk to them, and don't be afraid. Well, I was in Kansas City for a wedding, and I had to stop and get gas, and we were there in the ghetto of Kansas City. Well, I pulled over and got out to pump my gas. There I am in my tuxedo, drunker than shit with the tail of my shirt untucked. In my nice car. Well, there were three or four black guys sitting there, and I couldn't figure out the pump. So I say, "Hey, man! Come over here, and give me a hand." One of them comes over, and he helps me pump my gas, and we start shooting the shit. That's what you gotta do; you just have to talk to people.

Paul began by noting that black people are not dangerous, but drawing on the sort of racial double talk that characterizes a supposedly postracial America,[18] he then implied he was in danger because he was in the presence of black men. According to Paul, he was able to make it out of the city and safely back to his rural, white home only because he used his street smarts.

Beyond interpersonal interactions that made much of the significance of race, whiteness infused Foster's in subtler ways. Scholars from several theoretical traditions have found that the physical arrangement of spaces encourages particular people within those spaces to be present and then act in particular ways while there.[19] The hunting décor that adorned the walls of the bar is notable in this respect because hunting is linked to the reproduction of racial differences and inequalities.[20]

What animals are hunted and how they are killed are particularly important marks of racial difference and status.[21] Hunting is predominately a white activity in the United States, but duck and goose hunting have especially close links to the accomplishment of whiteness.[22] The U.S. Fish and Wildlife Service estimates that 94 percent of hunters in the United States in 2011 were white and that at least 96 percent of those who hunted migratory birds were white.[23] In addition to being a homage to the significance of waterfowl hunting in the history of the community, then, all the allusions to waterfowl hunting that adorned the walls and shelves around the bar indicated that Foster's was a space that welcomed white people.

The significance of race, and whiteness specifically, was evident throughout the community. As in other predominantly white rural and (sub)urban settings across the United States,[24] whiteness informed how residents arranged their lives and community. It informed how individuals thought of themselves and each other, how they went about their daily lives, and even how they conceptualized and manipulated the surrounding landscape.

Being white was something to be proud of, whereas being disrespected was akin to having one's whiteness challenged. For example, as I stood behind two men in their twenties during a Wild Goose Festival, one of the men spotted a friend wearing a T-shirt advertising the company for which they all worked. After the first man pointed this out, they both noted they had not received new shirts. The first man then asked, "What are we? A bunch of n——s?" His equating being disrespected to being black, suggests that he believed being fully worthy of and getting respect was part of what it meant to be white.

The comment also alluded to how individuals policed the boundaries of what it meant to be properly white as well as who could claim the respect associated with this status. Even though everyone in Sumner was white, being granted the respect that went along with being white was not guaranteed. If someone was not being properly white, others would call them out and degrade them for it. Though I heard women talk about and reference race, men seemed far more concerned with policing the boundaries of who should and should not be granted the respect that came with being properly white.[25]

Scott, Lee, and Jerry, all in their forties, had grown up in the area, and I had gotten to know them during Swan Lake Sportsman's Club meetings.

As we stood around the bed of a truck outside Scott's garage, Scott looked at me with a smirk on his face and asked, "Do you need some money?"

Unsure what he was getting at, I took the bait. "Do I need money?"

Gesturing toward my faded, sweat-stained Kansas City Royals hat, he explained, "That hat's filthy!"

"Well that's what happens when you actually do work. Your hat gets dirty! That's why your-all's are so clean," I responded, gesturing at their pristine caps as I drew on the links between manliness and manual labor[26] to lay claim to a respectable masculinity.

Playing along with Scott, Lee asked, "Don't you know how to shape the bill?" Clarifying the racialized dimensions of hats while denigrating how I wore mine with little to no crown in the bill, he concluded, "Old flat-bill homie!"

I may have been wearing a hat like most other men in the community, but according to Scott and Lee, I was doing it wrong. My hat was too dirty and the bill was too flat. It was associated with being white trash, or what Rebecca Scott calls the "specter of failed whiteness,"[27] while simultaneously calling to mind the racial other against which whiteness was constructed in Sumner. They gave me a hard time about it in a manner that questioned my whiteness. Those fully white were worthy of respect, but if they were being not quite white, they were open to criticisms that clarified the boundaries of what it meant to be properly white.

Political-economic institutions also reproduce structurally advantageous positions for whites and support the reproduction of whiteness.[28] How whiteness informed and was reproduced in Sumner was no different. State institutions were centrally important to whiteness and its structural advantages. In fact, whiteness was an institutional project permeating the surrounding landscape.

First, the landscape had been transformed in the surrounding area through agricultural and conservation techniques developed and legitimated by European societies dominated by whites for the benefit of whites.[29] Second, individuals and groups had transformed the landscape in the past and present at least in part to facilitate the accomplishment of respectable, white identities. Neither point can be considered separate and apart from the political-economic institutions that informed how the forests, fields, and marshes in the surrounding area were transformed.

Aside from the Swan Lake refuge and some smaller areas managed by the Missouri Department of Conservation, the surrounding landscape was privately owned. If it was behind a levee or out of a floodplain, heavy machinery and consistent doses of fertilizers and pesticides were being used to grow corn, soybeans, or wheat. This industrialized system of agricultural production is largely ubiquitous in the United States, but it is a relatively new method of producing crops that is distinctly European.[30] Private ownership of property for capitalist agricultural production is a European development less than three hundred years old,[31] and state-corporate actors from Western states have purposefully pushed for the development of highly mechanized forms of agriculture worldwide over the last century.[32] Without state institutions nurturing its development through subsidies and regulations favorable to industrial agriculture, this capitalist system of farming would not exist.[33]

This system of agricultural production has also been institutionalized in a manner that funnels resources and opportunities to white individuals and households. Each year nearly all the farm subsidies distributed through price supports, loans, and insurance programs go to white landowners. And this is not just because white individuals own the majority of properties from which a majority of agricultural products stem.[34] There has been and very likely continues to be discrimination in how federal agriculture subsidies are distributed.[35] Regardless of the pervasiveness of interpersonal discrimination, though, this is an institutionalized system of resource redistribution that allows racialized accumulation of wealth and privilege because official agricultural programs and policies channel resources primarily to white households in the United States.[36] Accordingly, white families in Sumner receiving agricultural subsidies were part of a national, institutionalized system reproducing white privilege.

The refuge itself was even a testament to white ways of relating to landscapes that facilitated the reproduction of white advantages. Originally a conservation practice in the United States, designating areas as largely off limits to humans was developed and forwarded worldwide by Western states and nongovernmental organizations.[37] Emblematic of how this system of conservation is predicated on white ways of relating to landscapes, elite white Americans mobilized understandings of private property, progress, and nature, which all had their roots in over two hundred years of European philosophy, to remove indigenous peoples from what are now Yosemite and Yellowstone National Parks.[38] It can be easy to overlook the racialized dynamics of this conservation strategy because it is ubiquitous in the United States today, but it is explicitly associated with white colonialism in places where this model of conservation has been imposed by Western states.[39] Even in the United States it is associated with whiteness in some contexts. In northern New Mexico, for example, many Latinos and indigenous peoples associate the management of federal forests with racial/ethnic exclusion and inequality.[40]

Since its inception the Swan Lake refuge has been an institutional project that aids white individuals and households in accessing and accumulating both exchange and use value. The white men in Company 1727 of the Civilian Conservation Corps dramatically transformed the refuge landscape from 1937 to 1942. This was undoubtedly hard, labor-intensive work, but it was also valuable work during the Depression era. The racial composition of Swan Lake staff did not change over the years. As of this writing, only white individuals have held full-time staff positions at the refuge. Further, the overwhelming majority of visitors to the refuge were white. Countless white faces are in the pictures of those enjoying the refuge that are included in annual refuge reports dating to the 1930s, but people of color are almost completely absent from these photos. During my twenty months of fieldwork at Swan Lake, I saw a person of color using the refuge on only four separate occasions.[41]

Swan Lake also contributed to the financial well-being of the white individuals and families living near the refuge. The goose hunting heyday significantly increased land prices and provided valuable sources of revenue to local residents. Even after the geese stopped coming, land adjacent to the refuge that was suitable for duck hunting continued to have inflated values because the refuge continued to draw ducks and duck hunters. In addition to being an institutional project founded on white ways of relating to landscapes, the refuge facilitated the accruement of opportunities and resources by whites.

In sum, the Swan Lake refuge and the fields of beans, corn, and wheat surrounding it were testaments to white ways of relating to landscapes that have been institutionalized over the previous centuries in ways that enhanced white individuals' and households' access to resources and opportunities. Interpersonal dynamics of whiteness in the community were somewhat obvious, but institutionalized projects of whiteness that reproduced white privileges were so ubiquitous they were nearly invisible. Whiteness was the neat rows of corn and beans that covered the surrounding fields. It was the barbed wire strung from the metal and wooden fence posts that separated privately owned parcels of land. It could even be found sitting behind the refuge boundary.

Class, Status, and Thinking Meritocracy

For the 2014 holiday season, a small Christmas tree was placed in the corner of Foster's beside the round table where Rachel, Jill, Stacy, and their friends sat each Thursday afternoon. Although an unassuming seasonal addition, the tree was emblematic of how Foster's was a working-class space. Instead of decorating the tree with more traditional lights and ornaments, crumpled cans of Miller Lite, Bud, Milwaukee's Best, and Busch Light were shoved onto the ends of the branches. These beer brands were a testament to the working-class tastes of those who drank at the bar,[42] and getting things done in a no-frills manner is part of what it means to be working class.[43] The cans did not bestow middle-to-upper-class distinction, but they still gave the tree some color and flair.

Who came into Foster's and when they did also indicated its class dynamics.[44] The retirees who filled the bar during the afternoon were primarily former lunch ladies and delivery drivers, carpenters and secretaries, bartenders and mechanics. Each evening what Mitch called "the after-work crew" trickled into the bar. Composed of women who worked in convenience stores or food services and men who worked on construction crews or assembly lines, the after-work crew had as many in working-class occupations as the retirees who filled the space during the afternoons.

Like Sumner more generally though, while Foster's had the trappings of a working-class space, it had class differences and inequalities linked to broader American processes of rural deindustrialization and agricultural concentration. Many who came in and out of Foster's labored in working-class occupations, but others who were upper class or were in poverty by most definitions also came in and out of the bar. And while patrons never actually said the word "class," they were mostly well attuned to where people fell within the class hierarchy in their community.

Kip made this apparent while we were talking at the bar one evening. In his forties, he had grown up in Sumner and was now working in a factory in a nearby town. Pointing to particular men in the bar, he explained that they were farmers who worked thousands of acres of land. It was obvious he had a considerable degree of admiration for them and thought of them as big shots in the community. Pointing to one man, Kip said, "See Paxton, there? He bought a new combine last year. Wrote a check for it. Can you imagine that—$350,000 in the bank? That's a lot of money!" Such a purchase was unimaginable to Kip because he worked a job for close to minimum wage, but he was well aware of those in the community who had been able to accumulate wealth through agricultural production.[45]

Kip was not the only one willing to draw my attention to these class differences. On numerous occasions, others indirectly or even directly noted the different degrees of income and wealth possessed by individuals and families in the community. Importantly though, residents of Sumner considered class differences and belonging to be determined by far more than just income and wealth.

Community members tended to consider class to be something that was determined by habitual behaviors: how people talked, what they wore, what they drove, what they ate, what they drank, the music they listened to, and what they did for fun. Consequently, class groups were often conflated with what Max Weber called "status groups," or groups whose membership is predicated on particular lifestyles.[46] While I acknowledge that individuals in Sumner usually considered class and status groups to be one and the same, I choose to use the language of class throughout this book because "status is too benign."[47] By this I mean that using status instead of class would distract from the significant ways that positions within institutionalized labor markets are crucially important to peoples' lives, including the status groups they can belong to by dressing, eating, and recreating in particular ways.[48]

How residents of Sumner understood class through the preparation and consumption of wild game is illustrative.[49] It is not surprising that individuals in a rural Missouri community with a storied history associated with hunting ate animals such as squirrels, ducks, and deer. What is significant is how they drew sharp class distinctions between community members on the basis of their consumption patterns of these animals. Being unable or unwilling to prepare and consume wild game was associated with being upper class. Preparing and consuming species understood as undesirable, such as particular duck species and fish like gar, marked one as being lower class. And preparing and consuming species deemed desirable, such as deer and catfish, distinguished one as being somewhere in the middle of these two poles.[50]

Community members mostly agreed that paying someone to butcher your ducks or being unwilling to eat your ducks was something upper-class individuals did. While Greg, Mitch, and I were sitting at the bar on a humid summer afternoon, Greg made this point after telling us about how he had recently shot and cooked some squirrels.

"I made squirrel gravy with the young ones, and the older ones I put into the crock pot. Squirrel gravy is a country boy's dream. Some women won't eat them, say they're rodents or whatever, but they're good. Anyone that's grown up in the country will tell you that. A lot of people just don't like wild game, but I think it's good."

Greg and Mitch then looked to me to hear my thoughts on the matter, likely curious to see where I would locate myself in the gendered country-city dichotomy Greg had constructed.

"I mean, there's things I'd rather eat than a duck, but they aren't bad by any means," I said, honestly, but also attuned to the significance of my answer.

Satisfied, Greg injected class into the discussion. "Those guys that hunt out at Habitat Flats won't eat them. They're mainly corporate, though. They come in to shoot ducks, and they just leave them at the lodge. I'll pick them up, and I'll eat 'em. They aren't going to cook wild game."

Like Greg's comments, many conversations about the customers of Habitat Flats concerned how they regularly left their ducks to be butchered and given away to local residents. A commercial hunting lodge that catered to high-end clients from out of state, Habitat Flats was located just east of Sumner. Residents tended to think of its clients as being from cities, so it was often impossible to disentangle whether butchering and eating your ducks was an indication of class or rurality. Nevertheless, though it is impossible to pull apart the importance of class, gender, and rurality in Greg's account, his statement that these were "corporate" men alluded to the class dimensions of preparing and consuming ducks. It evoked the image of a city dweller, but it was not just a statement about rural and urban men. It also evoked the image of a man in a suit in an office. These were not blue-collar city men who were not eating their ducks. They were upper-class men who came to Sumner, shot their ducks, and then returned to their suits and ties without butchering and consuming what they had killed.

Jay more directly addressed the classed dynamics of picking and consuming ducks while we talked outside the community general store one morning. Quiet and well respected throughout the community for his seemingly inexhaustible work ethic, Jay was his sixties and had lived in the area most of his life. I had gotten to know him from the bar.

"Sure was a lot of shooting from Habitat Flats and Broxton this morning," Jay noted, referring to a wealthy business owner who lived in the area and hunted next to the refuge.

"Is Broxton hunting that right now? I hadn't seen any decoys out there this year. I know last year he left like five Mojos on the stakes until March," I said. Mojos are a duck decoy with motorized, spinning wings that Mojo Outdoors was the first company to mass produce. Costing from $75 to $200 apiece, they are placed on metal stakes above the water.

"Broxton didn't do that! He doesn't do nothin'! He hires someone to do all the work for him. He just hunts," Jay corrected me. "I guess he was looking for someone to pick his ducks this year. There's no way I'd pick ducks for that asshole."

In this case there was no ambiguity as to whether rurality or class were at stake if someone did not butcher their ducks. Broxton was a rural man, but according to Jay, Broxton's desire to have someone else pick his ducks was just another instance in which he avoided the labors of duck hunting because he was upper class.

Additional divisions were made between those who butchered and consumed ducks. Although species such as mallard, pintail, teal, and wood duck were generally considered good to eat, men often claimed that other kinds of ducks, such as spoonbills and mergansers, tasted so bad that they were not fit for consumption. Class distinctions were made on the grounds of whether someone shot and ate these "shit" or "trash" ducks.

"You like the taste of duck?" I asked George while we were sitting at the bar one afternoon.

"Oh, yeah," George responded, nodding his head. In his forties, he worked as a heavy-equipment operator and regularly came into the bar.

"Now, I've heard all kinds of people tell me mallards are the best, but I swear I just can't tell the difference between them," I said.

"Oh man, no!" George disagreed, shaking his and laughing with disbelief. "Mallards, wood ducks, teal, they taste completely different than some of those other ones."

Chuckling, I doubled down, "I'm telling you, I can't taste any difference between a mallard and a spoony."

"No way!" George responded in disbelief, setting his beer down and looking at me as though I had questioned the word of God. "They're completely different. They don't—they don't taste the same. They just don't."

Whether it is possible to objectively determine which ducks taste better than others is somewhat beside the point. What is important is that some in Sumner declared that particular ducks tasted better than others, and as Pierre Bourdieu and Sidney Mintz have found, tastes are not just biological expressions of innate desires for particular foods that naturally taste better.[51] Food preferences are taught and learned in ways that both reflect class distinctions and allow individuals to make them. What a person prefers to eat, in other words, is political and involved in the reproduction of a multitude of meanings and inequalities.[52] The relative rankings of ducks such as mallards and spoonbills was important because it was an embodied effect of years of eating and being taught to prefer particular ducks invested with class meanings and stigmas. By eating ducks deemed desirable, one could position him- or herself as belonging to a respectable class.

Importantly, and related to how class involves individual actions set in relation to institutions, the preparation and consumption of wild game and fish are invested so strongly with classed meanings at least partially because their consumption is closely linked to a person's ability to eat other things.[53] Those in the upper class can afford to kill and not consume, but others do not have this luxury. While those who fall somewhere in the middle can afford to distinguish good from bad game, those with comparatively few resources do not necessarily have the luxury to avoid consuming stigmatized animals such as mergansers or gar. Thus, the treatment and consumption of wild game is not just about individual choices made to belong to particular groups. Class, as a labor market position associated with resources and opportunities, constrained and enabled how individuals understood and consumed wild game.

Sumner residents acknowledged that there were different class groups in their community and acted in accordance with their perception of them. Yet there was also general agreement that the distribution of resources and opportunities through labor markets did not determine what class someone belonged to. Such understandings, however, were not due to an unawareness of institutionalized processes that influenced the distribution of resources and opportunities. Many readily acknowledged that others had much different opportunities because of how they were positioned in labor markets. Nevertheless, they would contend that these discrepancies did not ultimately determine class. Instead, during my interviews with them and their everyday conversations, residents drew on broader American discourses concerning individualism and meritocracy to state that individuals' work ethics best explained class inequalities.[54] Consequently, class was talked about in ways that acknowledged how political-economic processes influenced individuals' opportunities, but residents mostly indicated that work ethic best explained economic success.

Residents consistently acknowledged the significance of broader political-economic processes for peoples' opportunities through comments about the decline of rural communities such as Sumner. Again and again, when I asked what they thought the community's biggest challenge was they said it was "dying," "fading away," or "turning to dust" because of the limited number of job prospects for present and future generations. This is a point that also came up during casual conversations between local residents.

"Guess what my daughter did today?" Gary hollered down the bar to Joe, in his fifties and wearing his customary faded overalls.

Joe responded, "I don't know. What?"

"She went to Kansas City and joined the army. That little shit joined the army," Gary crowed, clearly proud of his daughter.

"Nothing wrong with that," Joe noted.

"Hell no," Gary emphatically replied.

"How old is she?" I asked.

"Eighteen. She tested so high they'll let her do whatever she wanted," he added.

"At least that'll get her outta here," Joe replied.

"Yeah, there's nothing around here for her, that's for sure," Gary agreed.

Despite the sense that opportunities were lacking in Sumner, residents still argued that if someone was in poverty or using a social welfare program, it was because of a personal fault. And this was not a case in which those acknowledging declining job prospects were different from those who focused on individualistic explanations for poverty. The same residents who recognized the institutional dynamics of class often gave explanations for class differences and inequalities that were based on individuals' work ethic.

Mitch provides a telling example here. As I sat with him and Stan at the bar one afternoon, I asked what they thought the biggest challenges were to Sumner. Instead of answering my question, they explicitly rejected the notion that the community could be sustained.

"Well, as you can see, it's not [sustainable]," Mitch said.

"Yeah, sustaining itself? It's not," Stan concluded, emphasizing his point by mimicking the sound of an airplane crashing into the ground as he smacked his hand on the bar.

Nevertheless, Mitch argued that class inequalities stemmed from differences in individuals' work ethics and not the broader political-economic processes that contributed to depopulation in communities like Sumner. Another evening, when a man returned to his table after ordering a beer at the bar, Mitch said to me, "Always thought he was a loudmouth. His mom and dad worked their asses off their whole lives. They had seven kids, and besides one, they're all on disability. Not a fuckin' thing wrong with any of 'em. They're just fuckin' lazy."

Greg made remarkably similar comments during our interview. He had a stark awareness that broader, institutionalized political-economic processes affected rural communities and the people living in them. Nevertheless, he related a story about a set of men in the community who were supposedly cheating the welfare system to show that individuals were in poverty because they did not work hard enough.

I asked what he thought the community's biggest challenge was, and he said, "We're not going forward. Best-case scenario is just hanging in there. The community's made up of three societies anymore around this part of the country. You have the farmers, and their land has increased four times in the last few years, so they've become very wealthy. Won't tell you that, but they are very wealthy. And then you have the working class that drive to town and make just enough to get along. Then you have the disability, which has become the biggest thing we got. All small towns are the same way. If the people aren't working, they're either on disability or they're trying to get it because if you get workman's comp, well, you gotta fight [for] it. You get disability? Well, you're set. It's unbelievable."

"I mean, I dunno, I guess people just do what they gotta do," I responded, unsure how to follow up on Greg's comments.

Greg did not agree this was a viable survival strategy that stemmed from structural conditions, however. According to him, being poor and using welfare programs was probably a symptom of laziness. "Well, a lot of them could go to work if they wanted to," he said, reiterating that "a lot of them could work if they wanted to." To clarify and support his thoughts on the matter, he continued, "There's a lot that deserve what they get, but there's a heck of a lot of people that don't. I know two guys here that're on disability, but they still run big, long hoop nets and raise hundreds of pounds of fish. They've been on disability for years. Twenty years. And there's plenty of that." Because catching fish with hoop nets and raising them out of the water is physically demanding work, Greg was emphasizing that the men should not be receiving disability benefits.

Greg acknowledged that fluctuations in land prices had added to farmers' wealth and that depopulation as well as economic precarity often characterized rural communities in the region. Like Mitch, he was adamant that having to depend on disability to make ends meet was a personal fault, however. Even though Greg and others in the community were aware that broad political-economic processes such as agricultural concentration and rural deindustrialization made it harder for people to make a living, they still framed class in ways that detached class inequalities from these broader political-economic processes. Being in poverty or using disability were generally considered personal troubles that stemmed from an inadequate work ethic and not social issues that stemmed from the relation of individuals and households to historically contingent, structural processes.[55]

Good Times and Good People: Intersectional Delineations of Worth in a Rural Town

"Hey, I gotta get out of here pretty quick. I'm headed down to the bar," I said to a man who lived in the community as we talked outside his house one afternoon.

"The bar!" he exclaimed.

"Yeah, what's up?" I asked, somewhat surprised by his reaction.

"Have you ever *been* to the bar in Sumner?" he asked.

Beginning to laugh, I responded, "Yeah, I've been going up there the past couple of months. They have a fish fry on Thursdays. There's lots of people in there to talk to."

"Oh," he responded, somewhat taken aback. In a disapproving tone and with his gaze cast to the ground, he continued, "Well, that should be interesting."

Chuckling, I asked, "What's the big deal?"

"Oh, nothing. You're going to turn into one of those bar people up there," he concluded.

Although many in the community emphasized the good times that could be found at the bar, like this man, some saw Foster's as a sort of seedy place frequented by less-than-morally-upstanding individuals. Some community members even actively avoided going into Foster's because they did not like its reputation or the thought of being associated with it. A particularly memorable case was a woman who had lived in Sumner for over sixty years. During our interview, I asked if she thought there were any differences between the people who did and did not frequent the bar. "Well, I wouldn't know. I've never been in it, and neither have any of my children. I don't plan on ever going, either," she informed me. Although she had lived in the community for decades and clearly had an opinion on Foster's, her disgust for the bar and the people who frequented it—and the associated moral implications—was so strong that she claimed to know nothing about the bar. She even emphasized that her children would not know anything about Foster's, because she had raised them to be better than that.

Underlying such aversions to Foster's were preoccupations with being considered a good, morally upright person worthy of respect. By going to the bar, it was assumed, this status was put in jeopardy. Whether one is considered worthy of respect by peers is important regardless of residential context, but it is particularly important in small communities such as Sumner where there are limited resources outside of friendship and kin networks.[56] Because of the relatively scarce amount of public and private resources in rural communities, it is especially important to be respected by the relatively small number of community members who act as gatekeepers to the opportunities and resources that do exist.[57]

Whether community members considered someone to be a good person worthy of respect was generally far more complex than just whether they frequented the bar. Some who frequented Foster's were widely respected and thought of as upstanding citizens, and some who never set foot in the place were regarded as less-than-model members of the community. As I spent time in Sumner, I came to realize that what it meant to be a good person, what it meant to be a member of the community who was worthy of respect, was largely contingent on intersections of class, race, and gender that incorporated understandings of what it meant to be a proper rural person.[58] By this I mean two things. First, intersecting meanings associated with class, race, gender, and rurality informed how individuals understood what it meant to be a good person. Second, depending on one's class, race, and gender, there were particular criteria for achieving a respectable status as a good rural person.

These points correspond to feminist scholarship on intersectionality from the 1980s onward finding that racialized, classed, and gendered differences and inequalities never operate in isolation.[59] They overlap and intersect, which means individuals' lives and communities are never informed by just race, gender, or class. These differences and inequalities exist, matter, and are experienced simultaneously, and each is transformed by its links with the others. Men and women do not have race and class in addition to gender. How one goes about being a man or woman is fundamentally different for men and women of different races and classes. Gender, race, and class reciprocally affect each other in ways that alter how one goes about being a woman or man and the resources and opportunities a person can expect to access because he or she is a man or woman with a particular race and class. This is why scholars advocating intersectional analyses have eschewed additive approaches to considering multiple aspects of difference and inequality.[60] One is not white and a man, for instance; one is a white man because race and gender intersect to influence the experiences, resources, and opportunities white men are able to access throughout their lives. Both whiteness and masculinity are transformed through their convergence. In this and other cases, dimensions of difference and inequality are transformed through their intersections.

Complicating the significance of intersectionality is how intersections of gender, race, and class are often grafted onto perceived divisions between rural and urban people and places. Because rural and urban communities are often understood to be distinctly different kinds of places, individuals in rural communities must negotiate expectations regarding how they ought perceive and act like a proper rural person.[61] Put another way, meanings associated with rurality are integrally important to how rural individuals go about their lives and arrange their communities. Combined with intersectionality, individuals are not only expected to behave in particular ways because of their race, class, and gender but also held to particular standards because of their rurality. A white man in Sumner, for example, was not expected to behave only as a white man. He was expected to act as a white, *rural* man, and he was judged accordingly if he did not.[62]

Take Edwin. In his forties, he had a reputation in the community for being lazy, and he was regularly harangued inside and outside the bar because of it.

While Edwin was sitting down the bar from me one evening, Judd, a young man in his twenties, walked up and started harassing him. "Are you ever going to mow your damn yard, Edwin?" Judd's two friends looked on, snickering.

"I'll mow it when it needs it," Edwin replied, swiveling in his chair to face his tormentors.

"When it *needs* it?! Hell, are you going to let it get ten feet tall before it *needs* it?" Judd asked.

As Judd's two buddies started laughing, Edwin shrugged his shoulders and held his hands up without saying a word.

Not satisfied, Judd kept on: "You know, I think I'm just going to take care of that yard for you. I'm going to go down there at night and just spray it with Roundup. That way you won't have to worry about mowing it ever again. It'll be real nice and short."

Edwin shrugged his shoulders again, and this time Judd let it be. Waving his friends along, they moved down the bar.

This exchange highlights how class, race, gender, and rurality intersected to inform what it meant to be a good person worthy of respect in Sumner. Numerous scholars have noted that yard upkeep, and the control of vegetation more generally,[63] is invested with meanings associated with class, because having a tidy yard is associated with the work required to make it orderly.[64] As much as understandings of lawns are informed by class, they are also infused with meanings associated with race, gender, and rurality. A private residence with an orderly yard is widely considered a mark of proper whiteness in the United States.[65] Further, manipulating landscapes with machinery is centrally important to the accomplishment of masculinities in rural contexts in the United States.[66] Accordingly, Edwin violated assumptions regarding how a properly raced and classed rural man living in Sumner ought to behave because he was unwilling or unable to mow the vegetation in his yard.

That Carol and Mary Anne were widely respected throughout the community was equally indicative of the intersectional dynamics underlying who was considered a good person worthy of respect in Sumner. On numerous occasions, others indicated their high regard for the two women. Both in their seventies and retirees from working-class occupations, each was on the board of numerous organizations such as the park board and on the city council.

Jan and Fred, a married couple, explained this to me at the end of our interview after I asked if they would suggest other community members to interview. Like Jan, Fred was in his sixties and had lived in Sumner for over thirty years.

"Carol and Mary Anne were born and raised here. Lived here all their lives. If they're not there, by golly, it doesn't get done," Jan said. "They're involved in almost every organization, and they're—to me, I kind of look at them as kind of the matriarchs . . . as the core. . . . When somebody dies, we do some fabulous dinners. We'll have a great dinner for the family, . . . feed[ing] anywhere from 50 to 150 people, and they're the ones who make the phone calls. They're the ones that ask for the dinner. They're the ones that get the help. They do the cooking. . . . They go up there and cut up thirty chickens. Cut 'em up individually. I couldn't cut a chicken up if . . . somebody put a knife to my throat and said cut a chicken up. I'd go, 'Just shoot me now!' because it's over. They work their butts off. They've been on city council."

"Yeah, they were there when I was on it when we first got married," Fred said.

"They're good, hardworking people in the community," Jan concluded.

Although neither Mary Anne nor Carol had marks of wealth such as a large farm or a new house or car, both were considered good people and worthy of respect because of the countless hours they worked to reproduce their community. Being respected for this kind of work was not just about class and understandings of work ethic, however. It was also informed by intersections of gender and rurality. In a paradoxical twist of the ideology of separate spheres, and as I explore in greater detail in Chapter 3, women are often expected to do the bulk of the behind-the-scenes work needed to reproduce rural communities.[67] Accordingly, respect for these women was based on intersecting understandings of class, gender, and rurality. Carol and Mary Anne were considered respectable members of Sumner because they were hardworking rural women who cared for their community.

Community members' perceptions of Edwin, Carol, and Mary Anne resulted from residents' understandings of what it meant to be a good person worthy of respect and the intersecting meanings associated with class, gender, race, and rurality behind those understandings. Individuals had to fulfill particularized standards to be considered respectable depending on their own intersectional identities. Everyone was expected to be a good white, rural person, but as I illustrate in greater detail in following chapters, men and women who belonged to different classes were held to different standards that delineated how to be upstanding members of Sumner.

Conclusion: A Small but Complicated Community

Sumner was small, but it was neither simple nor homogeneous. Whiteness informed how individuals thought of themselves and manipulated the surrounding landscape, and the community was complicated by gender and class inequalities infused by the particularities of Sumner and by institutional processes operating at the regional, national, and global scales. This contradicts idealized representations of rural communities as homogeneous, harmonious, and isolated, but idealized understandings of rurality were still important to the residents of Sumner. They regularly strived to be good rural people, and they held other community members accountable to standards according to understandings of what it meant to be a good rural person.[68]

As I explore adaptations in greater detail in the subsequent chapters, we see that intersections of race, class, gender, and rurality informed how individuals tried to reorganize and sustain their culture and community in response to shifts in goose migration patterns. Recent analyses find that individuals in rural contexts are constantly reworking their lives and communities amid convoluted interplays of the meanings associated with rural people and places and the material conditions in such communities. Corresponding with this, political-economic institutions, the material landscape, and plants and nonhuman animals also informed how culture and community were being reworked in Sumner.[69] Individuals and groups were navigating convoluted entanglements of meanings associated with rurality, numerous institutions, and a range of nonhumans as they worked to reorganize and sustain their lives in response to the absence of geese.

An Intersectional Transition to Duck Hunting, a Degraded Sense of Community

A Community Still Defined by Waterfowl Hunting

In his twenties and known for having a good time, Petey had grown up in Sumner and worked a construction job. On a muggy Friday night in August, he came into Foster's Sportsman Inn with a goose call he had recently purchased.[1] At least ten men in the bar blew the call while Petey showed it off, including me and a man from Illinois who was in town working on a new hunting blind for Habitat Flats.

"It sounds too high to me," one of the local men grumbled after blowing it.

"No way! It sounds just how it ought to," Petey disagreed, snatching the call from him and giving it another go.

Once he was done, another one of the men asked, "Do you want to learn how to call? I'll teach ya if you want to."

"You wanna get it fired up? We'll get it fired up in here if you want!" Petey responded, letting loose on the call again.

Once he was done, Elizabeth hollered from a table in the back of the bar, "Don't start that stuff in August!" Referring to her husband seated beside her, she continued, "I tell him you can't start blowing those things until at least September!"

While the men in the bar laughed and continued to give Petey a hard time about his new call, the man from Illinois went to his truck to retrieve a duck call, and to Elizabeth's chagrin, the men in the bar proceeded to put on a display with it. All seasoned duck hunters, they easily made the call emit the notes and cadences of ducks. Because they did not know the man from Illinois as well as they did Petey, however, and because the call was not a new purchase, instead of talking trash, they talked about the intricacies of calling.

"A lot of guys like those loud calls, but I think you have to tone it down. [Ducks] don't like that loud stuff. Maybe if you're hunting open water, but otherwise I like something that you can really tone it down with," the man from Illinois explained.

"Have you ever heard of Richard Aniston?" Petey asked, referring to a man from Saint Louis who was known for making and tuning calls. "His calls sound awesome, but they freeze up almost instantly. I mean, it doesn't take anything to freeze them up. Especially when it starts getting a little cold," he explained, referring to how the reeds in some duck calls tend to stick together when they get wet and it is cold outside.

"You know what I do? I blow the spit out of my call every time after I blow it. I just turn it around and blow it out. I think it helps a lot," the man from Illinois explained.

Petey emphatically agreed, "Oh yeah! Some guys, they don't think they spit in there, but I don't care if you just give it one quick blow, there will be spit in there. You always get spit in them."

Later that night the man from Illinois exclaimed to anyone who would listen, "Beer drinking and duck calling. I don't think I've ever been in a place like this. It just doesn't get any better!"

Even for a newcomer to the community who had no interest in studying the links between the community and goose hunting, it was readily apparent waterfowl hunting was significant to Sumner and its residents. Besides the frequent conversations about duck hunting that took place inside Foster's, "H.Q. Wild Goose Capital of the World" was painted in white block letters across the outside of the bar, its plate glass window was adorned with ducks and geese, and the bench sitting by the front door had a resting goose for its back. Indicators of the importance of waterfowl hunting to the past and present of Sumner were also scattered throughout the community. Private residences had waterfowl prints as well as stuffed ducks and geese hanging from the walls. Driveways around town were filled with duck hunting boats and trucks adorned with waterfowl decals. Duck and goose decoys were also popular yard decorations, and some houses were still adorned with address plaques in the shape of a flying goose that were distributed in the early 1970s as part of a community betterment project. The giant goose in the middle of the town park was also hard to miss.

As apparent as these ties to waterfowl hunting were, equally as apparent was a shift that had occurred in the type of waterfowl hunting that was especially significant to the community. Sumner was organized around goose hunting from the late 1940s until the early 1990s, but there had been a transition toward emphasizing duck hunting as an activity around which the community was organized.

The landscape around Sumner readily attested to this transformation. Soybean and corn fields were pocked with goose hunting blinds now overgrown with weeds, and intersections in the area were still adorned with faded signs advertising businesses that had catered to goose hunters. Yet mixed with these vestiges of the past were indications of adaptation. Many of the agricultural fields adjacent to the refuge had been converted to duck hunting spots. Pancake flat and surrounded on all sides by small levees so that they could be flooded in the fall to attract ducks, these fields were easy to identify even before they had been flooded. The town's welcome signs also registered the shift from goose to duck hunting. While the older sign on the west side of Sumner featured Canada geese, four mallards landing into a marsh were on the much newer sign on the east side of town.

Those living, working, and hunting around Sumner also registered this shift. Without question, individuals were well aware of the change in goose migration patterns as well as the increased significance of duck hunting for their community. I regularly heard conversations lamenting the absence of geese, yet conversations about duck hunting were just as common. Describing Sumner over the 100.7 KMZU radio airwaves during the 2015 Wild Goose Festival, Richard Aniston said, "This is duck country. There's a lot of duck and goose hunters around here, so if you like the outdoors this is the place to be." Calling Sumner "duck country" would have been unthinkable just twenty-five years earlier when the community was still considered one of the better places in the country to hunt Canada geese, but by 2015 this was no longer the case.

As important as what people were saying about this transformation is what they were doing. The refuge provides some telling figures: 11,581 people hunted geese on the refuge in 1979, and an additional 9,952 were sent "sorry cards" because they had not been selected for a spot to hunt.[2] By the time I began fieldwork, hardly anyone goose hunted on the refuge. Only eighteen people tried hunting geese on the Swan Lake refuge in 2013, and the number rose to just twenty-eight in 2014. No one hunted ducks on the refuge while I was conducting fieldwork because it was illegal to do so, but the refuge perimeter was ringed with duck hunting blinds. During the legally prescribed duck hunting season from late October through December, volleys of shotgun blasts repeatedly shattered the quiet of mornings whenever hunters managed to lure ducks within shooting range.

It may seem that a shift from emphasizing one kind of waterfowl hunting to another is a natural or easy transformation with little significance, and men in the community often framed the transformation in this manner. They told me duck hunting was "just something you do," they were "born to duck hunt," or duck hunting was "in their blood." In this chapter, however, I problematize the seeming inevitability of the shift from goose to duck hunting.

Instead of being an inevitable process of adaptation, this was an adaptive process dependent on dramatic landscape transformations to accommodate ducks. In many cases, these transformations were even paid for by U.S. taxpayers. Desires to enable the continued achievement of masculinities associated with whiteness, heterosexuality, reputable classes, and rurality also informed this transition.[3] Put simply, the shift to duck hunting was contingent on a tangle of (non)human beings and things, federal institutions, and attempts to achieve masculinities considered respectable. This transformation also helped undermine the strength of social ties between people in Sumner. Instead of being inevitable or insignificant, this was an entangled process of adaptation that facilitated the rearrangement of the community.

Exploring how a mash of (non)humans, institutions, and rural masculinities complicated by race, sexuality, and class informed the rearrangement of Sumner is particularly significant because relatively little attention has been granted to the intersecting inequalities behind reconstructing and sustaining communities in response to climate change.[4] With few exceptions,[5] researchers have tended to focus on a particular dimension of inequality such as class or gender.[6] These contributions are important, but I argue it is necessary to consider how intersecting inequalities inform and are informed by responses to climate change.[7] As I detail in Chapter 1, inequalities pertaining to race, class, gender, and other forms of difference intersect to simultaneously affect how individuals think of themselves, go about their lives, and arrange their communities.

Over the next two chapters, I discuss two primary advantages to using an intersectional approach to inequalities when considering the reorganization of cultures and communities in response to climate change. First, we can better consider how the messy ambivalences and complexities of intersecting inequalities influence processes of adaptation. Second, we can also better consider the consequences of adaptations for particular demographic groups such as men and women *as well as* for differentially situated members within those groups such as men and women with different classes.[8] In sum, we can better understand how inequalities inform and are informed by efforts to reorganize communities by approaching adaptations with an eye toward several intersecting inequalities.

An Intersectional Transition to Duck Hunting

Before exploring the significance of masculinities complicated by rurality, race, sexuality, and class, I consider the divergent landscape preferences of Canada geese and ducks. These differences were integrally important to how the shift from goose to duck hunting had taken place. And subsequently, how the community was being rearranged because of this shift. Canada geese generally prefer agricultural landscapes for foraging during the fall and winter. The extensive tracts of land around the refuge that were already being used to grow corn, soybeans, and wheat provided effective places to hunt geese during the goose hunting heyday. Though some types of ducks will feed in dry agricultural fields, they tend to prefer landscapes with water. As a result, agricultural ground both on and off the refuge was being transformed to make it more suitable for the migrating ducks that still came through the area.

On the refuge, 450 acres that were being farmed when goose numbers were high had been transformed into wetlands by 2013, and an additional 500 acres were slated to be converted to wetlands through a $1 million grant from the federal North American Wetlands Conservation Act program. Beyond providing suitable duck habitat, the U.S. Fish and Wildlife Service (USFWS) supported such changes at the refuge because, in comparison to fields planted annually with soybeans or corn, wetlands increased biodiversity while decreasing fertilizer and pesticide use.

Off the refuge, landowners were also transforming agricultural fields to make them more suitable for ducks. Don explained this process to me when I formally interviewed him. He had lived and hunted near Sumner his whole life, and we had gotten to know each other through the Friends of Swan Lake, a civic group of local residents who partnered with the USFWS to promote public uses of the refuge. While driving us in his green Polaris Ranger along a levee on his farm, he said, "I've been hunting here since I was six. Dad was part of four guys that had [this area] as a goose hunting camp. I'm fifty-nine, so that tells you how long I've been hunting here."

"Was it always wetlands like this?" I asked.

"No, it was just dry ag fields when the geese were here. We had six blinds back here. That's one of the old blinds right there," Don said, pointing to the top of an old goose hunting blind whose top now stuck up out of a shallow pond. "We manage it completely different for ducks compared to geese. All this here, we don't hunt it. We use it all as a refuge. The only spot we hunt is back here. You'll be able to see it here in a minute," Don concluded, punching the gas on the Ranger.

Although Don had grown up hunting geese in these river bottoms, he had intentionally changed the agricultural landscape into wetlands to make it suitable for duck hunting. And he was not alone. So many were adding water features to dry agricultural landscapes that what amounted to a duck hunting arms race was taking place in the area.

Greg described the obstacles and added expense to access good hunting as we sat across from each other at one of the tables toward the back of Foster's during our interview. "We still have really good duck hunting, though it's getting more specialized—if you don't have the big spreads and the flooded corn and everything perfect, you know. The duck hunting thing, it's not like it was when I was a kid. It's changed *tremendously* in the last three or four years," Greg said, emphasizing how intense the competition to attract ducks had become.

"Why do you say the last three years?" I asked.

"Because it's become more specialized. The big dogs are the guys who really have the power and the money and can flood the corn and afford to have an area that's not in the WRP program, which that's the thing here. You're either in or you're out of the WRP, and if you're out of the WRP you can put as much corn as you want to flood because it's your own property. Of course, [under the] WRP you can only [plant] 5 percent [of the land] in [corn], which is still all right, but it's different."

The WRP, or Wetlands Reserve Program, enabled local landowners to transform the landscape to make it more amenable to duck hunting. A federal program administered through the U.S. Department of Agriculture, it was another example of a racialized agriculture/conservation program like those introduced in Chapter 1.[9] In place from 1990 to 2014, the program paid landowners to enroll landscapes in easements that stipulated that the land must be used primarily for conservation purposes. In addition to reimbursing landowners for any loss of property value that resulted from enrolling in the program, the WRP covered the costs involved in transforming agricultural landscapes into wetlands. Given the expenses associated with building levees and installing pumps to convert former agricultural fields into marshes, several landowners in the area had enrolled in the WRP program to cover the costs of transforming former goose hunting spots into duck hunting spots.

The transition from goose to duck hunting was neither easy nor inevitable. Because of the different landscape preferences of geese and ducks, this adaptation involved landscape transformations that, in some cases, were funded by the federal WRP. The question is why did men go to such great lengths to hunt ducks?

In some cases, such as Habitat Flats, the landscape had been transformed so that landowners could generate revenue by continuing to cater to waterfowl hunters, but this was not a universal trend. When I asked why they had transitioned to hunting ducks, men often talked about the importance of maintaining connections with the landscape and their friends. They also said in one way or another that the transition enabled them to maintain their senses of worth. In short, transitioning to duck hunting allowed men to continue doing masculinities associated with respect in their community.

In particular, transitioning to duck hunting enabled men in Sumner to accomplish rural masculinities. As I note in Chapter 1, scholars have written extensively on the topic of rural masculinities. They agree that there is no one way to be a rural man, but they also argue that there tends to be a set of standards that men are expected to achieve because they grew up or live in rural contexts.[10] In addition to being white, working to middle class, heterosexual, and not urban, rural masculinities—immortalized by songs such as Hank Williams Jr.'s "Country Boys Can Survive"—are often characterized by an ability to make a living through hard work and knowledge gained through hands-on experiences and male role models. Rural men are expected to be salt-of-the-earth types who can fish and hunt, do jobs that are physically demanding, operate heavy machinery, and have an in-depth knowledge of local environmental processes gained through years of working and recreating outdoors. There were undoubtedly numerous, complex reasons for transforming the landscape and transitioning to duck hunting, but I argue that the shift to duck hunting occurred, at least in part, because it allowed men in Sumner to achieve intersectional, rural masculinities that they considered respectable.

Don's comments about his goose-turned-duck-hunting spot provide an excellent starting point for illustrating how this transition enabled the achievement and reproduction of masculinities. "I don't do it for the money," Don explained proudly as we looked out across his duck hunting spot from his Ranger. "As I've got older I just like seeing others. The best is when you get to see someone get their first duck. That's something they'll never forget. That just makes my season when it happens. Had three of those this year. Yeah, there's nothing better than watching a young man [*pauses*] or woman—but they've all been boys—get their first duck out of my blind. I just love it."

Transforming the landscape enabled Don to continue hunting water-fowl, but it also allowed him to be an effective mentor who provided hunting opportunities for subsequent generations of potential hunters. Not surprisingly, given who tends to hunt in the United States and who tends to hunt in Sumner, this had been only boys.[11] By transforming the landscape and transitioning to duck hunting, Don could socialize boys to like an activity widely associated with rural men who provide for themselves and their families by shooting and consuming waterfowl.

The question still remains: Why go through all the trouble to transform the landscape to enable duck hunting? Why not hunt something else that did not require landscape changes, such as raccoons or opossums? After all, hunting is associated with rural masculinities in the United States regardless of what is being hunted.[12]

The answer revolves around hunting being not just about the reproduction of plain, simple rural masculinity. As I discuss in Chapter 1, what animals are hunted and what methods are used to hunt them are associated with varying degrees of status and worth.[13] Unlike other kinds of hunting that could have been taken up, the transition to duck hunting enabled the continued reproduction of a masculinity associated with respectable classes and whiteness.

Andy's explanation for why he had started hunting ducks after the geese stopped coming to the refuge helps draw out the racial and class dimensions of this transition. Andy was a middle-class man in his fifties with an average build and a thick brown mustache who came into the bar from time to time. He hunted geese in the area from the 1970s through the 1990s, but now he hunted only ducks. During our interview, I asked why he thought there had been a transition to duck hunting. He said, "Like me, when there weren't any geese around, they just switched to ducks. Once the geese were gone, that's all that was left to hunt."

Andy naturalized this process of adaptation by saying that he and others switched to ducks because that was "all that was left to hunt," but this was not entirely accurate. He and other men could have started hunting other animals during the fall. There was a sizable raccoon population in the area, for example, and it was legal to hunt them each fall. Importantly though, hunting raccoons would not have fulfilled the same social functions as ducks. Compared to hunting birds, which has predominantly been an activity carried out by working- to upper-class white men, in the United States raccoon hunting has historically been associated with poor white and black men. Stuart Marks explains this:

> Chasing the "coon," or ringtail, became the domain of slaves, freedmen, and the poorer whites who were into the practicalities of feeding themselves rather than impressing their neighbors. . . . There remains a dimension of racial stigma in the activity, in that rural blacks make up a large segment of the producers and consumers of raccoons.[14]

Ducks were not really the only thing left to hunt, but hunting ducks allowed men to continue doing a masculinity associated with a respectable class and race. In contrast, and given understandings of what it meant to be a good person who was worthy of respect in Sumner, hunting raccoons would not have enabled men to accomplish respectable rural masculinities as effectively. Perhaps it is not altogether surprising that Andy did not even recognize that transitioning to hunting raccoons was a possibility. To recognize this was an option, he would have needed to start from a different standpoint on what was and was not a desirable practice. According to Andy's white, middle-class imagination, ducks were all that was left to hunt.[15]

Carl's reaction when I asked if he ever thought about hunting raccoons instead of ducks shows that the stigmas associated with raccoon hunting undercut this potential avenue for adaptation even if men did recognize that hunting raccoons was an option. Sitting by me at the bar, he gave me a look of surprise and responded:

> Raccoons? Why in the hell would I ever do that? That's the stupidest fucking sport known to man. There's nothing worse than walking around in the dark in the woods with branches beating you in the fucking face the whole time. You're just walking along, and a branch smacks you in the face, and then you trip over another one and fall down in the mud. Then you have mud up to your tits. What a stupid fucking sport.

According to Carl, there was no ambiguity about the merits of hunting raccoons. It was not a commendable pursuit carried out by respectable men. After all, what respectable man would do something so completely undesirable?

Duck hunting can easily be described in similarly disparaging terms. It
often involves getting up at three or four in the morning to carry hundreds
of pounds of decoys through the muck and the mud in the hours before
dawn just to lure a bird within shooting range by using a kazoo-like instru-
ment, but I never heard duck hunting described in these terms. Descriptions
of duck hunting emphasized the beauty of nature, the skills of hunters, and
facilitation of connections with friends. As my dad liked to say when we did
not have any luck duck hunting, "A bad day in the duck blind is always better than a good day at work." In contrast to hunting raccoons, duck hunting
was a commendable pursuit carried out by respectable men.

Beyond enabling the accomplishment of a masculinity, with its atten-
dant rurality, race, and class, duck hunting facilitated the accomplishment
of a masculinity infused with heterosexuality even though it is an activity
predicated on men spending large amounts of time with other men. Unlike
hunting animals such as deer, which requires one to remain quiet, or quail,
which requires one to constantly move around, duck hunting is like goose
hunting in that it is generally stationary with only brief flurries of action
punctuating periods of sitting and waiting. To pass the time, duck hunters
often talk and joke about their jobs, families, and especially memorable
hunts. Like goose hunting, then, duck hunting is an activity that is particularly amenable to building homosocial friendships.[16]

A theme that emerged during interviews and everyday conversations,
especially for men over forty, is that they liked duck hunting because it was
something they could do to spend time with other men who were important
to them.

While sitting at the bar one evening, a conversation between Greg and
his son James, who was in his thirties, turned to duck hunting.

"You want to go duck hunting in the morning?" James asked his dad.

"We'll have to break ice, but if we can get some water movement, it'll be
good," Greg replied. "If we don't get any, we can just go sit by the woodstove
where it's nice and warm."

They had prospects for a good hunt, but this was not ultimately that
important to Greg. What was most important was that he could spend time
with his son. If they had no luck hunting, they could talk by his woodstove.

Ralph also emphasized the significance of homosocial bonding while we
talked at the bar one evening. In his seventies, he had been traveling from

southwest Iowa to hunt in Sumner since the 1980s. After we discussed shifting goose migrations and his transition to hunting ducks, I asked why he still came to Sumner since he could easily hunt ducks much closer to home.

"Just to get away really. I love it here. It's laid back and everyone has always just been really nice," Ralph said, before admitting, "I honestly don't really care that much about hunting anymore anyways, but I like to come down and spend time with my buddies."

Similar to Greg, for Ralph hunting was not what was ultimately most important. What was significant to Ralph was the ability to participate in an activity that allowed him to reconnect with local residents and spend time with his male friends. And duck hunting in Sumner provided a way for accomplishing both ends.

Like other kinds of hunting,[17] duck hunting was largely understood as an activity undertaken by overtly masculine, heterosexual men who were capable, paternalistic providers. Consequently, duck hunting did not draw men's heterosexuality into question, even though men were hunting ducks at least partly so that they could spend large amounts of time with other men.[18] Comments I heard community members make about hunters and their assumed heterosexuality are illustrative.

During an April 2014 Wild Goose Festival Planning Committee meeting, Susan proposed putting together a cookbook to sell at the festival. She had grown up in Sumner and was now involved with a number of civic groups. In her forties and the youngest member of the planning committee, Susan was particularly adept at suggesting new ways the group could generate interest in the festival. In the cramped city hall building, she said, "I was thinking about a community cookbook. I was looking back through and the last one made in Sumner was in the 1980s as far as I know."

"Everyone buys cookbooks!" Carol said, excited about the idea.

"Well, I printed off some things as far as information about production goes," Susan said.

As the stack of papers detailing printing costs and logistics was passed from person to person, Susan expanded on her rationale for wanting to make a cookbook, "When the guys come hunting they always want to take something back to their wives. There's never anything like that for them to take from the festival."

Liz, who was in her fifties, offered a strikingly similar appraisal of goose and duck hunters' sexuality during our interview. A resident of Sumner for more than forty years, when large numbers of hunters still came to the community, Liz, along with her husband, had operated a goose- and duck-picking business for over twenty-five years. As we talked about their business, Liz clarified her role, "I always cleaned the birds because I wanted them to be oven ready for . . . the hunter's wife because my theory was if that bird wasn't clean, the wife wouldn't let the hunter come back. So I wanted it to be oven ready." Like Susan, Liz believed goose and duck hunters coming to town were heterosexual. They came to Sumner to spend time with other men, but hunters were assumed to have a wife waiting for them at home. Like goose hunting, duck hunting provided an effective outlet for homosocial bonding that also enabled the accomplishment of heterosexual masculinities.[19]

Duck hunting was a kind of hunting that allowed men to continue to bond with other men while doing rural masculinities infused with heterosexuality, respectable classes, and whiteness. Much in the way that intersectional masculinities have informed responses to shifting social and ecological conditions in other contexts,[20] accomplishing intersectional masculinities helps explain why many men were willing to go to such great lengths to transition to hunting ducks after goose migrations shifted. Unlike other contexts, though, in which culturally legitimated ways of being men were fundamentally transformed so that men could accomplish respectable masculinities as social and ecological conditions shifted under their feet,[21] the terms and conditions of masculinity remained largely the same in Sumner. Hunting had been and continued to be centrally important to masculinities. Men just changed the ground under their feet to enable the continued accomplishment of respectable rural masculinities through hunting.

The transition to duck hunting enabled the continued accomplishment of intersectional masculinities, but there were important class differences in how men hunted ducks. It was also apparent that these class differences were not as pronounced as with goose hunting. As a result, and what Greg meant by his reference to "the big dogs" who could afford not to enroll landscapes in the WRP, the transition to duck hunting had facilitated the emergence of new ways of reproducing classed inequalities among men in the community. The transition to duck hunting enabled new ways of doing intersectional masculinities in Sumner.

Class Inequalities by Any Other Name

"With the ducks this year, there just wasn't any water anywhere in those [river] bottoms," Kurt said to me as we sat at the bar following the 2013 duck season. Kurt had grown up in Sumner, moved to Kansas City for work, and then returned after retiring. In his fifties and usually wearing blue jeans, a flannel shirt, and a camo hat, he was an avid duck hunter who liked to talk about the ins and outs of hunting and cooking wild game.

"Which bottoms?" I asked.

"The ones north and south of here. Well, I shouldn't say there wasn't any water. There was some. Those guys at Habitat Flats had it. That's another thing," Kurt said.

"What do you mean that's another thing?" I prodded him.

"Well, they have quite a bit of land around here. I guess it's good that they pull some ducks in, but there's some anger towards them. Growing corn, pumping it, and shooting all the ducks around here, you know?" Kurt explained.

Kurt was not the only one with animosity toward Habitat Flats. Other working-class men in the community often disparaged the operation and those who hunted there.

Simon, for example, berated Habitat Flats while we sat at the bar talking about his recent duck hunting experiences. In his twenties, Simon was born and raised in Sumner. During the week, he drove back and forth to a construction job in Kansas City, but he spent most weekends hunting or fishing around Sumner.

Curious about the reason for his animosity, I asked him, "Because they suck all the ducks with their flooded corn?"

"No. It's because they make it so damn expensive for everyone else to hunt around here. They're out leasing up all the fields before the year. Giving a farmer $300 with the agreement they can have access in case there are some birds in it later in the year. And you'll try to go and get permission, and the farmer will tell you no because they already have it leased," he said.

"Oh yeah?" I asked.

"Yeah. Then I guess opening weekend they had two guys down there. Came in with brand-new, in-the-box guns. Couldn't even put them together. Had to get someone else to put them together for them. Then, evidently they went through two cases of shells in three days!" Simon said, dismayed that the two hunters needed five hundred shotgun shells to kill their combined limit of thirty-six ducks.

"Two cases in three days?!" I asked, equally shocked that any hunters could be such bad shots.

Beginning to laugh, Simon continued, "Yep. Two cases. Fuck, blindfold me and let me shoot left handed and I could shoot their ducks with less shells than that."

Kurt's and Simon's comments and other opinions on Habitat Flats carried an awareness of the classed disparities influencing where men were able to hunt ducks in the area. Those with enough money had access to large fields of flooded corn where they could shoot ducks regardless of their skills as hunters, while others had access only to wetlands, sloughs, and ponds. And it was not just where men hunted that helped reproduce class differences and inequalities. How men hunted ducks was equally indicative of class disparities.

Some men in the area used water pumps or machines called Ice Eaters to keep water open once temperatures dropped below freezing toward the end of duck season.[22] This was an important advantage because ducks are generally repelled by frozen water. An Ice Eater alone was roughly $800, and they required a power source. Some hunters used generators, but others paid large sums to run electricity to their duck hunting spots. One couple I talked with who owned some duck hunting locations near the refuge said they had spent $70,000 to install electricity so that they could keep water open when temperatures dropped. Obviously, not everyone had $70,000 or even $800 to spend on such amenities, so those without access to this equipment were literally and figuratively frozen out of hunting toward the end of duck season.

Political-economic institutions inform the reproduction of class inequalities,[23] and similarly, duck hunting regulations facilitated the reproduction of class inequalities among duck hunters. Regulations regarding corn were especially significant. According to state and federal regulations, growing corn and then intentionally flooding the field up to the unharvested ears was legal. Consequently, it was legal to spend tens or even hundreds of thousands of dollars to build levees around fields, install water pumps and wells, and then plant hundreds of acres of corn just to flood it each fall. On the other hand, buying a ten-dollar bag of corn and then dumping it to attract ducks was illegal baiting. If intentionally flooding corn were illegal or if hunting over dumped corn were legal, it is reasonable to assume that hunting over flooded corn would not be integrally important to class differences and inequalities among men. However, because it was legal to hunt over flooded corn and illegal to dump a ten-dollar bag of corn, hunting over flooded corn enabled class inequalities among men. Upperclass men legally hunted large fields of corn that had been grown and then intentionally flooded, while those who could not afford such amenities were relegated to hunting without bait.

WRP regulations also contributed to this classed disparity in hunting. As Greg noted, there were drawbacks to being in the WRP because of the use stipulations that came along with the funds accessed through the program. Because the WRP sought to enhance biodiversity and reduce pesticide use, 5 percent or less of the area in the easement could be cultivated annually. If landowners could afford to, they avoided the WRP, left their ground in agricultural production, and paid to build levees around their fields themselves. This way, they could continue planting large tracts of corn and flood it in the fall after the crop matured.

This provided a decided advantage for duck hunting compared to land in the WRP, because large fields of flooded corn amount to an all-you-can-eat buffet to migrating ducks, as an owner of Habitat Flats described it in a Twitter post. "With rain on the way tonight, time is of the essence! #duck-buffet." The post included a photo of a corn planter being pulled behind a tractor with a massive, tilled field in the background. Duck season was still five months away, but by October the field would be a large tract of flooded corn ready to attract ducks.

Kurt and Simon, making their remarks about the patrons of Habitat Flats, indicated that hunting ducks over flooded corn had become part of what it meant to be upper class. Conversely, not having such access implied to men that they were not part of this class. Ben and Darren's conversation before the start of a Friends of Swan Lake meeting highlights this point.

"I've been watching ducks tornado into Habitat Flats the past few nights," Ben said to Darren excitedly, in a reference to how large flights of ducks landing into a small area can look like a tornado. "I mean, they're just funneling in there!" Ben, in his thirties, and Darren, in his forties, had grown up in the area and currently worked in agriculture.

Nodding his head knowingly, Darren agreed, "Oh yeah."

Beginning to laugh, Ben concluded, "If I hunted there it'd have to just be one shot each time a group came through. That's the only way you'd get your money's worth!"

By fantasizing about intentionally prolonging a hunt at Habitat Flats because of how expensive it was to hunt there, Ben linked an ability to hunt over flooded corn with being upper class. To him, not being able to afford such hunting meant that he was not part of this class.

Understandings of rurality often infused how local men thought about the classed dimensions of hunting over flooded corn and about those who hunted at Habitat Flats. I do not know whether the patrons of Habitat Flats were primarily from rural or urban areas, but according to many local men, those who hunted at Habitat Flats were primarily urban men described as "corporate," "suits," and "city boys." By portraying themselves as better duck

hunters than the supposedly urban men at Habitat Flats, local men constructed respectable rural masculinities even though they usually did not
have access to the best hunting spots in the area.[24] Simon's comments are
telling because he was emasculating the men who hunted at Habitat Flats by
emphasizing their inability to properly assemble or use their fancy new
guns. Jay had a similar take, saying he would not want to hunt at Habitat
Flats because the men who hunted there were "New Yorkers who probably
didn't know which end of the gun to shoot." According to such accounts,
those hunting at Habitat Flats were not really any better than local men even
though they had better hunting opportunities. In fact, they were lesser men
because they needed the added, classed advantages of flooded corn to kill
their ducks.[25] After all, Simon could have shot his limit of ducks at Habitat
Flats "blindfolded" and "left handed."

Although some in the community were angered by the privileges enjoyed by those who hunted over flooded corn, not everyone saw problems
with it. Fred described attracting ducks with flooded corn as "part of the
game," for example. Meritocratic understandings of work, wealth, and class
championed in the United States informed why some in Sumner thought
this arrangement was acceptable.[26]

After acknowledging that the WRP use stipulations angered some in the
community, Greg said, "I don't see anything wrong with it myself. My thing
is, if you make enough money to buy whatever you want to, you should be
able to enjoy it." Instead of being upset, Greg felt that men with money had
worked to earn it and should therefore be able to enjoy it however they liked.
Of course, explaining disparities in hunting practices through work ethics
ignores the realities of wealth accumulation in the United States as well as
how state regulations concerning corn were centrally important to the class
disparities of duck hunting.

Class disparities in hunting methods were not as apparent with goose
hunting from the 1950s until the early 1990s. Besides a gun and some shotgun shells, no specialized equipment was required to hunt geese. Stan put
this succinctly at the bar one afternoon. He recalled, "Hell, all you'd have to
do was go stand out in a fencerow and wait for some geese to fly over. You
didn't need decoys or calls or any of that stuff." Similarly, I can remember
using worn out tires cut into thirds as decoys when hunting geese near the
refuge with my dad as a small boy. Used tires were not exactly high-cost,
high-tech, high-quality hunting equipment, but that did not matter, because
even during the early 1990s there were enough geese that expensive equipment was not required. Because attracting geese to hunting locations did

not require additional landscape transformations beyond annual cultivation practices, goose hunting in the area was relatively inexpensive. The going rate for a spot in a blind near the refuge was just two dollars a day.

Although shooting geese as they flew by had been an effective strategy, trying to do the same with ducks is less effective because they are much faster and tend to cruise at altitudes well out of shooting range. To lure ducks within shooting range, hunters use decoys that cost from $50 to more than $200 a dozen and duck calls that cost from $20 to more than $150 apiece. Combined with the costs involved in landscape transformations, this made duck hunting far more expensive than goose hunting ever was. Three days of hunting at Habitat Flats at $2,100 was on the high end, but even on the low end, hunters from out of town paid between $100 and $200 per person for a single morning of hunting in a blind with a guide. If hunters shot their limits of mallards and pintails, which are the largest duck species, this works out to roughly $116 to $16 per pound of duck meat.

Perhaps unsurprisingly then, residents indicated that duck hunters tended to be from a higher class than the goose hunters who used to come to the community. Though residents were aware of these class differences, they very rarely labeled them as such. Similar to how residents obscured the significance of the institutional dimensions of class in Chapter 1, they only alluded to, purposefully talked around, or even explicitly denied there were class differences between goose and duck hunters.

During our interview, I asked Don if there had been any consequences for the community because of the transition from goose to duck hunting. He said, "Yeah, people would come in and the goose hunting was so much— you know, I'm tickled to death that we've got the ducks, and I hope we can continue to have them, but the goose hunting brought in so many more people, you know, because there was three blinds on every 160 acres. Where the duck hunting, you know, is more . . . clubs. It's an expensive deal. You know, where all the property is owned and it's not leased out [*trails off*]." Don tried again, "Duck hunting is a [*trails off*]." He paused to think. "It's more of a [*trails off*]." Finally he said, "I'm trying to think how to say it." Failing to find the words to convey what he was thinking, he changed course and quickly concluded, "It just costs a lot more money to duck hunt than it did [for someone] to come up here with [their] dad in 1970."

It was as if class were an unspeakable or potentially unthinkable word. Although Don was directly referring to the classed dimensions of duck hunting and how it could be cost prohibitive to the working- and middle-class men who used to come to the community, he did not say "class." He pondered for some time how to convey that goose hunting had not involved such clear class disparities before concluding that duck hunting "just cost a lot more money."

Similarly, during my interview with Fred and Jan, Jan came to a point where she was talking about class differences between goose and duck hunters. Seeming to imply that duck hunters tended to be from a higher class than goose hunters, she then explicitly denied this was the case.

"You know, the thing with the goose hunter, typically we've seen, or at least I think I've seen, is goose hunters are a little different breed than duck hunters," Jan said. "Goose hunters, they're a little more laid back. They're a little more involved. You know, they want to go hunt, and then they'd go to town and they spend a little money in town and they get acquainted with people. . . . Duck hunters are very private people as a whole, I see. They're more money. They seem to be a higher—and I don't mean—I don't mean a higher class. They just spend more money."

Though Jan denied there were class differences between the goose hunters of the past and the duck hunters of the present, she brought up these differences later in our interview when she said that goose hunters "tended to be a little more blue collar." While Jan denied there were class differences between goose and duck hunters, her use of "blue collar" highlighted the shift in the classed masculinities enabled by the transition from goose to duck hunting. Working- and middle-class men living in Sumner still accessed duck hunting spots by drawing on their connections throughout the community, but a large portion of the working- and middle-class men who used to come to town to hunt geese were priced out of hunting ducks near Swan Lake.

Class was talked around, but residents were right about the classed dynamics of the shift from goose to duck hunting. There were undoubtedly upper-class goose hunters in the past, and a few working- and middle-class men still came to the community to hunt ducks, but a comparatively large proportion of the men who had come to the area to hunt geese were from the working and middle classes. Upton Henderson's study of the economic impacts of goose hunting around the refuge supports this point. Of the 181 hunters he surveyed during the 1963 and 1964 hunting seasons, 28.2 percent were laborers, 5 percent were civil servants, 4.4 percent worked for schools, and 1.7 percent were servicemen. Conversely, just 21 percent were described as professionals or businessmen.[27]

The shift to duck hunting refashioned the meanings of waterfowl hunting as well as class in the community. Goose hunting was a relatively inexpensive undertaking accessible to men from a spectrum of classes, but duck hunting was a much more cost-prohibitive activity that was wildly expensive if one wanted access to the best hunting spots and equipment. Consequently, waterfowl hunting was now associated with class inequalities. Further, what it meant to belong to the upper class had also been transformed. In large part because of hunting regulations that concerned corn, the ability to hunt over large swaths of flooded corn had become part of what it meant to belong to the upper class. To those like Kurt, Simon, and Ben, not having access to such hunting spots meant they were not part of this class.

The shift from goose to duck hunting also undermined what Emile Durkheim refers to as social integration, or the degree to which individuals feel as if they are part of a broader community of people.[28] Recognizing this consequence of the shift from goose to duck hunting further highlights that an adaptation tied to masculinities with intersections of race, class, sexuality, and rurality had important ramifications for how community was rearranged and sustained in Sumner. In other words, it draws further attention to how intersecting inequalities, adaptations, and community are linked.

A Degraded Sense of Community

Jack was a farmer who had spent his entire life in Sumner. In his late sixties, he had an unwieldy shock of white hair that poked out from under his ball cap, and he talked in a slow, contemplative style that suited how much he knew about the community. We had spent the last hour feeding his cattle on a cold and snowy winter afternoon, but now we were warming up by the fire in his living room as we talked during our interview. Eventually I asked him what it was like growing up in Sumner. Similar to others I talked with, he immediately jumped into a story that focused on coming together with others.

Jack recalled, "Well, every fall, about right after Labor Day, about the 20th of September, the geese would start coming, and the hunters would come from all over the world to fix their blinds, enjoy each other, and get together. And it all culminated in the Goose Festival about the 20th or 25th of October. And everybody would come to that. Then the season started, and it ran clear through Christmas at that time."

"Do you think there was a sense of pride with that? Being from the Goose Capital?" I asked.

"Absolutely. People were proud of where they came from. I remember my mom took me to Kansas City dress shopping with her. I was about five or six, and the sales lady says, 'Now, where are you from?' I said, 'Sumner.' And she said, 'Well, where's that?' And I said, 'Well, don't you know?!'" We laughed as Jack continued, "I thought everybody in the world knew where Sumner was because it was the Wild Goose Capital of the World!"

Carol provided a similar account of togetherness and pride in her community during our interview. Carol was especially well liked by other community members and was involved with several civic groups. With shoulder-length salt-and-pepper hair, she always seemed to be laughing.

As we sat at her kitchen table with the evening news on in the background, I asked if she had any memories of the era of high goose numbers that she considered particularly special. She recalled, "Oh, I don't know. We had a lot of fun. Especially in the bicentennial year. Then raising the money for Maxie and having the dedication. Having the governor come and speak and do that. That was, you know, really, that was Kansas City news." Carol laughed, "That was in the Kansas City papers, so that was big news. Then winning—Maxie, when we had her erected, we won first place in the Missouri Community Betterment Conference in Jeff[erson] City that year. And we won, I think it was $1,000. We won first prize. That was quite a thrill," Carol said, obviously proud of what she had helped accomplish.

"So it sounds like it's kind of safe to say that you enjoyed how, you know, it was busy, but at the same time it's almost like the geese being around and raising money for Maxie and that sort of thing almost facilitated people coming together?" I asked.

"Yes!" she emphatically agreed.

"A sense of community, maybe?" I asked, hoping she would expand.

"Sure!" Carol agreed. "Because the whole community, we went together to raise the money. We had all kinds of little things to raise money. We sold 'I gave'—what was it that it said?—'I gave towards Maxie' or something on the bumper stickers. I mean, you know, we had a lot of stuff like that and had dinners and things and raised money."

Todd, who was in his seventies and worked at Swan Lake during the goose hunting heyday, also mentioned how the geese provided the glue that held people in the community together. As we sat in his truck looking out across a cut cornfield during our interview, I asked if there was anything particularly special about working at the refuge. He recalled, "The part that really made that special was the fact that, you know, that whole community just revolved at that stage, at that time of year, around goose hunting and the geese being there. Of course, they did that because it was pretty economically lucrative during that period." Chuckling, he continued, "So they had a selfish interest, but at the same time, that was neat. I mean, I became friends with a lot of the people up there."

It was striking how often people, as in Jack's, Carol's, and Todd's accounts of the past, noted that practices related to goose hunting facilitated ties between people and a prideful sense of community in Sumner. Residents, hunters, and former conservation officials often related stories about the awe-inspiring presence of so many geese, but just as often they talked about the lifelong friendships they formed because of activities associated with the geese. Shared ways of relating to the geese facilitated senses of solidarity between members of hunting clubs, landowners, conservation officials, and community members.[29]

Stories of the past and how the geese brought people together often revolved around the Honey House. Owned and operated by Betty Ponting, the Honey House was a restaurant located between Sumner and the refuge where hunters and local residents stopped for a cup of coffee, something to eat, and a story. Though Betty had passed away by the time of my fieldwork and the Honey House had closed, the old menu board still hung on one of her son's barns. An order of coffee and biscuits and gravy ran $1.80. But for the person with an appetite, two eggs; ham, bacon, or sausage; biscuits and gravy; and "plenty of coffee & hash browns" could be had for $3.00.

Frank recalled the Honey House while we talked during the 2014 banquet for refuge volunteers. A taller-than-average and balding man in his sixties, Frank was a lifetime resident of the area. He was a dedicated waterfowl hunter with many memories of when the geese still showed up in large numbers. After discussing the ongoing duck season and how my project was coming along, he began to reminisce. "I can't believe how much things have changed. It's just so different. I was thinking about how much it's changed while driving in, past the main gates down there. I was thinking about how the Honey House used to be right there by that gate. I used to be excited to get my geese shot just so I could go eat at the Honey House. It was so good."

"Breakfast or lunch or dinner?" I asked him.

"All of them!" Frank enthused. "The food was just always so good, and you'd go in there and see people you hadn't seen for a while."

Catching up with friends after hunting was one of the things Frank most looked forward to each year. In fact, his remarks implied that spending time with others during goose season was at least as important as hunting.

More than just being a recreational activity that contributed to the local economy, the geese and all the activities associated with them facilitated interpersonal attachments, lifelong friendships, and feelings of togetherness for those in the community. Consequently, residents often indicated that the shift in goose migration patterns undermined ties between people in the community. All the preceding comments, for example, are about the past and how integrated the community *used to be*. Comments Fred and Jan made about the Honey House during our interview help make this point.

"Obviously the geese are missing, but is there also maybe a sense of almost like togetherness or people getting together that's also missing?" I asked. I had been working in Sumner for over a year at the time of our interview, so I had begun to purposefully ask about this after listening to so many residents' statements and stories on the topic.

"Oh, absolutely!" Jan responded immediately. "Go back to the restaurants. The Honey House was owned by Betty Ponting. And you would go down and there would be hunters. And they would come in at four o'clock in the morning to go eat biscuits and gravy. Then we would go down and have a cup of coffee and a piece of pie and have lunch."

"It was a good place to go visit; you'd see your friends," Fred said.

"And that's where the community kind of gathered, and you'd sit in," Jan continued, before rhetorically asking, "And now where do you go and have a cup of coffee to visit? No place. There's no gathering place anymore. There's no place to go sit."

"And the duck hunters don't come to town," Fred quickly interjected.

"The community, that sense of get together, we have lost that I think," Jan concluded.

As Fred's comments concerning duck hunters hint, while the absence of geese had undoubtedly undermined social integration, the loss of interpersonal connections was also linked to the shift to the relatively more exclusive activity of duck hunting. As Don said, fewer people came to the community to hunt ducks because of the relatively exclusive way that duck hunting was organized. Duck hunters, especially those who did not come to the area when goose numbers were still high, also tended to belong to private clubs where they spent time among themselves instead of interacting with local residents.

Contrasting goose and duck hunters during our interview, Greg explained, "The goose hunter came to town to drink some beer, smoke his cigars, and kill a goose and all that. The duck hunter comes, builds his nice lodge. He goes to that lodge, and he eats himself a really nice rib eye steak, smokes his nice cigar, and has a good shot of good bourbon. Goes to sleep and gets up the next morning and goes out there, and he's after that duck from before daylight until evening time. The goose hunter was, 'Ahh, hell! If we make it, all right. If we don't, who cares!' You've seen it!"

I laughed. "Yeah. My dad took me ever since I was a little boy, and I remember I didn't understand why half the guys didn't make it out to hunt in the morning."

"They liked to play!" Greg explained, letting out a loud laugh.

Like other residents, Greg never called the distinction what it was, a difference in class between former goose and current duck hunters. However, his comparison of goose and duck hunters still emphasized the classed dimensions of this transition. When he said that duck hunters built lodges, ate nice steaks, and drank good bourbon before sleeping and then hunting all the next day, he was talking about class without actually saying it. The duck hunter was an upper-class man who partook of fine food and beverages while keeping to himself in his private lodge. Goose hunters of the past, on the other hand, were more working to middle class. They drank cheap beer while spending time with local residents and other hunters at Foster's. Greg never explicitly stated the connection, but by contrasting duck and goose hunters in this manner, he linked the classed dimensions of this transition to the degraded sense of social integration in the community.

My observations supported these kinds of comparisons. Duck hunters who had originally come to the area when goose numbers were high still occasionally came into Foster's alone or in small groups, but duck hunters who did not have long-standing ties to the area were generally absent in the bar. This was a change compared to residents' portrayals of the past, when the bar was said to have been so jam-packed with hunters during goose season that it was nearly impossible to get in or out. Further, while a few groups of hunters who had been coming to the community for decades still came to the Wild Goose Festival every year, duck hunters who had not been coming to the community for years were mostly absent from the festival. This was also a change compared to residents' portrayals of prior festivals, which were described as events typified by throngs of camo-clad hunters flooding into town.

The absence of the geese and the interpersonal activities their presence had enabled contributed to a degraded sense of community among local residents. This sense of loss was also related to the shift from the relatively more inclusive activity of goose hunting to the relatively more exclusive activity of duck hunting. As the transition to a more exclusive, expensive activity occurred, fewer hunters came to town. And even those who did come to Sumner tended to avoid its working-class residents. As a result, the strong sense of togetherness that was tied to the presence of the geese had faded. The degradation of interpersonal ties and feelings of togetherness in Sumner was related to the absence of geese as well as to the shift to a more exclusive kind of waterfowl hunting less accessible to men from a wider range of classes.[30]

Conclusion: Entanglements, Inequalities, and Communities

Relating to nonhuman animals, plants, and objects in particular manners is centrally important to how people organize their communities,[31] so we should anticipate dislocations and disruptions to communities around the world as nonhumans' ranges continue to transform in response to climate change.[32] This happened in Sumner, and there is evidence it is happening elsewhere.[33] This chapter illustrates that communities will be rearranged in response to such disruptions through entangled mashes of social and ecological things, beings, and processes.

Far from being an inevitable, easy transition, the shift to duck hunting required dramatic landscape transformations because of the different behaviors of Canada geese and ducks. Part of the reason men were willing to go to such great lengths to hunt ducks was because duck hunting allowed them to continue to achieve rural masculinities associated with worth and respect. State programs and institutions were also integrally important to how and why men in Sumner transformed the landscape. Without the assistance of the WRP, many men could not have afforded to transform their property to accommodate ducks. It also would not have made sense to transition to duck hunting if the USFWS had not been pouring money into Swan Lake to provide habitat for tens of thousands of ducks. By capitalizing on a set of racialized conservation programs, men transformed the landscape to enable the continued reproduction of intersectional masculinities associated with respect.

Recognizing that intersectional masculinities informed the shift from goose to duck hunting is especially important because analysts and policy makers have given little consideration to the relation of intersecting inequalities and responses to climate change.[34] Acknowledging that masculinities complicated by race, class, sexuality, and rurality influenced the rearrangement of the meanings of class and social integration in Sumner is especially important. Others have started analyzing how intersecting in-equalities inform individual or household responses to climate change, but the broader, community-level consequences of intersecting inequalities re-main largely unexplored.[35] Individual- and household-level effects matter a great deal, but if we continue to focus solely on individuals or households, we will miss the effects that intersecting inequalities have on how commu-nities are reorganized in response to climate change. We will also miss see-ing how intersecting inequalities can be remade, at the communal level, because individuals rearrange their relationships with each other and the landscapes in which they live as they adapt to climate change. In Sumner, the transition to duck hunting had facilitated a reorganization of the com-munity and the intersecting inequalities that underpinned it.

On the basis of this chapter, one could think that adaptations will result in distinct groups of winners and losers. After all, the shift from goose to duck hunting had made it more difficult for some men to participate in an activity that enabled the accomplishment of respectable masculinities. And similar dynamics have been identified in other communities where adapta-tions have facilitated the intensification of inequalities.[36] But we should not expect adaptations to result in distinct groups of individuals who are either winners or losers. Drawing from scholars who find that individuals and groups are often simultaneously (dis)advantaged in ambivalent manners because of the complexities of intersecting inequalities,[37] I argue that we should expect individuals to be simultaneously (dis)advantaged as their communities are reorganized in response to climate change. In Chapter 3, I focus on a group of women who rearranged inequalities in Sumner in messy, ambivalent ways as they worked to sustain the Wild Goose Festival and their community despite the lack of geese and hunters coming to town.

The Buyers and the Bakers

Rearranging Messy Inequalities

Held annually since 1955, the Wild Goose Festival was incredibly important to those living in and around Sumner. By mid-October it was the hot topic of conversation. Residents discussed who was coming to town for the festivities and what would be the main attraction for the year. "You better make sure to come to the Goose Festival," they would tell me before going on to explain that it would be important for my project. They were undoubtedly right. The festival was the social event of the year that both reflected and helped remake their community.

The women in the American Legion Auxiliary kicked off the festival every year with a chili supper on Friday night. Charging eight dollars per person for a drink, bowl of chili, and sizable piece of pie, they coaxed crowds of men, women, and children into the legion hall. By Saturday morning, vendors lined both sides of the main street through Sumner selling everything from fried pork loins to duck calls to weight loss programs. The hundreds of adults and children in attendance meandered from vendor to vendor asking questions, inspecting the wares for sale, and occasionally buying something. Smells of fried food and kettle corn wafted through the air, and the ambient noise of conversations was cut by the joyous screams of children playing, boys and men wailing on their duck calls, and announcements coming from the public address system that stood beside the flatbed trailer used as the festival grandstand. Annual attractions included the parade, the baby and queen contests, the duck and goose calling contests, the quilt show, the gooseberry pie contest and auction, numerous activities for kids, and a band that played from the late afternoon until eight or nine at night. Main attractions included lawn mower races in 2013, the Dock Dogs in 2014, and laser tag in 2015. Figures 3.1, 3.2, 3.3, and 3.4 show some events.

The Goose Festival provided a tremendous economic boost for the few businesses left in town as well as the numerous civic groups that arranged raffles and dinners. In addition to the Legion Auxiliary's chili supper, the American Legion and the Swan Lake Sportsman's Club served food, the Sportsman's Club raffled guns, and the Friends of Swan Lake and the Fulbright Museum raffled quilts pieced by older women in the community. Attesting to the economic importance of the festival, the Wild Goose Festival Planning Committee distributed over $13,000 to community groups in 2014 from funds received through donations and festival memorabilia sales. Recipients included the American Legion Auxiliary, the American Legion, the Sumner Fire Department, the Sumner park board, the Missouri Community Betterment group, the Sportsman's Club, the Fulbright Museum, the United Methodist Church, and the City of Sumner.

Beyond economic impacts, the Goose Festival was a key way residents and visitors continued to construct a sense of community and their place in it.[1] It was an annual homage to the community's unique past during which people came together and enjoyed each other's company. But just as Sumner was not an idyllic, homogeneous community more generally, intersecting inequalities informed and were reconstructed through the festival. People came together and paid tribute to their roots, but they also reproduced differences and inequalities pertaining to race, class, gender, and sexuality because of how they arranged and participated in the festival.[2]

Before the festival began, teenage women entered the Goose Festival Queen contest, older men spit shined their antique tractors for the parade, and a group of women worked for months to ensure everything was in order for the event. Once the festival started, women entered their pies in the pie contest, men bid on the pies at the pie auction, women showed off their quilts at the quilt show in the church, and men participated in the *Duck Dynasty* lookalike contest on the festival grandstand. Race, sexuality, and class complicated these gendered dynamics of the festival. Like Foster's Sportsman Inn, the festival was a white space. Virtually all those who took part in the festivities were white, and the Confederate flag became noticeably more

Figure 3.1 Classic cars, trucks, and tractors composed large portions of the parades. Foster's Sportsman Inn can be seen in the background.

Figure 3.2 The *Duck Dynasty* lookalike contest on the 2014 festival grandstand.

Figure 3.3 A crowd looks on as John Wayne takes flight during the Dock Dogs competition.

Figure 3.4 Quilts pieced by women in Sumner are displayed as the stories behind the quilts are told during the quilt show.

visible on floats and clothing after the massacre in 2015 of nine black church-goers by a white supremacist led to national controversies over the meanings and uses of the flag. The festival was also purposefully designed to attract heteronormative families composed of a man, a woman, and children. On numerous occasions, the women organizing the festival said, "There's some-thing for the whole family at the festival," before noting that there were ac-tivities for a husband and wife and their kids. Men and women of different classes were also encouraged to participate in different ways. After all, not every man could pay more than a hundred dollars for one of those goose-berry pies at the auction. The festival was the boiled-down, emergent essence of Sumner. It was an annual enactment of community that reflected *and* helped reproduce all the intersecting inequalities on which the community was built.

This chapter explores how a group of women drew on their rural femi-ninities to rearrange and sustain the Goose Festival in response to dra-matically fewer geese and hunters coming to the community. As they reor-ganized the festival, they also contributed to the simultaneous reproduction and subversion of intersecting inequalities. This was an ambivalent rear-rangement of inequalities in other words.[3] Research on other rural com-munities has consistently found that rural women often do femininity in ways that involve them prioritizing the well-being of the men in their lives.[4] Similarly, women in Sumner reorganized the festival in a manner that re-produced patriarchal privileges. Nevertheless, they were also drawing on skills associated with the domestic sphere and homemaking to reorganize the festival in a manner that, at least in some respects, subverted inequalities between men and women. A small group of women now called the shots on what events happened at the festival, and women in the community were also much safer and more welcome at the newer Goose Festival. Further, men and women with various, intersecting arrangements of sexuality and class were differentially (dis)advantaged by the newer rendition of the festival.

The festival and the women who were in charge of organizing it illus-trate how individuals can creatively leverage the complexities and contra-dictions of inequalities to sustain and even improve their communities.[5] They also show how adaptations can result in ambivalent rearrangements of inequalities in which individuals and groups are simultaneously (dis)advan-taged. Both are important insights because up to this point research on adaptations to climate change has regularly missed the mark on inequali-ties.

Researchers have often framed inequalities as zero-sum games, in which individuals and groups are portrayed as either empowered or marginalized, privileged or oppressed. Instead of diving into how the complexities of inequalities will inform and be informed by adaptations, many have argued that individuals will win or lose because of how their communities are rearranged and sustained.[6] But inequalities are not zero-sum games. As I discuss in the preceding chapters, inequalities neither operate nor are they experienced in such neat, dichotomous manners. Individuals and groups can simultaneously experience both privilege and oppression because of who they are and how they are positioned within exceedingly complex, institutionalized systems of intersecting inequalities.[7] A white woman, for example, enjoys the institutional advantages of being white while simultaneously being disadvantaged by her gender. To consider how inequalities inform and are rearranged through adaptations we must start acknowledging such ambivalences. If we continue to conceptualize inequalities as zero-sum games, we will miss how the convoluted complexities of inequalities inform and are informed by rearrangements of ways of life and community.

By illustrating how the reorganized festival contributed to the reproduction of a convoluted, ambivalent empowerment for women in Sumner, I emphasize that adaptations can simultaneously (dis)advantage particular demographic groups. To continue drawing out the complexities of inequalities, I also illustrate that some women and men were differentially disadvantaged by the newer renditions of the festival because of their sexuality and class. The chapter concludes by exploring how the complexities of inequalities will be centrally important to whether and how communities are rearranged in response to climate change.

Drawing on Intersectional, Rural Femininities to Make a Rowdy Festival Family Friendly

In her eighties, Becky had white, shoulder-length hair that was usually draped across a cardigan or denim button-down. Because she had lived in Sumner her whole life and was involved in a number of civic groups, other residents repeatedly noted that Becky was a leader in the community who was also an expert on Sumner's history. We got to know each other through the Friends of Swan Lake group, so when I spotted her sitting with three of her friends at the Legion Auxiliary chili supper I took the opportunity to hear their thoughts on the festival. Two of Becky's companions were a married couple who had also lived in the area for over eighty years, and her other friend was a woman in her sixties who had grown up in Sumner and was back in town for the festival.

After we talked for a while I asked if the Goose Festival had changed over the years, and they all exchanged knowing looks. Then Becky explained, "Well, it depends on what time [of the day] you were up here. If you were here until four or five you would have been all right, but the later it got—"

"I remember one year," Vicky, the younger woman, cut in. "The most—." Letting her body language speak for itself, she shook her head, took a deep breath, and let out a long sigh before continuing, "—thing happened. About thirty guys from Iowa came down here, and they just set up shop out there in the middle of the street. They made big towers out of beer cans!"

I began to chuckle as I imagined the scene, but I quickly stopped when I noticed everyone's reactions. The man in the group was sitting quietly with a sly grin on his face, but it was clear the three women at the table did not think this was a laughing matter.

Beth, the other woman Becky's age, then said, "Those dang hunt—." Cutting herself short, she concluded, "Iowegians!"

I am not sure if she stopped herself before she said "hunters" because she knew I hunted, but the point of the story was clear. Goose Festivals used to be rowdy affairs where large groups of men came to town, got drunk, and started trouble. And this was not a good thing.

The festival began to die out when Eastern Prairie Population geese stopped migrating as far south. As goose numbers dipped, so too did the number of hunters coming to the festival. This was especially concerning to many in Sumner because of the economic and social importance of the event. To reinvigorate and sustain it, a small group of women in their forties, fifties, and sixties took control of the festival and transformed it. In contrast to the men in the Sportsman's Club who had organized the Goose Festival as a big party that catered to hunters, the women converted it into a family-friendly event inviting to men, women, and children.

Rick summarized these changes when we were at the bar one afternoon. In his sixties and of average height, he was burly and usually wearing one of his striped Wrangler button-downs. He had spent his entire life in Sumner working in agriculture and was a local historian who took a tremendous amount of pride in the community's past. He had taken an interest in my project, and he brought in a stack of festival programs from the 1960s and 1970s for me to look through. As we flipped through the books, I asked why the Sportsman's Club had stopped organizing the festival as it had during the years covered by the programs.

"Well, the Sportsman's Club used to have five, six hundred members, but then it got down to where there just weren't many active members. The women said it was the town drunks, and they were pretty much right. They said they wanted to do it, and that really tickled us because we didn't have to anymore. They really changed it anyways to be more family oriented instead of a big party," Rick said.

"So it used to be a little more wild and crazy?" I asked.

"Yeah, I mean, you'd be out there and the whole street would just be lined with hunters in their camo. Then at night the riffraff would come into town. You know, guys looking for a fight, and there would always be someone to oblige. The women did a good job of it too. It was petering out when they took it over, and they took it over and did a good job bringing it back."

Carol, Jan, Patti, and Susan were the core of the group that had rearranged the Goose Festival as a family-friendly event, and they carried out the vast majority of tasks associated with organizing it while I was conducting fieldwork. All middle age or older, they had long-standing ties to Sumner and were deeply invested in the continued reproduction of civic groups and social integration in the community. Meeting once a month in city hall, they organized a sprawling array of events, services, and infrastructure for the festival. Insurance, Porta Potties, bleachers, a public address system, a grandstand, someone to sing the national anthem, an auctioneer, prizes for festival contests, vendors, the parade, and entertainers, as well as festival shirts, Koozies, buttons, and programs, had to be arranged. This is to say nothing of the labor needed on the day of the festival to sell memorabilia, direct vehicle parking, and pick up trash left by festival attendees. Except for me, men rarely came to these meetings, and when they did it was only briefly to ask whether they could host a particular event at the festival such as a golf cart race.

Intersections of rurality and gender help explain how and why these women undertook so much unpaid, behind-the-scenes work to successfully transform the festival. As I discuss in Chapter 1, the ideology of separate spheres was integrally important to how residents in Sumner went about their lives and arranged their community. It was especially important to how and why Carol, Jan, Patti, and Susan rearranged the festival. They regularly and creatively drew from the ideology as though it was a gendered toolkit to formulate strategies for enrolling men and women to help organize and participate in fundraisers and events.[8] Men were encouraged to donate money to the festival in order to be breadwinners for their community; women in Sumner were encouraged to be caretakers who did the work necessary to organize and then implement events such as the princess tea and beauty pageant.

The cookbook Carol, Jan, Patti, and Susan assembled and sold for ten dollars apiece as a fundraiser provides an excellent example. Women in the United States have used cookbooks as a way of organizing and sustaining communities for at least the last 150 years.[9] With their overtly feminine appearance, cookbooks are an outlet for women to safely gather their knowledge and put it into texts that can be distributed throughout communities and then passed from generation to generation. These texts do not necessarily subvert gendered inequalities, but they are testaments to gendered ways of knowing and being in the world. They are texts that are informed by and aid in the reproduction and subversion of gendered inequalities. Analyzing the cookbook produced to commemorate the sixtieth rendition of the Goose Festival as a text that both reflected and helped reproduce gendered inequalities allows us to see how this group of women drew on the ideology of separate spheres to sustain the festival.

After Susan floated the cookbook idea at the April planning committee meeting, over the next five months the women in charge of the festival gathered recipes to fill the book. With names like Apple Dapple Salad, Grandma's Cinnamon Rolls, Dorito Chicken Salad, and Knock You Naked Brownies, the 167 recipes collected for the book covered everything from appetizers to desserts. Not surprisingly, women contributed 152 (91 percent). Of the remainder, men contributed 9 (5 percent), and tandems of men and women contributed 6 (4 percent). If not for a chocolate zucchini bread recipe contributed by me, men would have submitted only 8 recipes. That nearly all the recipes came from women is important because it highlights how the women organizing the festival used a gendered toolkit to sustain the festival. In a community underpinned by the ideology of separate spheres, women drew on their gendered networks to obtain recipes for the traditionally feminine activity of cooking to create a book to sell as a fundraiser.

Even after the books were printed, the women organizing the festival continued using the ideology of separate spheres to their advantage. To get men to purchase the books, they encouraged men to be good providers for their wives, who presumably liked to cook.

Walking up behind Mitch, Stan, Paul, and me as we sat at the bar one afternoon, Carol began to put the hard sell on Mitch. "Your wife said she needed one of these," Carol said, holding out one of the cookbooks.

"What is it?" Mitch asked, feigning ignorance.

"It's the Goose Festival cookbook!" Carol explained cheerily, seeming to know Mitch's game.

"How much is it?" Mitch crankily asked.

"Just ten dollars," Carol assured him.

"I thought they were twenty, weren't they?" I asked, to Carol's and Mitch's amusement.

"She doesn't cook, does she?" Paul asked, needling Mitch about his wife's femininity.

"Yeah, what's she need a cookbook for?" Stan asked, piling on.

"You ought to get one for your wife too!" Carol said to me.

"Oh, I'm planning on it, but I'll get one at the festival," I replied, though I really wanted one for me and not my wife.

"Well," Mitch sighed as he caved to the pressure and pulled out his wallet to buy a book.

The gendered dynamics of the interaction are readily apparent. Carol, Stan, and Paul were all drawing on traditional understandings of gender to try to get Mitch and me to buy a book. While Carol was trying to get Mitch and me to be providers for our wives, Stan and Paul were questioning the degree to which Mitch's wife adhered to the supposedly feminine duty of cooking and, by association, the degree to which he and his marriage also adhered to gendered ideals.

By the end of the 2014 festival, the cookbooks made nearly $2,500, an impressive amount of money that would not have been produced and then distributed to civic organizations without Carol, Jan, Patti, and Susan using the gendered division of public and private spheres to their advantage.[10] As I discuss in greater detail shortly, this also draws attention to how they were simultaneously undermining the ideology of separate spheres in somewhat convoluted and paradoxical ways through their civic engagement.

Like women in other contexts who have several motivations for becoming community activists,[11] festival committee members had many reasons for becoming involved with reorganizing the festival. Jan noted she "didn't want [Sumner] to have the [bad] reputation [it] had," for example. Most commonly, though, Carol, Jan, Patti, and Susan indicated that they were willing to do the immense amount of work required to reorganize the festival because it was part of being a good woman.[12] Again and again in interviews and everyday conversations, they positioned themselves as caretakers for their community who should be the ones responsible for doing the time-consuming, largely invisible work needed to put on the festival.

Conversely, men were generally portrayed as breadwinners for the community who were not obligated to participate in this work.[13] Men, especially those who owned businesses or farmed large amounts of land, were expected to participate by donating money or prizes to support festival events. To help fund the Dock Dogs event in 2014, for example, the committee raised over $3,000 in donations almost exclusively from men. If men who were known to have money were not willing to donate, they were disparaged as "tight-asses" or worse.

This understanding of women as caretakers and men as breadwinners was so taken for granted that the women organizing the festival were somewhat taken aback when I asked them why no men came to their meetings or helped organize the festival.[14] During a lull in conversation before one of their monthly meetings officially began, I asked, "Now, how come none of the men in the community help organize the festival?"

The women gave me a puzzled look and then looked from one to another to see who would answer my question. Carol finally ended the awkward silence by saying, "They're probably over there at the bar."

I was not sure how to respond but was well aware I had questioned an unstated assumption about who ought to be organizing the festival.

Then Jan said, "They help. They help put up the big tent every year!"

Though true, this belied the clear disparities between the few hours it took to set up the tent and the months it took to organize the festival. Regardless, Jan's comment still points to the significance of the gender dichotomy. Men were generally not expected to care for their community through behind-the-scenes tasks, so it was especially noteworthy and memorable when they did.[15] Further, when they did this kind of work, it was the physically demanding, outdoor work that is often associated with rural men.[16]

But more than understandings of gender informed why members of the festival committee were doing the immense amount of work required to reorganize the festival. As in other rural contexts, perceived links between femininity and rurality informed why these women stepped in to do the work necessary to sustain their community during a time of need.[17] Being good rural women meant prioritizing others' needs and taking on large amounts of unpaid civic work to help sustain the festival and community. Carol's explanation for why she dedicated so much time to the community generally, and the festival specifically, highlights these interconnections between understandings of femininity, rurality, and civic activism. During our interview, I asked why it was important for her to participate in so many community groups. She explained:

Oh, I just, I enjoy it. I like to help and do things and be involved. . . . That's what [my partner] says: "You're the happiest when you see all those little kids go over there to the park and play on all that new park stuff." . . . You know, you're a small community. Moms have to be doing it.

Carol's claim that in a small community "moms have to be doing it" is telling because it underscores the understanding that in this rural community, and elsewhere, good rural women were moms who also mothered their communities.

Jan framed her involvement on the festival committee in strikingly similar terms. As we talked during our interview about all the work she did to help organize the festival, she said, "I think for a little town we do a pretty darn good job. I hope it can continue. I just—it's—." She paused to think. "Do I buck [hay or straw] bales? No, but it's a lot more work than I think people realize it is. . . . I've got my leather gloves, and I'm just trying to do what I can as an old worn-out woman." Her invocation of small towns, bucking bales, and leather gloves are all unmistakable allusions to rurality. Jan was not doing work traditionally associated with rural masculinity, which meant this work was largely invisible and underappreciated,[18] but she was doing all she could as a good rural woman to sustain her community. And this was a lot of work.

Women on the festival committee framed their community engagement as being an expression of a particular kind of femininity complicated by rurality, but others have repeatedly found that women in (sub)urban locations across the United States usually do the unpaid work necessary to reproduce their communities. And they also regularly draw on understandings of motherhood and caretaking to frame their civic activism.[19] Women working to reproduce communities and then framing this work as a form of caretaking is not restricted to rural communities in other words. Phyllis articulated this widespread connection between femininity and community work during our interview. In her sixties, she had worked closely with the women on the festival committee in other community groups. After I asked why she thought only women organized the festival, she said, matter-of-factly and pointedly, "Well that's easy. Women are the most involved because they're expected to care for the community." Although similar to Carol's and Jan's, Phyllis's explanation for why women were organizing the festival was a more generalized statement on the links between femininity and community activism.

Then why were the women on the festival committee linking their civic engagement to rural femininity? Why not just frame their work as something women did? I believe they framed their work in terms of rurality at least partly because they were transgressing the ideology of separate spheres by organizing the festival.

Women must reconcile extra work they take on during times of need with expectations for how women in their communities ought to behave. In other words, they must navigate historically contingent, locally acceptable ways of doing gender when they step up to sustain their communities.[20] By working in the public sphere to reorganize the festival, the women in Sumner were actively transgressing their legitimated positions within the domestic sphere. Further, this work could have easily been construed as a feminist effort to undermine patriarchal privileges given that the women on the committee were using their power to make the festival more welcoming to women.

By framing their work outside the home as the kind of care work proper country women did for the sake of their community, the women aligned this work with expectations for how rural women ought to be going about their lives. Rural people and ways of life,[21] and rural women in particular,[22] are also often associated with moral purity beyond the pale of politics and self-interest. By invoking a femininity that was supposedly particular to rural women, the women organizing the festival also framed their work in the public sphere as just another example of an apolitical course of action regularly undertaken by good country women. They were in the public sphere, but they were depicting their civic engagement as how gendered individuals ought to behave in Sumner.

Age also informed why Carol, Jan, Patti, and Susan were organizing the festival. Carol's claim that "moms have to be doing it" brings up the age dimensions of this work, but equally as pointed were the comments made by community members who told me I needed to talk with the older women in the community who "ran the organizations" and were "the matriarchs" of the town. According to such portrayals, the community was a family in and of itself, and the middle-age and older women in Sumner were expected to act as (grand)mothers who did all the reproductive work necessary to sustain their community.[23]

Again, the tensions between the public and private spheres and women's proper place in this dichotomy are apparent. In this case, the community legitimated the women's engagement in the public sphere by depicting it as a form of domestic caretaking. Although this work could have been considered evidence that the ideology of separate spheres was an arbitrary division, framing it as (grand)motherly caretaking feminized it and allowed the ideology of separate spheres to remain intact. Women were working to rearrange and reproduce the public sphere, but metaphors of the community as a family recast this work in the public sphere as an extension of women's domestic duties.

As the preceding examples reveal, the significance of gender, rurality, and age cannot be understood independent of each other. Understandings of femininity, rural communities, and age intersected to inform how and why Carol, Jan, Patti, and Susan were rearranging the festival. An interaction that took place following the 2014 Goose Festival emphasizes this point. It was the only time I ever saw anyone directly and forcefully challenge the gendered and aged dynamics of festival organization. And in their defense of how they organized the festival, the committee drew direct attention to how intersections of gender, age, and rurality guided their work.

In their fifties, Alice and Wallace were longtime residents of the community. They generally did not attend festival planning meetings, but they came to the committee's wrap-up meeting following the 2014 festival to declare that they wanted to see some changes.

"It just gets old, you donating so much money to groups and not getting any help in return," Wallace said, upset that other community members did not help organize the festival even though they often benefited financially from the event.

"Yeah, there's no support," Alice agreed.

"They *do* support us, though," Jan said, pleading, "They might not be here, but they donate money, let us use buildings—"

Cutting Jan off, Alice asked, "Why does the Goose Festival donate to people doing fundraisers?"

"Community betterment. Our goal isn't to build money for the Goose Festival. It's so we can donate back to the community because it can't fund itself. It's small and limited," Jan said.

"Those fundraisers draw people to the Goose Festival. Like the fish fry, people come just for that," Susan noted.

"They come for the gun raffle. It's been going on for thirty years. Some come just for that," Jan added, highlighting the Sportsman's Club contribution to drawing a crowd.

"All I know is, you do *a lot*, and you don't have the support," Alice disagreed.

"But we do!" Jan pushed back.

"If we don't get support from the bar, go to the park. Just move it off [the] main street. I mean, the only one it supports is the bar!" Wallace exclaimed, referring to the financial benefit the bar owner received from the crowds the festival drew despite not helping organize the festival.

"If you want to be family friendly, move it down there! No family wants to see a drunk falling out of the bar," Alice said, playing to the family atmosphere the committee had been promoting.

"Yeah! If *those* people don't want to help—" Wallace started.

"But the legion has the fish fry!" Jan said, resisting their suggestion to move the festival from the heart of Sumner because this would undercut groups' efforts to generate revenue.

"Don't make excuses for them!" Alice retorted.

Wallace added, "The young kids have to be involved. . . . Everyone says they want to help. But when it comes down to it, the young ones, twenty-six and down, they just don't care."

"They have to get to a certain age to realize. Now the tent, everyone helps do that," Jan said, invoking the significance of age and again using the tent to support her argument that the community really did support the committee.

"But there's more to it than putting up a tent!" Alice rightly noted.

The importance of gender, rurality, and age were all on the table because Wallace and Alice were questioning the assumptions that guided Carol, Jan, Patti, and Susan's organization of the festival. And at every turn the members of the committee had an explanation for why things were the way they were. Younger individuals would step up and start helping eventually. The men? Well, they helped too, Jan assured Wallace and Alice. They donated money, let the festival use buildings they owned, and even helped put up the tent. Even if they did not put in time to help organize everything, it was seemingly okay. After all, Sumner was a rural community that was "small and limited," so someone needed to be doing the work to make sure it was sustained.

Along with the links between gender, rurality, and age, this interaction also draws out the tensions between having the power to organize the festival and being required to do all the labor associated with that power. Scholars studying rural communities have debated whether this kind of civic work empowers women or if it is just another case of women doing extra care work. Like many of these authors, I believe the answer is both.[24]

In some respects, organizing the festival was empowering for the women who composed the committee. To an extent, they controlled what events would be happening, which vendors would be invited, and how money from sales and donations was distributed. I say to an extent because, presumably, the men in the community would have pulled their support for the festival if the committee had done anything too disagreeable. Wallace emphasized this when he said that if he had been one of the men donating to the festival he would "never donate again" because he was so displeased with how it was being organized. In a community with limited infrastructure and resources that were generally controlled by men, the festival likely would not have been rearranged and sustained if such negative feelings had been more widespread.[25] Further, as Alice and Wallace's comments stress, organizing the festival was not purely empowering for the women who did it. They were doing a lot of unpaid work to organize a festival in a community underpinned by understandings of gender that often devalued work associated with femininity. Remember, this was work Rick had said he was "tickled" he no longer had to do now that the women were organizing the festival.

This was an ambivalent empowerment in which Jan, Carol, Patti, and Susan were simultaneously (dis)advantaged. They undoubtedly had more power than in the past when men were organizing the festival, but this power came with a price—the obligation to do lots of tedious, behind-the-scenes work. This convoluted empowerment was just the beginning in regard to how the reorganization of the festival was helping reorganize and reproduce convoluted arrangements of empowerment and marginalization. Besides facilitating the continued reproduction of inequalities between men and women, the festival also facilitated the rearrangement and reproduction of intersecting inequalities among men and women, respectively.

Ambivalent Inequalities: (Dis)Advantaging Men and Women

"I've never been to the quilt show because I never saw it," Susan informed Jan and Carol as they talked before one of their monthly planning meetings.

"Yeah, but the people that're interested always make a point of going," Jan said, defending the decision to host the quilt show in the town church, located well away from the heart of the festival.

Carol, agreeing with Jan, added, "It's always full, and there are some real neat stories with those quilts a lot of times."

Jan and Carol were right that the quilt show was well attended, but Susan's point that many might not even know it was occurring was also accurate. When I was writing my field notes and analyzing the festival program following the 2013 Goose Festival, I realized that I had absolutely no information on the quilt show. In fact, I had no information on events that focused on women and girls such as the beauty pageant and princess tea. This was not intentional but was instead due to these events always being held in places well away from the festival grandstand. I had spent my time on the main street of the festival because that is where it seemed the action was, but I had missed all the events focusing on women by doing this.

Feminist scholars have long and rightly noted that how individuals arrange and are made to arrange themselves in space is crucially important to the reproduction of gendered inequalities.[26] In this respect, whereas events that focused on women were always held on the margins of the festival where one had to purposefully seek them out, events focusing on men were always held on the festival grandstand. To see the *Duck Dynasty* lookalike or duck calling contests, one did not have to seek these events out. They and the men who participated in them were at the very center of the festival.

Arranging events in this manner contributed to the perception that events focusing on men were what was really worth seeing at the festival, while events focusing on women were not really all that important. As Jan and Carol noted, if someone wanted to see the events focusing on women, they could seek them out, but they did not need to be on the festival grandstand. As a result, every time men in the community took to the festival grandstand they were placed on a literal and metaphorical pedestal of importance over and above women in the community, who were pushed out of sight to the edges of the festival.

A key exception to this gendered arrangement of space was the festival queen. Each year, the teenage women who entered the beauty pageant were judged by a panel of women in a building well away from other festivalgoers. It was only after the winner was chosen that she was displayed on the festival grandstand and in a convertible during the parade.

Although the queen was very visible at the festival, this was more of an affirmation of the gendered arrangement of space as opposed to being an example of its subversion. After all, it was only after the queen was vetted by a panel of experts and found worthy of a crown that she was allowed to assume a prominent public presence. Further, with their bedazzling crowns, flower bouquets, and prom dresses, the pageant contestants visibly embodied and modeled an ideal of femininity that is often cast as appealing to heterosexual men.

This spatial arrangement of events was emblematic of how the festival helped reproduce gender differences and inequalities in a manner that was underpinned by the ideology of separate spheres. Repeatedly, women were offered opportunities to do gender in manners that affirmed their roles as heterosexual homemakers, while men were provided opportunities to do gender in manners that affirmed their roles in the public sphere. Women and girls were encouraged to take part in the princess tea, beauty pageant, and quilt show. On the other hand, boys and men were given opportunities to show off their hunting skills in the calling contests, march in the color guard at the front of the parade, promote businesses and political causes during the parade, and show everyone just how closely their appearances paralleled the patriarchs of the Robertson family from A&E's *Duck Dynasty*.

The gendered dynamics of these activities often went unstated, but at times they were made more explicit. As I sat in the bleachers opposite the festival grandstand, for example, Jan took the microphone and announced, "The tea party's starting right now. The tea party's starting right now for any little girls."

The yearly gooseberry pie contests and auctions are also particularly notable. Once the pies had been judged, they were publicly auctioned on the grandstand as a community fundraiser. Winning bids ranged from $100 to $800, and the festival committee received roughly $2,000 annually from the auction.

Women and men participated in the pie contest and auction in substantively different ways. Women who were predominantly middle age and older were the only ones who baked and entered pies in the contest. On the other hand, it was primarily men—business owners, farmers, and politicians—who were bidding on the pies. Women rarely bid on and won pies. And when they did it was as representatives of businesses such as Ray-Carroll County Grain or Brunswick Distributors. I never saw a woman who was not representing a business win a bid on a pie, in contrast to the men. By participating in this community fundraiser in starkly different ways, a binary was being reproduced in which middle-age and older women were positioned as behind-the-scenes, domestic caretakers for their community, while high-status men were positioned as highly visible breadwinners for Sumner.

How people were encouraged to bid on the pies by the auctioneers also helped reproduce this gender dichotomy. When a woman in the crowd began to bid on a pie, in one instance, the auctioneer jokingly exclaimed, "Ma'am, you start moving like that [and] you'll be buying one of these pies! Is this your first time doing this?" After a round of laughter from the crowd, the bidding fired back up. Eventually the same woman bid again. Playing off the ambiguity involved in the act of bidding and that women did not typically bid on the pies, the auctioneer again used this as an opportunity to question whether the woman knew what she was doing or whether she was just a ditz. "There you go again! You know you're bidding on this pie, right?" the auctioneer chided her, to the delight of the crowd. Though men were competent members of the public sphere worthy of the auctioneer's trust, women might not be prepared for the fast-paced, high-stakes world of bidding on gooseberry pies.

The auctioneers also routinely tried to get men to bid more by drawing on the assumption that men should be the breadwinners for Sumner. Following a bidding war between two men, the auctioneer looked at the man with the losing bid and exclaimed, "You're shaking your head the wrong way! Like I said, all the money goes back to Sumner! It's good for the community! It's just money; they print it every day, you know!" When a bidding war stalled on another occasion, the auctioneer looked at the man with the lowest bid and pointedly exclaimed, "I won't tell her, fella!" The implication being the man ought to more fully embrace his role as a community breadwinner and not worry about his hypothetically restrictive spouse who would not want him to spend so much on a pie. In both cases, the auctioneer encouraged the men to bid by questioning their masculinity.

The interconnections between gender, the pie auction, and reproducing the community are best illustrated by the auctioneer's comments at the end of the 2014 pie auction. When the champion pie was brought out, he enthusiastically announced, "This is Mrs. Fanny Foster's first-place pie, folks! Here's your time to shine! Thanks for putting it in!" Once the bidding began, the price quickly jumped from $100 to $200, and then to $300, $400, and $500, before reaching the winning bid of $525. After the auctioneer had learned the winner's name, he announced to the crowd, "$525 for Mrs. Fanny Foster's first-place pie; [it] goes to Buzz at Franklin's Auctioneer Service! Give a great big round of applause to the buyers and the bakers! Thanks so much, ladies, for putting them in!" Whereas the bakers were the middle-age and older women who had participated in the auction by doing the domestic work of baking pies, the buyers had all been men who had participated in the fundraiser as community providers.

The festival promoted the continued reproduction of a traditional gender dichotomy informed by the ideology of separate spheres, but the festival cannot accurately be described as a clear, straightforward example of patriarchal privilege—especially when more recent renditions of the festival are compared to the rough-and-tumble ones of the past. Women and children were far more welcome at the festival now than when goose and hunter numbers were high. Over and over again, both men and women in the community emphasized that this was the case. Further, women were now in charge of the festival, and at times they explicitly rejected proposals brought forward by men in the community.

To focus only on the festival's facilitation, in some respects, of gender inequalities would miss two key points, then. The festival was much more inviting and safe for women now than in the past, and women in the community now had far more say in how the festival was organized. A more accurate understanding of the festival is to think of it as an event that facilitated the reproduction of both empowerment and marginalization for women in the community. Inequalities inform individuals' lives in incredibly convoluted and messy manners,[27] and other scholars have similarly found that rural women are (dis)advantaged when they take on extra work to sustain their communities in times of need.[28] Highlighting such complexities is especially important because much research on adaptations to climate change and other socioenvironmental challenges facing communities views inequalities as zero-sum games in which individuals are reduced to winners or losers.[29] But neither inequalities nor adaptations can be described in such simple, dichotomous terms.

It is not just that women were simultaneously (dis)advantaged by the rearrangement of the festival that helps illustrate how reorganizations of communities result in ambivalent rearrangements of inequalities. It is also clear that women and men with particular sexualities and classes were differentially (dis)advantaged by the festival reorganization. In other words, the rearranged festival helped reproduce inequalities among women and men, respectively.

Those who adhered to a wholesome ideal of heterosexual monogamy were the kinds of women and men most welcome at festivals. One of the more memorable instances in which it was readily apparent that the women organizing the festival wanted to organize it to cater to heteronormative families comes from Wallace's remarks at the meeting following the 2014 festival. In his opinion, there needed to be more things happening on the Friday and Saturday nights of the festival to draw in younger people, in their teens and twenties. Carol disagreed because she thought this would undermine the committee's efforts to attract men and women deemed desirable. Wallace proposed having a dance or a concert, but Carol replied:

We had to quit those dances. It was horrendous. We didn't have 15 kids in this town, but we'd have 150 drunk ones down there at those dances. The highway patrol just lined up waiting for them. . . . I'm not for the night stuff. After seven you get drunks and you get *trouble*. You get trouble. [In] the past, that's all we had. Out there drinking whiskey in the streets. Now we got it more family oriented.

Like the other women in charge of the festival, Carol did not think they should try to draw in a younger crowd at night because this could jeopardize the specific kind of inclusiveness they had worked so hard to achieve. The dance would bring in younger men and women, but these were not the kinds of men and women the festival committee wanted at a family-oriented festival.

The husband-calling contest, an event featuring women calling their husbands to the grandstand much as an owner would call their dog, was also now excluded from the festival proceedings because it threatened the family-friendly atmosphere. Describing the final husband-calling contest, Jan recounted:

We used to have adult games. The women would get up there and they had a husband-calling contest. . . . The last time we did it that I can remember, somebody got up there and got very offensive on the microphone calling her husband. It was like, this is over because you don't know what a good time is, people. Look at the crowd! Look at who's standing in front of you, people. And so we decided, you know, if they can't do something right, we just wouldn't do it.

Though the husband-calling contest helped reproduce a heteronormative conception of how men and women should relate to each other, Jan's belief that the woman was inappropriate given the audience illustrates an expectation for a morally upright heterosexual order. Women were more welcome than in the past, but particular femininities were conceptualized as inappropriate to the family-friendly atmosphere. As a result, the committee purposefully excluded events that might enable women to behave in undesirable manners.

It was not just the women organizing the festival who helped enforce this exclusivity for particular kinds of women. Regular festivalgoers also helped police the boundaries of which femininities were most welcome at the festival. Two instances in which women were stigmatized for violating the monogamous, wholesome ideal are notable.

In contrast to the vast majority of women who wore T-shirts or sweat-shirts, jeans, and a pair of boots or tennis shoes, one year there was a woman wearing a low-cut, cheetah-print top; skintight jeans; and tall, red heels. Combined with her relatively more sexualized wardrobe, her teased up, hairsprayed hairstyle made her look distinctly different from the other women in attendance. This appearance elicited numerous disapproving looks and comments from both men and women. As she walked by the group of middle-age men and women I was sitting among on a set of bleach-ers, for example, one of the women turned to her friend and whispered, "Well, would you look at *her*?"

A vintage convertible driven by an older man with a group of five women in masquerade masks elicited similar, negative responses. The masks hinted at something outside the bounds of wholesome monogamy, and a large sign on the side of the car read "German's Harem," making the sexual undertones unmistakable. As the convertible crept by during the parade, I quickly turned my attention to the married couple with children standing beside me to see their reactions. Without saying a word, the two looked at each other after reading the sign. Her raised eyebrows and mouth set in a hard line of disapproval made the woman's opinion unmistakable. Even though the festival was safer and more welcoming to women than in the past, it was most welcoming to particular women doing femininities that adhered closely to a certain heterosexuality. Sexualized wardrobes and in-nuendoes were outside the bounds of respectability for good rural women.

Particular men were also privileged by the newer renditions of the fes-tival. In contrast to previous festivals that were typified by physical alterca-tions, which would have provided numerous opportunities to achieve mas-culinities associated with physical strength and toughness, current festivals were more amenable to achieving family-man masculinities. If a man was in a heterosexual relationship and had children, the festival was now an event to which he could bring his partner and children without fearing for their safety. It was clear these kinds of men were taking advantage of the opportunity. Sizable portions of festival crowds were heterosexual couples, and men pushing strollers or holding their small children's hands so that they would not get lost in the shuffle of the crowd were a common sight.

Men with different classes also had divergent opportunities to achieve respectable masculinities at the festival. The pie auction is again notable.

Most men at the festival did not have a spare hundred dollars. Consequently, most men in the community did not position themselves as breadwinners for Sumner by participating in the pie auction. Richard's comments are illustrative.

"Now, how come you're bidding on all these pies?" I asked Richard as we stood shoulder to shoulder during the pie auction.

Laughing, he feigned shock and joked, "You aren't supposed to see me doing that!" As I started to laugh along with him, he continued, "I just like to give back to the community. See the town make some money, and it's all for fun anyways."

"Now, are you running people up, or do you really want to win?" I asked.

"Oh, I don't mind winning, but running Bud's tight ass up doesn't hurt either!" Richard said with a laugh.

Bidding may have been fun and for the good of the community according to Richard, but participating in the auction undoubtedly helped reproduce masculinities infused with class. Richard's apparent lack of concern over having to pay hundreds of dollars for a pie if he happened to win while trying to get others to pay more draws direct attention to the resources needed to participate in this event. Most men could not afford to be unconcerned about having to pay hundreds of dollars for a pie, but for Richard and a few other well-off men the auction was an opportunity to compete to be community breadwinners.

It is tempting to read the festivals as events in which upper-class masculinities were privileged over and above working- to middle-class masculinities, and to a degree this is an accurate understanding because working- to middle-class men generally did not have the same opportunities to act as highly visible, monetary providers for their community. Further, the newer festivals with their fewer physical altercations were less amenable to masculinities couched in physical strength, which are often exuded by working-class men.[30] Nevertheless, the festival provided working- to middle-class men with some opportunities to do rural masculinities associated with worth and respect.

Men from these classes regularly drove their trucks and all-terrain vehicles in the parades. They also tended to be the ones participating in the duck and goose calling contests and the *Duck Dynasty* lookalike pageant. Consequently, they portrayed themselves as capable operators of machinery and adventurous masters of nature who were capable providers for their families. They did not buy pies as their upper-class counterparts did, but they still acted as community breadwinners in a less visible and status-laden way by buying the five-dollar raffle tickets community groups sold as fund-raisers.[31] The festival was being organized in a manner that privileged particular kinds of masculinities, but it still provided opportunities for men from a range of classes to accomplish respectable masculinities.

Conclusion: Working with and Reproducing Messy Inequalities

By drawing on their rural femininities to guide their rearrangement of the festival, the women on the festival planning committee both undermined and facilitated the reproduction of inequalities between as well as among men and women. Carol, Jan, Patti, and Susan had more power than they had when the men in the Sportsman's Club organized the festival, and they had made Goose Festivals more welcoming and safe for women. Nevertheless, the power to reorganize the festival came at the cost of the obligation to do a lot of unpaid, largely invisible work. The committee also continued to organize the festival in a manner that often excluded women from the public sphere. While boys and men were given opportunities to reaffirm their abilities to be good breadwinners on the festival grandstand, girls and women were presented opportunities to reaffirm their roles as homemakers on the largely invisible margins of the event. The newer festivals also privileged those who exuded a heterosexuality perceived as wholesome and upper-class men who were provided with especially visible opportunities to reaffirm their dominant positions within the community.

These findings support research emphasizing the need to consider how inequalities inform and are informed by adaptations to socioenvironmental disruptions such as climate change.[32] More specifically, though, they also reject analyses supporting zero-sum approaches to inequalities.[33] Inequalities are incredibly complex and cannot adequately be described in dichotomous, either-or terms.[34] Effects were not universal for all members of a particular demographic group. Men and women were fragmented by other, intersecting dimensions of difference and inequality that informed the degree to which they benefited from the festival reorganization. Some individuals and groups were even simultaneously (dis)advantaged because of how the festival was reorganized and sustained in response to shifts in goose migration patterns.

In addition to informing the outputs of adaptations, the messy complexities of inequalities also informed how adaptations unfolded. Although social heterogeneity can undermine adaptations in some circumstances,[35] numerous researchers have found that social heterogeneity can increase the likelihood that communities can be sustained in response to climate change and other socioenvironmental disruptions because this diversity presents avenues by which communities can be rearranged.[36] Various outlooks and ways of getting things done can be tapped like a reservoir for adaptations, for example.[37] Debra Davidson complicates this perspective by noting that inequalities can undermine the positive benefits of social heterogeneity.[38] Though communities may be diverse, the positive influences of diversity can be muted if a majority of individuals and groups are marginalized.[39]

This chapter corroborates this previous research in two key ways. First, the festival was sustained because women in Sumner took control of it. If women had been excluded from the festival committee, it is much less likely the festival would have been repurposed and sustained. Women were doing all the behind-the-scenes work needed to reorganize the festival, and men in the community were supporting this work by providing access to community infrastructure and financial backing for entertainment and fundraisers. Second, the festival was sustained because the women rearranging it managed to leverage the demographic heterogeneity in their community. By drawing on their rural femininities to attract a group of people who were less welcome at previous festivals, Carol, Jan, Patti, and Susan reimagined, reinvigorated, and sustained a major source of revenue and social integration in Sumner.

This is not to say that inequalities are good. Far from it. Intersecting inequalities can create "vortexes" in which individuals and groups become trapped and unable to reorganize and sustain their communities.[40] Nevertheless, the messy ambivalences of inequalities are part of the complexity that individuals can creatively draw on to rearrange and sustain their communities. By modifying and repurposing meanings and practices that underpin inequalities, individuals and groups can even reorganize their communities in more just and equitable manners.[41] The women reorganizing the festival drew on sets of knowledge and skills associated with homemaking to rearrange the Goose Festival, for example. Making cookbooks and encouraging men to be financial providers probably are not the first strategies that come to mind to reorganize a community in a manner that empowers women. Nevertheless, by creatively using knowledge and skills that are often associated with the domestic sphere and marginalization, women in Sumner sustained their community while also rearranging it in a manner that, at least in some respects, benefited some women in their community.

Scholars calling for greater attention to social heterogeneity, inequalities, and power when analyzing adaptations are absolutely correct. As long as communities are conceptualized as homogeneous entities, the social inputs and outputs of adaptations will be obscured. Importantly, though, we must move away from zero-sum approaches to inequalities, which frame individuals and groups as either empowered or marginalized, winners or losers. The messy complexities and contradictions of inequalities are integrally important to how and whether communities can be sustained in response to climate change. We also should not expect clear groups of winners and losers following a community's reorganization. A way to account for such complexities is to consider the multiple dimensions of difference and inequality that intersect with and transform each other. But even if only a single dimension of inequality such as gender is being considered, it is still important to keep in mind that particular dimensions of inequality inform individuals' lives and communities in messy, ambivalent manners. We can be both winners and losers because of how our lives and communities are reorganized in response to climate change.

Part II

Institutions and Adaptations

4

Swan Lake National Wildlife Refuge

A Contact Zone Infused with Cultural Convictions

Residents of Sumner widely considered Swan Lake National Wildlife Refuge (NWR), just a mile south of town, to be significant to the past, present, and future of their community. It was no longer the epicenter of Eastern Prairie Population goose migrations, but the refuge continued to be an important resource for the community. It drew swarms of ducks to the area each fall, and many community members now used the refuge as a place to gather for activities related to environmental education. It also evoked pleasurable memories of times spent hunting geese, fishing, and passing time with friends and family. Thus, local residents cared a great deal about how Swan Lake was being repurposed in response to the relative lack of geese coming to the area. Its history was centrally important to the ways many thought of themselves and their community, and it continued to be significant to how residents arranged their relationships with each other and the surrounding landscape.

In subsequent chapters I explore how community members were rearranging the meanings and uses of the refuge in response to fewer geese, but before doing so, it is important to have a better understanding of the refuge. I begin this chapter by introducing the refuge staff members and how they worked to transform the refuge. Then I discuss how materials, plants, and nonhuman animals transformed the way people understood and related to the refuge. Swan Lake NWR is best thought of as a space that emerged through entanglements among (non)humans within and far beyond the boundaries of the refuge. Next, I focus on how community members understood the refuge and the methods used to manipulate it. In line with findings in Chapters 1 through 3, the meanings local residents associated with rural people and places informed how they perceived the refuge. Interrelated understandings of progress, conservation, and governance popularized in the United States over the previous centuries also informed how refuge staff and members of the public understood Swan Lake.

I conceptualize the refuge as a "contact zone." According to Donna Haraway, contact zones are the omnipresent instances in which differentially empowered (non)humans continually remake each other through their constant interactions.[1] Thinking of the refuge as a contact zone is important because it forces us to acknowledge how it emerged, and continued to emerge, through swirling entanglements of (non)humans who constructed the refuge through interactions that were informed as much by materiality as they were by culturally legitimated meanings. In later chapters I continue to draw attention to how a mash of (non)humans and culturally legitimated meanings pertaining to rurality, progress, conservation, and governance informed how the refuge was repurposed in response to shifting Eastern Prairie Population migrations.

The Sort of Wild Life

Four full-time staff members were at Swan Lake NWR while I was conducting fieldwork—two maintenance workers, an office administrator, and the refuge manager. Neither a biologist nor a law enforcement official was on staff, which many members of the public found troubling. To them, this implied that the refuge, and by association their community, was low on the list of priorities of the U.S. Fish and Wildlife Service (USFWS).

Of average height and usually sporting a USFWS ball cap, Larry liked to talk hunting and fishing, though he never seemed to have much luck at either. Indicative of the fraternal atmosphere he liked to promote at work, he referred to himself and the other permanent staff members as "the boys." Aside from loving to give the other employees and me a hard time, Larry especially enjoyed it when groups of schoolkids came to the refuge so that he could ham it up for them. His whitetailed buck impressions were especially popular with the kids, who would howl with laughter whenever Larry imitated a deer rubbing his antlers on a tree.

Ray was far less likely than Larry to give anyone a hard time, but he was just as likely to laugh at a good joke. Tall and gangly, he usually had a full beard, and every now and then he wore a cowboy hat to work. Once he started talking about something it was hard to get him stopped. An avid morel mushroom hunter, he was always pumping others for tips on where the prized fungus could be found when it was "popping" from the ground from late April through early May. Although Ray was eager to hear others' tips, he guarded his morel mushroom spots as though they were state secrets. As hard as I tried, I never once got him to divulge any information on the topic during the twenty months I was at the refuge.

Pete was tall with an average build, and he had a thick push-broom mustache. Always talking in a measured tone and at a steady pace, he liked to discuss gardening but had little patience for anything else that might be associated with a liberal political stance. He knew my project was related to climate change, so whenever we saw something out of the ordinary at the refuge he would sarcastically suggest it was proof that climate change was real. Conversely, to get him wound up and grumbling, I would jokingly threaten to slap a Hillary Clinton bumper sticker on his truck.

Russ was Larry's accomplice, regularly setting him up for a joke or following through on one of Larry's assists. Of average height and stocky, he often spent his weekends fishing or hunting. Like Pete, he was a staunch conservative, and the two of them often teamed up to try to goad me into politically charged discussions on topics such as taxation and health care systems. I mostly avoided these engagements, but every now and then these playful conversations presented opportunities to probe their thoughts on the USFWS.

All four staff members were middle-age white men who exuded a "country-masculine habitus,"[2] meaning they had a gendered knowledge and set of skills that stemmed from spending a considerable amount of time in rural settings as boys and men. They had an intimate familiarity with things such as operating farm equipment and fishing and hunting, for example. They took such knowledge for granted and assumed that others should be able to do things like chaining down heavy equipment to a trailer, so whenever I failed to display such knowledge they gave me a good ribbing. The day I could neither start nor drive a work truck with a manual transmission they sarcastically asked, "Don't they teach you anything in school?"

Aside from the four permanent staff members, temporary workers were hired to help from the spring through early fall. The refuge partnered with the Student Conservation Association and Youth Conservation Corps programs to hire recent college graduates and local high school students for the summer. These workers were usually given the dirtiest, most labor-intensive jobs, such as weed whacking, brush cutting, and power washing mud-caked farm equipment. The student crewmembers were all white, but a roughly even number of women and men filled these positions while I was conducting fieldwork. The refuge also operated a work-camper program in which people with camper trailers and RVs were granted access to utility hookups in exchange for part-time work. The white, retired couples that participated in this program primarily helped around the visitors center by picking up sticks, mowing, and staffing the center on weekends.

These permanent and temporary staff members were charged with managing the largely flat fifteen square miles that composed Swan Lake NWR. Situated between the confluence of Yellow Creek and Grand River, the refuge was a patchwork of agricultural fields, lakes, prairies, hardwood forests, and wetlands. As one might expect given this habitat diversity, it was an excellent place to see a large variety of birds, mammals, bugs, reptiles, amphibians, and fish in a relatively small area. At least partially because of this biodiversity, Swan Lake was a favorite spot for birders, wildlife photographers, and local residents who liked to "take a ride" through the refuge in their vehicles just to see what they could see.

Nevertheless, it was not a preserved wilderness unaffected by humans. The entirety of the landscape as well as the plants and animals there bore the traces of humans' actions both on and far beyond the refuge. Many buildings and a fleet of heavy equipment were at refuge headquarters just south of Sumner, and another smaller set of structures was located at hunting headquarters on the northern edge of the refuge. Figures 4.1, 4.2, and 4.3 show some of this infrastructure.

Areas of the refuge that looked more natural were not beyond human influence either. The tall stand of timber with dense undergrowth on the northern side of Swan Lake is notable. With an array of towering trees and lush, green vegetation, it conformed to images that are often associated with wilderness. Nevertheless, I continually came on traces of peoples' prior actions while walking through it looking for morel mushrooms. Benches next to a defunct trail sat overgrown with moss and vegetation, an old metal clothesline ran between trees, and a rusty hand-operated water pump still stood attached to the top of a well. Even the trees themselves could have been survivors or descendants of the 110,235 trees planted on the refuge from 1938 to 1942.[3]

Wilderness untouched by human hands was actually antithetical to the refuge's institutional mandate to provide habitat for migratory waterfowl. How staff transformed the refuge landscape through a technique called

Figure 4.1 The refuge visitor center.

Figure 4.2 The refuge bunkhouse.

Figure 4.3 The maintenance shop, multibay garage, and a few of the pieces of heavy equipment used by refuge staff.

moist soil management is particularly notable. By manipulating water levels and vegetation around the refuge through the use of forty-two water control structures, thirty-five miles of levees, and heavy equipment, refuge staff enhanced nearly two thousand acres of wetlands.

At the beginning of fall each year, staff opened a set of water control structures and moved water from Silver and Swan Lakes into the wetlands around the refuge. Water remained in the wetlands (called units) through the fall so that waterfowl had places to safely eat and rest. Eventually the marshes froze over as fall turned to winter, and nearly all the one hundred thousand ducks using the area continued south. When marshes thawed at the beginning of spring, refuge staff opened a different set of water control structures to slowly drain water out of the units. Tens of thousands of migrating waterfowl and shorebirds such as sandpipers, avocets, and yellowlegs used the exposed mudflats and shallow waters during this period as they headed back north. As the heat and humidity ratcheted up throughout the summer, the wetlands became covered with a thick green carpet of vegetation that was interspersed with the bubblegum pink of smartweed blossoms, brilliant white of hibiscus blooms, and canary yellow of partridge peas. Almost no waterfowl used refuge marshes during this period, but bright yellow warblers and fluorescent blue buntings darted among the thick vegetation. If and when units became dry enough, staff mowed and disked portions to kill woody vegetation that crowded out plants such as smartweed that provided more food for migrating waterfowl. Disking also encouraged expansions in invertebrate populations—another key food source for migrating waterfowl. When fall arrived, the units were again filled with the seeds and invertebrates waterfowl liked to eat.

Maintaining and using this system of levees, water control structures, and fleet of heavy equipment required constant work, but through this work staff provided excellent habitat for migratory waterfowl. Tens of thousands of ducks regularly used the marshes during migratory periods, and passing cold fronts sometimes pushed numbers well over a hundred thousand. Figure 4.4 provides a rudimentary idea of just how many ducks could crowd into the wetlands, but it does not really do the scene justice because a key part of the spectacle was the raucous chorus made by mallard hens calling to other ducks. The glossy heads of the mallard drakes also turned the now dull wetlands a vibrant green. As Ray excitedly said to me when I walked into the office after a big push of ducks had arrived overnight, "It's just solid freakin' green out there!"

Alterations that had been made to privately held lands off the refuge also affected Swan Lake NWR. The two massive levee systems that ran along the southern boundary of the refuge were particularly important because they had influenced refuge hydrology since it was established in the 1930s. Because the levees created a bottleneck on the Grand River floodplain just downstream from Swan Lake, the refuge and surrounding lands turned into a lake whenever large volumes of water flowed down the Grand River and met the pinch point created by the levees.[4]

These floods also help illustrate how landscape uses far beyond Swan Lake influenced the refuge environment. Intense corn and soybean production in the Grand River watershed, which stretches into southwest Iowa, was particularly important to refuge hydrology. Because croplands soak up less water than prairies and wetlands, relatively high amounts of runoff quickly entered increasingly channelized streams and tributaries. The runoff barreled south toward Sumner and the refuge whenever rain fell in the watershed, and the refuge frequently flooded when areas hundreds of miles north received heavy or even moderate rainfall.

Southern portions of the refuge protected by relatively small levees regularly went under water from the spring through the fall. A major flood also inundated the refuge in September 2014. One of the top five floods in Sumner's recorded history, most of the refuge went underwater for three days after thunderstorms dumped over half a foot of rain in large portions of the Grand River watershed. The damage to the refuge was extensive. Entire levees were chewed up and washed away, large fields of soybeans were turned into masses of rotting vegetation, and the carpets of smartweed in the moist soil units were flattened and killed. One of the main refuge levees is being topped during the flood in Figure 4.5, while some of the aftermath is depicted in Figures 4.6 and 4.7.

Human influences on the refuge were readily apparent, but it was also transformed by nonhuman beings, plants, and materials. Consequently, while Swan Lake was not a pristine wilderness untouched by humans, it was wild in the sense that it was being reproduced through interactions between people and nonhumans beyond their control.[5] Lotus, reed canary grass, buttonbush, bulrush, sericea lespedeza, and willows crowded out vegetation deemed more desirable. Beavers jammed up water control structures with logs. Raccoons broke into and wrecked buildings. Dogs chased coyotes onto

Figure 4.4 Mallards take flight from a refuge marsh.

and around the refuge. Mice immobilized heavy equipment by chewing through wiring. And floods continually wore on refuge infrastructure.

Staff members were often frustrated when nonhumans disrupted manipulation of the refuge environment, but they also considered these disruptions to be part of the job. Ray talked about this as he drove us across the refuge one afternoon.

"You know, so far we've been lucky . . . that the upper levels of bureaucracy have been hands off with [our moist soil management]," Ray said.

Having been at the refuge long enough to realize how complex moist soil management was, I replied, "I mean, how could they try to regulate it? It's too variable. You say it's kind of simple, but I never realized how much goes into it and how much it depends on how much it rains, how fast things dry out, and how much it has to be worked with constantly."

"It's more of an art, and not a science," Ray said. Drawing on his rural masculinity, he then spoke of how much he valued knowledge he had gained through hands-on experiences with the refuge landscape, "You know, there's just things you can't write down or read about in a book. I'm always learning more about these units each year." Pointing out the driver side window to a wetland we were driving past, he expanded on this: "Like this

Figure 4.5 Backwater flooding from the Yellow Creek tops a major refuge levee.

Figure 4.6 A refuge staff member assesses damage to a levee following the flood.

one here. We'll draw it down and expose that mud flat out there and it'll be good habitat. Then we'll get a spring flood and it'll all go underwater."

Floods often complicated staff members' management plans, but to Ray the ability to respond to floods was a skill gained through years of firsthand experiences at Swan Lake NWR.[6] Managing the refuge effectively, in other words, required learning how to work within the shifting webs of entangled (non)humans that created it.

Figure 4.7 Pumping out a pit blind after the flood.

The entangled landscape that emerged through a convoluted mix of so-cial and ecological things, beings, and processes was often beneficial to the nonhumans that used it. If not for these entanglements, Swan Lake would not have been suitable for one of the most interesting species there. The presence of massasauga rattlesnakes, one of the three confirmed popula-tions in Missouri, on the refuge was a direct artifact of the entangled land-scape. The only place the snakes were present was in a field that had been terraced for agricultural production sometime in the past. Though it was no longer being cultivated, the terraces still caught enough water to sustain a crayfish population in whose burrows the snakes survived the cold winters. Without the manmade terraces that gathered water or the crayfish that colonized the previously cultivated field, it is unlikely the rattlesnakes would have been on the refuge.

More common species also used the manipulated landscape to their advantage. Deer thrived in the agricultural fields and prairies interspersed with timber and thick fencerows. Ducks swarmed refuge wetlands. Feral cats loved the mice-infested buildings around refuge headquarters. Bees and butterflies enjoyed the pollinator garden in front of the visitor center. Lotus, bulrush, willows, smartweed, wild millet, and buttonbush also grew especially well in units being manipulated through moist soil management techniques.

Progress and Landscape Manipulations

Although I knew staff manipulated the refuge landscape before I began fieldwork, the intensity of landscape interventions at Swan Lake surprised me. Water levels were constantly altered in the lakes and wetlands. Fields were disked, planted, and harvested with hulking farm equipment. Maples and other trees were killed with powerful herbicides to promote the growth of trees considered more desirable, such as oaks. Beaver dams were ripped out of drainage ditches to allow water to flow through them. And refuge staff always seemed to be mowing something.

Instead of being surprised by the human interventions occurring at Swan Lake, the overwhelming majority of community members I talked with passionately expressed the need for more intensive management strategies. According to common wisdom, there was seemingly always more vegetation that should be destroyed, crops that should be planted, or water levels that should be adjusted.[7] I particularly remember a phone call to the refuge during duck hunting season.

"Swan Lake, this is Braden," I began, mustering as cheery a voice as I could at seven thirty in the morning.

"Hi, this is Allen Maples," the man on the other end of the line responded. "I'm looking at the S and T units right now and was just wondering what you guys had going on down here. We're not getting anything hunting by S and T. What're you guys doing over there? Why isn't there any vegetation? Are you planning on planting something?"

I was caught off guard by the implication that the wetland units, which were designated by letters, ought to be manipulated for Allen's duck hunting, but I explained, "Uh, well, we had that fall flood, and it really set everything back."

"Well, what about now?" Allen replied, not dissuaded by my explanation.

Not understanding what he expected me to say, I responded, "Well, nothing's really going to grow in the unit now, sooo . . . ?"

"Well, I know that!" he retorted, his irritation evident. "I thought maybe you'd drain it and get some kind of mud flats out there. Right now it's just a bunch of open water. Right now it just looks like hammered dog shit. Mud flats would be better than nothing. Right now all the ducks are headed east out of the refuge, and we aren't getting any shooting whatsoever."

Having been in the S and T units just the day before, I knew it was not just open water, but it seemed that Allen would not be satisfied with anything I said unless it involved confirming that the refuge landscape would be more intensively manipulated. Consequently, I informed him that the refuge manager would be in later that day, and he was welcome to call back and talk to him if he liked.

Despite Swan Lake being a national wildlife refuge, and wilderness often being conceptualized as an environment that has not been influenced by people, locals supported visible, dramatic transformations to the refuge environment.[8] Though some residents wanted to see more landscape interventions because of more individualized concerns like duck hunting, locally accepted understandings of progress that equated improvement with agricultural production also help explain why residents generally favored more intensive landscape manipulations.[9]

Conforming to the belief that agricultural production improves land by lifting it out of wilderness, which has informed understandings of progress in the United States and the West for more than two hundred years,[10] community members widely considered the amount of land being cultivated on the refuge to be a barometer of how well the refuge was being managed by the USFWS. Accordingly, members of the public and refuge staff regularly found it particularly egregious that fewer refuge acres were being cultivated than during the 1970s, 1980s, and 1990s.

Fred and Jan brought this up during our interview. As we sat around their kitchen table, both told me they were disappointed that less of the refuge was in agricultural production than in the past.

"There's no way . . . [having more moist soil] is going to hurt the longevity of that refuge," I said, referring to an area on the refuge that was going to be converted from crops into moist soil wetlands through a North American Wetlands Conservation Act grant.

"It'll be great," Jan agreed.

"Now, I don't see—they're not going to go the other way," Fred said.

"As far as?" I asked, not quite sure what he was getting at.

"More crops," Fred clarified, before continuing, "Doing a better job. That isn't going to happen."

"Yeah, that's dead as far as now," I agreed, knowing that the USFWS had no plans to farm more refuge ground.

"So they're going to go with let it grow up and whatever grows up out there. Well, okay, fine, but that's not really a very progressive—that's not progressive at all in my opinion," Fred said.

Fred's contention that converting the landscape to wetlands was the opposite of "doing a better job" reveals the conceptual links between agricultural production and progress. Moist soil management completely depended on extensive levee systems, water control structures, and a fleet of heavy equipment to intensively manipulate the landscape for the benefit of ducks. Fred did not consider this to be a good management practice, though. "Whatever" would be growing instead of row crops, and "whatever" made up a landscape that was not being improved as best it could.

Swan Lake staff also had especially negative sentiments about the locusts, willows, cottonwoods, maples, and grass species that grew in places where corn, wheat, and beans were previously cultivated.[11] On several occasions, Larry even fantasized about burning formerly cultivated areas on the refuge that were now covered with reed canary grass. One such occasion was when Larry, Russ, I, and a reporter from the Missouri Department of Conservation were passing time in the maintenance shop during a managed deer hunt.

As Russ and Larry pored over a dated aerial photograph of the refuge that was hanging on the shop wall, Russ pointed to the photo and said, "We don't farm any of this anymore, and it's just a mess, a bunch of willows and trash growing up in there." Pointing to another area, he drew attention to how USFWS staff in the regional office wanted to keep pulling refuge ground out of agricultural production. "They think it'll grow back to grassland if we stop farming it. No way! It'll be a bunch of willows and locusts. They say, 'We want it to be the way it was,' but how far back do you go? Columbus? The dinosaurs? They don't say."

"See this area up here?" Larry pointed to another spot on the refuge. "We don't farm any of that anymore either."

"Yeah, because of those snakes," Russ said, referring to the massasaugas.

Turning to look at the reporter, who was wandering around the shop, Larry asked, "Do you smoke?"

"No?" the reporter responded quizzically, unsure why Larry asked.

"Oh, well, that's too bad. I was going to say, if you did, you should just throw your cigarettes out the window while you're driving by. Yeah, that would really help us if you could have thrown a butt or two out into the grass over there on your way out of here."

Much like Fred, Jan, and other community members, Russ and Larry wanted the vegetation destroyed to restore order and improve the landscape. In addition to touching on the conceptual links between agricultural production and progress, Russ and Larry also made plain how local residents often contended that regulations coming from supralocal levels of the USFWS made commonsense manipulation of the refuge harder.

They were undoubtedly right that USFWS regulations informed how the refuge was manipulated. However, best practices for transforming the refuge environment were not necessarily inevitable or common sense. Taken-for-granted ways of relating to environments are social constructions having convoluted meanings that can and do change over time and from place to place.[12] In addition to the conceptual links between progress and agricultural production, refuge staff and members of the public regularly drew on meanings concerning governance and conservation to call for more intensive landscape interventions, which they viewed as common sense. Meanings associated with governance and conservation also played a part in Sumner residents' conceptualizations of the refuge and how it ought to be manipulated.

The USFWS as an Out-of-Touch, Urban Bureaucracy

Swan Lake NWR was at the end of a long chain of command that stretched from USFWS headquarters in Washington, D.C., to Region Three headquarters in Bloomington, Minnesota, to complex headquarters in Columbia, Missouri,[13] and finally to Swan Lake NWR in Sumner. What this meant in effect was that refuge staff had to interpret and follow a long list of policies and directives coming from USFWS officials working off-site. For anyone who has worked in a bureaucracy or business with multiple management levels, it probably is not surprising that refuge staff generally agreed that directives coming from the federal, regional, and complex levels of the USFWS often made it harder for them to do their jobs. Staff took these regulations seriously and did their best to follow them, but they consistently grumbled that these directives undermined their ability to more effectively perform work tasks.[14] Perhaps no other staff member expressed such frustrations more succinctly than Larry when he shouted from his desk one day, "You have to get a form signed just to take a crap around here!"

Members of the public also were frustrated with USFWS regulations. During our interview, I asked Greg if he thought there should be any changes to how the refuge was managed. In his usually direct manner, he said:

There's some people here really doing their job. It's the advice coming from upstairs, way upstairs, from people that . . . wouldn't even
know how to get across the refuge! And they spent billions of dollars, or millions and millions and millions. We watched them for
years down there, and they've wasted tremendous amounts of
money and accomplished nothing with it! . . . Now you got me fired
up a little bit; I guess I did it to myself, but I'm giving you the consensus of most of the folks.

On another occasion, as Greg and I caught up at the bar one afternoon,
I told him about my preparations to take the strenuous pack test so that I
could be certified to help with prescribed burns at the refuge. "You know
just how to get me going!" he exclaimed, gesturing as though he was stab-
bing a knife into something and then twisting it around. "Yeah, you're getting me fired up! That's the idiocracy again! They spend so much time and
money on testing this and that, when all they'd have to do is just put you on
four-wheelers and you'd be fine! Hell, they'd probably have enough money
to buy you all four-wheelers, as much money as they spend on testing!"

Having heard his viewpoints on certification courses and regulations
over the preceding year, I began to laugh.

"Yeah, you know just how to wind me up!" he exclaimed, throwing his
hands up in despair.

Still laughing, I replied, "I mean, I understand having some sort of physical test. Now, should it be as strenuous as this test? Well, I don't know about
that, but you'll love this: Larry was saying that they've actually had more
people die trying to pass the test than in actual fires."

"My god!" Greg practically shouted, his disdain for such regulations
presumably vindicated.

Such portrayals of the USFWS correspond with conservative, neoliberal
views of the federal government as an overly intrusive, wasteful, bungling
burden. Popularized in the United States since the 1980s, neoliberalism
holds that federal agencies should take a much more hands-off approach
and let individuals or the market solve problems. Neoliberalism is predicated on a general push to roll back regulations and government spending,
including government involvement in conservation, except when these facilitate the accumulation of capital.[15] According to advocates of neoliberal

conservation strategies, environmental protection and the sustainable use of resources is best achieved through individualistic, market-based solutions such as green consumption and ecotourism.[16] On the other hand, and as Greg suggested, money tends to get wasted, and matters supposedly go awry whenever federal agencies such as the USFWS get involved in conservation.

As I describe in Chapters 1 through 3, perceived differences between rural and urban people and places were particularly important to individuals in Sumner. As the preceding examples allude to, beyond a generic, neoliberal rejection of government, community members regularly linked USFWS mismanagement to differences between rural and urban people and places.

For example, although not all men in the community blamed the USFWS for causing the geese to stop migrating to Sumner, those who did often emphasized that overly educated, urban-based bureaucrats and their misguided management practices at Swan Lake NWR were behind the lack of geese. Discussions of organic farming programs implemented during the 1980s were particularly telling. While sitting at the bar one afternoon, Kurt invoked these programs to explain why the geese stopped migrating to Sumner:

> There's no geese around here now, as you know. Those fuckers. Some guy that has never been here and doesn't know what the fuck is going on around here running things. There was one manager that was in there [at the refuge], didn't even want to fertilize the fields! Said the earthworms would take care of it. The earthworms!

By blaming USFWS officials for the lack of geese, local men like Kurt positioned their knowledge (and their rural masculinities) as superior to the formally educated officials running Swan Lake and the USFWS. USFWS officials "did things by the book" and "studied things to death" while implementing inappropriate management strategies. Conversely, according to Kurt and others I talked with, the geese might have continued coming to Sumner if rural men who relied on experience-based knowledge and industrialized agriculture techniques[17] had been managing the refuge.

Members of the Friends of Swan Lake also asserted that the USFWS mismanaged Swan Lake because it favored refuges near urban population centers. During their monthly meetings, Friends members frequently said USFWS officials "up there in their offices in Minneapolis" were not all that invested in supporting public involvement "out here in a small town like Sumner."[18]

Divergent Understandings of Conservation

USFWS regulations were considered particularly troublesome also because they often violated assumptions about the purpose of conservation.[19] Justin Farrell's analysis of Yellowstone National Park is especially useful here. He is careful to note that political-economic and institutional factors are part of the reason for conflicts over conservation strategies in and around the park, but he argues that the conflicts have been underpinned by divergent understandings about humans' proper relation with nature. Conflicts concerning the management of Yellowstone, in other words, have been moral conflicts informed by socially constructed assumptions about how people ought to relate to environments and the nonhumans therein.[20]

Farrell makes the case that three moral stances are primarily behind these controversies. Utilitarianism considers particular plants, animals, and materials important if they are useful for people. Usefulness can be contingent on economic value, but nonhumans can be useful for other purposes, such as ducks being useful for accomplishing masculinities in Sumner. While nonhumans deemed useful by and for humans are considered worthy of efforts to retain them, others that are not can be destroyed to promote the well-being of, or access to, useful plants, animals, and materials. In contrast, biocentrism considers the environment to be an interconnected web that can become an uninhabitable dystopia for humans and nonhumans if it is disrupted. Consequently, nonhumans are important and worthy of protections because the degradation of any one species could throw environmental systems out of balance. Finally, spiritualism considers nature useful because humans can escape the perils of modernity and urbanism by communing with environments and the nonhumans in it.[21]

I heard bits and pieces of the spiritualist understanding of the relation between humans and environments during conversations and interviews, but utilitarianism versus biocentrism came up far more frequently when refuge staff and members of the public were discussing management practices at Swan Lake. Members of the public and refuge staff overwhelmingly advocated conservation strategies that were grounded in utilitarianism. They found particularly egregious the regulations that were based on a biocentric approach to conservation. Controversies over river otters and the massasauga rattlesnakes are illustrative.

People had more or less eliminated river otters in Missouri by the 1930s, but the Missouri Department of Conservation began an otter reintroduction program in the 1980s to restore ecological complexity. Swan Lake was ground zero for the project because its waterways and wetlands made it ideal otter habitat. The effort ended up being wildly successfully, so that by 2013 it was not unusual to see otters on the refuge and in the surrounding area.

Although nature shows and children's cartoons often depict otters as cute, cuddly, and playful, local residents saw otters in starkly different terms. While sitting at the bar one afternoon, I mentioned to Carl and Greg that I had seen some otters earlier that day. Instead of expressing pleasure at hearing my report, Carl immediately began to criticize the Missouri Department of Conservation for reintroducing otters in the 1980s.

"I tell you what," he began, his eyes widening and his face growing red with anger, "I hope they shove every goddamn otter they let loose up their fucking asses!"

"I caught one of the first ones they let loose in one of my traps," Greg recalled. "Had a tracking device and everything. Told the [conservation] agent and he got all pissy with me about it. It's not like I could help it, and at least I told them about it. Could have just left it there in the weeds."

"I was sitting out in my backyard and I saw five or six of them humping it over the hill behind my house. Just hauling ass across my field," Carl recounted, still visibly irritated. "Well, within a couple weeks they'd eaten every damn fish out of my and everyone else's ponds. I just shot the fuckers. Well, the conservation agent came down and was giving me a hard time, and I asked him, 'Are you gonna stock my pond for me?' He said, 'Well, no.' So I said, 'All right, well, that's my pond, and I'll do whatever the hell I want. I'll shoot every one of the fuckers I see from now on.' I don't try to break the law; I mean, I pretty much follow it, but I don't give a shit on those motherfuckers. They'll ruin every damn pond there is, so I'll shoot the fuckers on sight."

Carl was not alone in his desire to eliminate otters. Whenever I said I had seen an otter, residents asked whether I had managed to kill it, before going on to explain that otters ate all the fish out of ponds. Otters needed to be eliminated, in other words, because they undermined the utilitarian objective of people catching and consuming fish. Their reintroduction may have helped restore the biological complexities of the Missouri ecosystem, but this was not a good thing according to local residents, because the otters hindered them in catching and using species they found useful.[22]

Reactions to policies and directives pertaining to the massasauga rattlesnakes were equally indicative of the tensions between utilitarianism and biocentrism at Swan Lake NWR. I never once heard a positive word said about the rattlesnakes by members of the public who lived near the refuge, but remarks about the "damn snakes" were commonplace. Statements that juxtaposed desires to promote species considered useful with the USFWS's efforts to protect the snakes were especially notable.

During our interview, Grover, a farmer in his eighties who had grown up and spent his entire life next to the refuge, explained that he was displeased that agricultural production had been rolled back on the refuge. An avid waterfowl hunter, he argued that fewer crops would mean fewer ducks and even fewer geese coming to the area. Sitting across from me at a small desk pushed against the wall in his kitchen, he rolled his eyes and said, "But they'll do anything for them damn snakes!"

Some refuge staff had similar opinions. Though the massasaugas were on only a small part of the refuge, they caused many conflicts between refuge staff and USFWS staff in the ecological services office in Columbia over management of that portion of the refuge. There was disagreement over whether to burn the area as part of a prescribed burn plan. Then staff members in the ecological services office raised objections to spraying sericea lespedeza in the area from a tractor because the snakes could get run over. Swan Lake staff members' general distaste for regulations as well as their rural masculinities informed how they reacted to these concerns, but equally as important was their utilitarian take on conservation that privileged particular species as more worthy of consideration.

As I leaned against Pete's office door one morning, he gave me a mischievous grin and said, "I got a job for ya."

Rightly suspicious because of his tendency to try to assign me humorously ridiculous tasks, such as the time he and Larry tried to convince me to climb a tree to look in an eagle nest "for the advancement of science," I warily asked, "What is it?"

"We're going to be spraying that lespedeza, and we were getting a spray rig for it, but the snake people in the ecological services office don't want a tractor or even a four-wheeler out there," Pete explained, obviously annoyed. I gave him a wide-eyed look of disbelief, and he continued, "Chyeah. They want us to backpack spray two hundred acres."

I began to laugh incredulously, before saying, "Well, I guess they can do it if they want. That's a big area! Plus those snakes will be out there with you. No way I'm doing that!"

To Pete and me it was inconceivable that tractors could not be used to spray the area. Two hundred acres was a large area, and we considered tractors to be perfectly suitable tools for manipulating landscapes. But our incredulity was also from rattlesnakes being the reason that tractors could not be used. Unlike deer and waterfowl, snakes are not usually considered useful. It seemed ridiculous to us to go to such great lengths to avoid killing a poisonous snake when destroying undesirable vegetation.

On another occasion, while Ray was driving Larry and me back to the visitor center after working in the area with the massasaugas, Ray directly linked conflicts over the snakes to tensions between the utilitarian and biocentric approaches to conservation. He said, "If those snakes were other places on the refuge, it would make it where we couldn't do anything anywhere those snakes are. The thing is, people around here don't care about those snakes. But if you'd get a [refuge manager who focused on snakes] here, I guarantee things would change." The snakes and directives protecting them, in other words, presented roadblocks to more intensively altering the refuge landscape to benefit species local residents considered useful.

Programs and policies that were implemented to promote otters and rattlesnakes tended to evoke a considerable degree of anger and frustration from members of the public and refuge staff. By protecting species that local residents did not consider useful, such policies violated local residents' assumptions about the purpose of conservation. Put more generally, these policies often angered community members because they violated commonsense understandings concerning how people should relate to environments and the nonhumans in them.

Conclusion: A Contact Zone, an Inhabited Institution

While the refuge landscape and its nonhumans had been influenced by humans' actions, nonhumans also complicated how people related to Swan Lake. The refuge was not a wilderness untouched by human hands, and it was not perfectly controlled by people. It is better thought of as a contact zone that continued to be reproduced through interactions between social and ecological things, beings, and processes. Further, understandings of progress, governance, and conservation were particularly important to how refuge staff and members of the public conceptualized the (non)human entanglements of the refuge.

In Chapter 5, I examine these linked understandings of progress, governance, and conservation and their importance to the reconstruction of the meanings and uses of Swan Lake in response to the lack of geese. More-over, I consider power and inequalities in my analysis. Critical theorists have repeatedly shown that power, inequalities, and culture are intricately wound together.[23] Culturally legitimated ways of perceiving and acting in the world are informed by *and* involved in the reproduction of power and inequalities in other words. This is especially true in how individuals un-derstand and relate to environments. Scholars from a range of disciplines have repeatedly shown that different individuals and groups often associate divergent meanings with particular places, and that individuals and groups are (dis)advantaged when their ways of understanding an environment are (de)legitimated in informal and legal terms.[24] Swan Lake NWR was no dif-ferent.

The following chapters address these links between power, inequali-ties, and how individuals and groups interpreted the refuge by seeing the USFWS and Swan Lake NWR as "inhabited institutions."[25] This approach to studying institutions such as the USFWS emphasizes that institutions are made up of individuals who are constantly interpreting and negotiat-ing how to get things done.[26] Bureaucrats are not robots following ready-made rules that tell them exactly how they should do their jobs. Further, and returning to the significance of power, this approach posits that previ-ously established ways of getting things done[27] and the organizational ar-rangement of institutions influence how officials go about doing their jobs.[28] The actions and interactions that are centrally important to institu-tions do not occur independently of previously established ways of solving problems or (in)formal authority structures within institutions. By ap-proaching the refuge and the USFWS as an inhabited institution in subse-quent chapters, I focus attention on how efforts to repurpose the refuge in response to the lack of geese were informed by an entangled mix of cultur-ally legitimated meanings and perceptions, interpersonal interactions, and individuals' and groups' locations within the organizational structure of the USFWS.

Although USFWS staff up the chain of command from Swan Lake NWR had a considerable amount of power in how the refuge was being repurposed, they did not control how the meanings and uses of the refuge were being rearranged. Representatives of other institutions, refuge staff, and members of the public interacted to creatively leverage the organiza-tional structure of the USFWS and the meanings associated with progress, governance, and conservation to influence the repurposing of the refuge. In some cases, they even successfully resisted and undermined policies and programs being pushed by USFWS representatives at higher levels of the organization. Also complicating how the refuge was being repurposed were (non)human interactions. The refuge, in other words, was an institution that was inhabited by far more than just people.

5

Repurposing the Refuge

Adaptations amid Conflicts over the Future

Russ let out a startled, "He-yow!" as we walked along a levee through matted vegetation well up over our waists.

Just ten feet to his left, I managed a surprised, "What?" before hearing something moving toward me through the tangled grass and smartweed. After being startled by snakes I had stepped near, over, or on all morning, I knew what was coming my way, so I scampered up the levee to the relative safety of its gravel top.

Russ excitedly exclaimed, "I about stepped on that dang snake!" Holding up his hands to make a circle the size of a Pringles can, he continued, "That thing was huge! I'll tell you what, Larry would be out of here after that." We both started laughing as Russ continued, "He'd be done! I'm starting to think we've walked enough of this levee too."

Not a fan of snakes, I emphatically agreed.

It was a sunny morning in mid-May, and Russ and I were walking a refuge levee marking washouts from the September flood with fluorescent orange flagging tape so that staff members would not hurt themselves by accidentally dropping off into one of the sizable holes when they mowed the levee later that day. Daily work like this at the refuge routinely involved practices meant to avoid risks, or negative outcomes that could happen in the future.[1] Taking certification courses on all-terrain vehicle operation and prescribed burning, wearing protective glasses and earmuffs while mowing, always buckling seatbelts, wearing steel-toed boots, and being subject to routine safety inspections are excellent examples. Nevertheless, it was often unclear what was risky because it was not possible to know the future.

Was it risky, for example, to walk a recently burned field looking for rattlesnakes? It may sound risky, and I certainly thought so while I was doing it, but it was too early in the year for the snakes to emerge from their wintering dens. Was it risky to wade into black, stagnant floodwater that reeked of sulfur and had bloated fish floating in it to open a water control structure after a flood? I am not really sure, but I am glad I did not trip and fall because, to the bemusement of Russ and Pete, the smell of the water alone had me dry heaving repeatedly. Was it risky to walk around the bed of a truck with a board sitting across it? Apparently, because an injury report had to be filed after a refuge staff member walked smack into the board. Because of this inherent uncertainty about the future, refuge staff members frequently discussed, and sometimes disagreed over, the risks involved in work tasks like spraying herbicides, building handrails on boardwalks, and removing feral cats from the barns around refuge headquarters.

Beyond informing daily work routines, understandings and conflicts over risks were centrally important to reconstructing the meanings and uses of Swan Lake National Wildlife Refuge in response to the lack of geese. During the year and a half I was at the refuge, conflicts continually erupted among members of the public and U.S. Fish and Wildlife Service (USFWS) staff in response to policies implemented to lessen the risk of lawsuits. Because these policies tended to undermine community members' efforts to repurpose the refuge in response to the lack of geese, and because local residents were less concerned about lawsuits, the policies prompted a considerable degree of conflict between the USFWS and local residents.

At the heart of these conflicts were divergent frames of risk that portrayed the future in manners that foregrounded particular risks as worthy of attention.[2] Members of the public and refuge staff tended to combine conservative takes on governance with utilitarian approaches to conservation to frame the future in ways that focused attention on the risk of decreased public use of the refuge. In contrast, USFWS staff working off-site drew on a biocentric understanding of conservation to frame the future in ways that emphasized risks posed to and by webs of interconnected humans, materials, plants, and nonhuman animals. Both frames were based on divergent, taken-for-granted understandings of the environment and how humans ought to relate to it.[3]

The relation between divergent frames of risk and adaptations at the refuge aligns with over thirty years of research in environmental sociology. Numerous scholars have found that perceptions of risks influence responses to socioenvironmental disruptions, harms, and dangers,[4] and analyses have even determined that the ways that potential hazards are framed is especially important to our responses to them.[5] Scholars have argued that perceptions of risk specifically influence adaptations to climate change.[6] Though I agree that perceptions of future harms inform adaptations to climate change, my examination of conflicts over risks at the refuge leads me to a different conclusion from most about *how* perceptions of the future can inform adaptations.

There is general agreement that adaptations to climate change are undermined by climate-related risks being thought of as in the distant future.[7] We might assume that people would take measures in the present to avoid the negative impacts of climate change if they were more concerned with the distant future or if they believed climate risks were more immediately threatening. This explanation seems reasonable, but it is fundamentally flawed. Assuming that individuals consciously weigh the pros and cons of different courses of action when deciding what to do erases the significance of emotions and habits to perceptions of and responses to risks. Further, adaptations to climate change involve risks other than those associated with climate change.[8] A focus on individuals' responses to climate change, or lack thereof, ignores the other risks they face and the baggage from living in social relationships with others, which also influences individuals' responses to risks associated with climate change.[9]

The key questions are not how to get individuals to think more long term or how to reframe climate change so that its current, dramatic consequences are recognized. Instead, the questions are: How do individuals, groups, and institutions with different amounts of power manage to adapt to climate change in a world filled with a dizzying array of risks? How and why are some risks considered more important and therefore worthy of action in the present than others? How do conflicting understandings of the future become reconciled to a degree that cooperative actions facilitating adaptations become possible? I address these questions in the following two chapters.

Adaptations at the refuge were not being undermined by a lack of concern for risks that could happen in the relatively distant future. In fact, the opposite was true. Complex-, regional-, and federal-level USFWS officials' focus on the risk of being sued sometime in the future undermined community members' repurposing of the refuge. Further, as I illustrate in Chapter 6, an eye to the immediate future actually enabled members of the public to continue working with Swan Lake staff even as anger grew over the implementation of new policies designed to avoid lawsuits. Instead of stressing that a focus on the distant future is needed to enable adaptations to climate change, over the next two chapters, I emphasize the opposite. A focus on the relatively distant future can undermine adaptations, and a concern for the more immediate future can enable collective efforts to remake ways of life and communities so that they can be sustained in the face of shifting climatological conditions.

This chapter begins with the repurposing of the refuge in response to the lack of geese and newly implemented regulations. Next, I discuss divergent frames of risk and how they informed efforts to rework the meanings and uses of the refuge. Using behind-the-scenes details of the USFWS, I extend my analysis to consider how multilevel institutions organized across multiple regions inform processes of adaptation.

I found that the multilevel institutional arrangement of the USFWS complicated adaptations at Swan Lake, but this chapter is not evidence that such bureaucracies necessarily undermine localized adaptations as some have argued.[10] Finding bureaucratic inefficiencies and then concluding that peoples' lives would be better without that bureaucracy is a logical leap. The institutional arrangement of the USFWS did undermine adaptations at Swan Lake in some respects, but it also enabled adaptations in other respects. I and others ultimately contend that multilevel governmental institutions can facilitate adaptations to climate change.[11]

Redefining the Refuge: An Emergent, Conflictual Process

Swan Lake was primarily understood and used as a space for observing, researching, and hunting geese when they were there in significant numbers, but the shift in Eastern Prairie Population migration patterns undermined community members' abilities to relate to the refuge in this way. Hardly anyone attempted to observe or hunt Canada geese on the refuge by the time I began fieldwork. Just eighteen people went goose hunting on the refuge in 2013, a significant decrease compared to the goose hunting heyday, when well over ten thousand would hunt on the refuge in a given year.[12] There was also no ongoing research concerning geese, another significant shift compared to previous eras when an extensive amount of research on geese was carried out by officials from the USFWS, Missouri Department of Conservation, and University of Missouri.[13]

Local residents were still using Swan Lake but in ways different from the period of high goose numbers. Similar to their remaking of the Goose Festival (see Chapter 3), local residents had worked together to repurpose the refuge from a place that catered primarily to goose hunters to a place that catered primarily to heteronormative families. By redefining Swan Lake as a place where families could gather for environmental education activities, local residents reconnected their community with a place that was important to them. They also continued to create and renew connections with each other every time they gathered at the refuge. In short, local residents sustained their community by rearranging how they defined and related to the refuge.

The refuge had been hosting events such as the Eighth Grade Environmental Education Day, the Youth in the Outdoors Day, and hunter safety certification courses to repurpose the space. First Fridays at the refuge were especially important to bringing about this change. Sponsored and paid for in large part by the Friends of Swan Lake, the group of local residents that partnered with the USFWS to promote public uses of the refuge, these events were held on the first Fridays of summer months. Attracting primarily families, they featured environmental education activities such as canoeing, an archery station, and presentations about eagles. Given the relatively low population in the area, that First Fridays regularly drew as many as three hundred attendees speaks to how significant the events had become.

Like others I talked with, during our interview Jack pointed to cooperation between members of the public and refuge staff as being especially important to organizing these events and repurposing the refuge. I asked whether he thought the refuge had been transformed into a place for community involvement. Leaning forward in his chair and answering in his slow, contemplative style, he said, "Right. That wasn't the case in the past. If you weren't a hunter, you didn't go down there. Except to drive through. And there was no community involvement in it to speak of, except what money there was to be made off the hunters and whatever they did. But there was no community involvement until the last ten years or less."

"Now why do you think that was?" I asked.

"Well, I think it was," Jack began, before pausing to think. "It wasn't encouraged. There was no encouragement from the feds as we call them or the [Missouri Department of Conservation] for anything else besides hunting. When the season was over that was it. You didn't go back down there, and you weren't really invited to."

In addition to refuge staff and community members working together to repurpose Swan Lake, refuge infrastructure afforded reinterpretation of the refuge as an appropriate space for hosting over three hundred people for activities related to environmental education.[14] Most likely, the public events that were centrally important to repurposing the refuge would not have taken place if it did not already have a visitor center, gravel roads, parking areas, picnic tables, and bathroom facilities. Refuge staff often had to stretch their budget to maintain existing infrastructure,[15] so it would have been cost prohibitive to install this infrastructure to allow public events.

The longer I spent at Swan Lake, the clearer it became that its meanings and uses were still being reworked through conflicts over appropriate public uses of the refuge that pitted local residents against the USFWS. Crucially important to these conflicts were newly instituted and more rigorously enforced policies that restricted locally accepted ways of building community. These policies undermined local residents who were working to remake the meanings and uses of the refuge, and they put increasing strain on the cooperative relationships between refuge staff and members of the public.

Sitting at a group of tables in the visitor center with the refuge manager and a handful of Friends members during their April 2014 meeting, I watched as the manager told the civic group that they would no longer be allowed to sell raffle tickets for a quilt pieced by one of the women in the group because the USFWS considered selling raffle tickets to be gambling.

Almost instantaneously, Diane let out a disgusted, "Get real!" Diane was generally quiet at Friends meetings—except when she thought the USFWS was doing something particularly egregious to the refuge. Now in her seventies, she had lived next to the refuge her entire life. Involved in numerous civic organizations in addition to the Friends, she was deeply committed to her community and maintaining a connection between it and Swan Lake.

"Who makes these rules? Is it a group of people? Just one person?" Cindy asked. Less than five feet tall and also in her seventies, Cindy was an unimposing figure. But she was also a savvy veteran of civic activism who was as committed as Diane to maintaining a connection between local residents and the refuge she had lived next to for over seventy years.

"A great big bureaucracy," Tim answered. Generally easygoing and middle age, Tim had lived and hunted near the refuge for the last decade.

"A bunch of people who have never even been here! That's who makes them!" Ben added from under his customary Beretta ball cap.

"A lawyer, or a bunch of them!" Chris said with comparable conviction. Both in their thirties and responsible for working their respective family's farms, Ben and Chris were equally adept at criticizing the USFWS.

"This Friends group started as a way to help the refuge, and now they are starting to tie our hands with all of these regulations," Tim noted in an aggrieved tone.

"But the refuge is supposed to be for everyone, isn't it?" Cindy asked rhetorically. Then, the passion growing in her voice, she concluded, "It's publicly owned, so it's supposed to be for the people!"

"No, it's owned by the government and they'll determine just how you spend your time here," Ben disagreed.

When the Friends were filing out of the visitor center after their meeting, Tim said to me, "I mean, really, is this gambling? I guess you're technically buying a chance, but does anybody get addicted to buying raffle tickets to a quilt that some little old lady has made for a nonprofit organization? I mean, really? It's not like we're playing roulette or black jack. It's a raffle for a quilt!"

Friends members were absolutely furious about the new regulation. Raffling a quilt was a key fundraiser to support events promoting public uses of the refuge, and it was a standard form of fund raising for other civic organizations in Sumner. Part of the reason this policy generated so much anger, then, was because it violated assumptions about how gendered individuals ought to participate in maintaining their community. As I describe in Chapter 3, men and women drew on gendered strategies and skills to participate in the reproduction of their community. Women piecing quilts and men buying raffle tickets to try to win the quilts was a standard way that community members generated funds to sustain Sumner. A policy decreeing that raffles were unacceptable contradicted many residents' understandings of how to go about being good women, men, and community members.

USFWS policies undermining locally acceptable ways of organizing community events created an even greater conflict in May. Because of liability concerns regarding allergens and microorganisms, refuge staff informed the Friends that they would no longer be allowed to serve homemade cookies, grilled hot dogs, or fried fish at any community events unless they developed and documented USFWS-approved standard operating procedures for handling, cooking, and serving these food items.

The new food regulation was interpreted as directly discouraging a public presence on the refuge. Free food had attracted families to the refuge and then kept them there for longer periods. Homemade cookies, hot dogs, and fried fish were also explicitly associated with family and community gather-ings in Sumner. As Ray said to Pete and me, "I'll tell you what. Around here, you get yourself a pot of grease and throw some fish in it, and people will show up from places you've never even heard of." Given this understanding, it is unsurprising that anger toward the USFWS was only intensified by the implementation of the new policy.

Three days after the Friends learned about the new policy at their monthly meeting, members of the Swan Lake Sportsman's Club were in-formed about it. Sitting at one of the two long lines of tables that ran the length of their meeting hall, I watched the jovial mood of the gathering quickly turn hostile. Mike stood at the front of the hall to address the forty to fifty men in attendance about the upcoming Youth in the Outdoors Day at the refuge. A burly man in his fifties who regularly sported at least two pieces of camouflage clothing, Mike had a reputation in the community for being a strong advocate for youth involvement in hunting and fishing.

"The refuge system is pretty much getting—" Mike began.

"Fucked!" Bill shouted from a chair just down the table from me. Tall, lanky, and in his twenties, Bill had a penchant for interjecting loud com-ments and jokes during meetings.

Mike paused, seemingly caught off guard by the outburst. "Well, they aren't letting us have trap shooting or BB guns or anything this year, so it's probably the last time the event will be taking place at the refuge. It looks like they aren't going to let us have hot dogs on the refuge for the kids this year either."

"My god!" Greg shouted.

"Yeah," Mike agreed, shaking his head and pausing for effect. "I don't really know what's going on."

"If we can't do hot dogs . . . !" Kurt said, exacerbated.

Mike then informed everyone it was not just hot dogs that were on the line. "They also aren't letting them have any pies or cookies from the ladies around here."

Instantaneously a chorus of "What the fuck!" "What the hell!" and "Why!" rang out from men around the hall.

"I was thinking about maybe just providing some ham and cheese sand-wiches," Mike continued calmly.

Not one to avoid bluntness, Greg shouted, "They can kiss my ass!"

"It's getting to be ridiculous," Mike agreed, before somberly adding, "They can't even sell raffle tickets at the refuge for the quilt that the ladies make every year because that's supposedly gambling."

Again, a chorus of "My god!" "What the hell!" and "What?!"

After the outbursts had died down, Mike continued, "The fish fry. That's off too. It's really just getting out of hand."

Standing up from his chair, Greg looked around the room and shouted, "It's getting to be time to stand up and just say kiss our ass!"

"It boils down to them wanting to shut [the refuge] down. Let it happen! What's the point if you can't be on it?" Kurt agreed from his seat.

As a storm of side conversations and mutters filled the hall, Mike tried to steer the group in another direction by emphasizing the need for group cohesion, "If we don't stick together, we'll be down the tubes."

Greg was not buying it, though. According to him, no matter what the group did, the USFWS was set on undermining any connection between the community and the refuge. "The gates will be closed down there in ten years. Just you wait and see."

"We worked our asses off to save Silver Lake, and now they're shutting it down anyways. The Friends are working their asses off, but what can we do?" Kurt asked, referring to a previous USFWS plan to drain Silver Lake.

"I couldn't give a damn!" Greg shouted. "We work our asses off, and it's for nothing!"

"If you can't do anything down there, then what can you do? It just seems like we're pissing in the wind," Kurt lamented, aptly summarizing the frustration that had boiled over during the meeting.

As Table 5.1 illustrates, concerns over decreased public involvement at the refuge were not unfounded: the number of events and attendees in 2014 were much lower compared to previous years. This decline was related to a lack of funding to hire a refuge employee to organize visitor services, but increasing regulations that undermined the number and variety of events also decreased visitor numbers. The annual Youth in the Outdoors Day, for example, was moved from the refuge to a nearby Missouri Department of Conservation area in 2014 because of the new food policy.

Scholars studying conservation agencies have rightly called for policy makers and land managers to consider the meanings and emotions that the public associates with particular places.[16] Meanings and emotions associated with the refuge undoubtedly informed residents' reactions to USFWS policies, but residents' understandings of practices used to connect with the refuge were also significant. After all, residents were angry about the new raffle and food policies not only because the policies undercut their ability to maintain a connection with a place that was important to them. They were also deeply upset because frying fish, baking cookies, and raffling

TABLE 5.1. REFUGE EVENTS AND EVENT ATTENDEES, 2010–2014

Year	Number of events	Number of attendees	% change in attendance from previous year
2010	15	2,198	—
2011	61	2,710	+23.3
2012	61	3,812	+40.7
2013	38	2,406	−36.9
2014	11	856	−64.4

Source: Handout distributed by Swan Lake National Wildlife Refuge manager at February 2015 meeting with Friends of Swan Lake.

quilts were all considered acceptable, gendered ways of facilitating the reproduction of community in Sumner.

Beyond being ways of life associated with community cohesion, these practices were understood as perfectly safe and devoid of risk, and this also contributed to community members' anger. Tim's take on hot dogs during a Friends meeting is notable. He said, "It's okay to have those regulations, but you need a balance, you know? Now we're just saturated with regulations. It's hot dogs, not skydiving or bullfighting!" As others in the community had made clear, requiring a standard operating procedure detailing how to cook hot dogs seemed ridiculous because consuming hot dogs was not considered dangerous. Consequently, resentment toward the USFWS continued to intensify as this and other policies meant to avoid future harms were implemented over the next year.

Risky Frictions: Entangled Institutions and Divergent Frames of Risk

Officials at the upper levels of the USFWS sought to reduce the likelihood of litigation by trying to limit harms to refuge visitors and by ensuring that management practices were in line with federal regulations. The new food policy, for example, was instituted to reduce the likelihood of the USFWS being sued if someone got sick after eating contaminated or allergenic food at a refuge event. According to the members of the public I talked with and observed, though, the risk of litigation was not as significant as the risk of decreased public use of the refuge that could result from these very policies. Consequently, conflicts often emerged over which risks USFWS officials should focus on.

Previous research on risk has found that which risks are considered legitimate concerns is fundamentally cultural.[17] By this I mean that individuals and groups draw on culturally legitimated meanings and perceptions to understand the future and its risks. Further, individuals' and groups' prior experiences also influence understandings of and responses to the future.[18] Given the infinite number of cultural meanings as well as experiences that can be used to interpret the future, it is not surprising that there are often very different understandings of risks.

Divergent perceptions of the future rarely carry equal weight, however, because perceptions of risks are political. Some can tap into culturally legitimated meanings to validate their portrayals of risk as correct more effectively than others.[19] Further, and relatedly, individuals and groups have different degrees of access to the institutionalized levers of power to support their understandings of the future.[20] The risk of destroying the Appalachian environment and its inhabitants through coal extraction, for example, has been obscured by corporations and politicians claiming that environmental regulations threaten jobs for white, male breadwinners. In turn, Appalachia has been turned into a "sacrifice zone"[21] that can be destroyed, while the representatives and supporters of energy corporations proclaim their love of both coal mining and the environment.[22] This example also illustrates that portrayals and perceptions of risks are political because they regularly facilitate the reproduction of a range of inequalities. As long as coal continues to be extracted under the pretense of providing jobs, any who remain near coal production facilities will have elevated risk for a range of negative health outcomes. Perceptions of risks are informed by inequalities and also inform the reproduction of inequalities.[23]

At the refuge, a mash of culture, politics, and the particularities of individuals' and groups' relations with Swan Lake informed how they understood and took action in response to risks. The considerable institutional power exercised by USFWS representatives at the supralocal levels of the organization made it possible for them to formulate and implement policies based on their understandings of the future, often despite community members' opinions on the matter. Nevertheless, it would be a mistake to characterize USFWS responses to risks as a top-down process in which representatives at upper levels determined which risks mattered and how the refuge would be used as a result. Entangled understandings of rurality, progress, conservation, and governance; emotion-infused relationships and interactions among people and places; the organizational structure of the USFWS; the absence of Canada geese; and even institutions far beyond the

USFWS informed how the refuge was being repurposed through conflicts that hinged on divergent understandings of the future.

I use the concept of risky frictions in my understanding of the significance of these entanglements. Drawing on the work of Ulrich Beck, who argues that individuals and institutions with different degrees of power jockey to define risks as worthy of attention and action,[24] I note that interactions between differentially empowered (non)human beings, things, and institutions informed understandings of and responses to potential future harms. Bureaucrats in the upper levels of the USFWS had a considerable amount of authority to influence which visions of the future were acted on at the refuge. However, spiraling connections between representatives of other institutions, Swan Lake staff, members of the public, and nonhumans also influenced responses to risks at the refuge. Using Anna Tsing's concept of friction, which posits that social and ecological processes play out through combinatory contacts (or frictions) between (non)humans across space and time,[25] I draw attention to the ways that frictions between differentially empowered (non)human beings, things, and institutions influenced definitions of and responses to risks at the refuge. In addition to underscoring how frictions between entangled (non)humans influenced responses to risks, I use a more colloquial understanding of friction, in which conflict exists between two entities, to highlight that processes of defining and responding to risks at the refuge regularly involved conflicts over competing visions of the future.

The following sections illustrate how risky frictions informed two ongoing processes of remaking the meanings and uses of the refuge. I investigate the influence of risky frictions on the implementation of cooperative farming agreements at the refuge.[26] Then I consider the influence of risky frictions on the public events being held to transform the refuge into a space for community involvement. Each section addresses the interconnections between (non)human beings, things, and institutions across space and time that informed responses to risks and discusses the divergent frames of risk that underpinned conflicts over these ongoing processes of adaptation.

Cooperative Farming Programs

Although local residents tended to downplay the significance of lawsuits being brought against the USFWS, the refuge was tangled in litigation during my time in Sumner. It was one of five areas in USFWS Region Three that were named in an injunction filed in the U.S. District Court for the Northern District of California in August 2013.[27] Filed by the Center for Food

Safety, Public Employees for Environmental Responsibility, the Sierra Club, and Beyond Pesticides, the complaint alleged that the five areas had allowed genetically engineered crops and pesticides to be used in cooperative farming programs without proper documentation. The plaintiffs claimed that this violated the National Environmental Protection Act and the Administrative Procedure Act. According to the suit, the use of pesticides such as 2,4-D; dicamba; neonicotinoids; and glyphosates put countless (non)humans at risk of physical harm and even death.

In March 2015, the U.S. District Court, District of Columbia, gave a mixed ruling, finding for the USFWS on some complaints and for the plaintiffs on others.[28] The court ruled in favor of the USFWS on the use of pesticides such as 2,4-D and dicamba even though proper National Environmental Protection Act paperwork on site-specific impacts of their use was never filed. Regarding neonicotinoids, though, the court ruled in favor of the plaintiffs and issued an injunction against the use of seeds treated with these chemicals.

Measures were taken throughout Region Three in response to the lawsuit even before the decision was handed down. Staff from across Region Three formulated a new farming policy that banned the use of neonicotinoid-treated seeds in cooperative farming programs. The policy did not prohibit planting corn on refuges, but as a side effect local farmers who had agreements with the USFWS to cultivate areas of the refuge were unable to grow corn in 2014. Exploring why illustrates the frictions between (non)human beings, things, and institutions that informed processes of repurposing the refuge.

The new farming policy was undoubtedly important to the move from corn to soybean production in 2014, but the shift in the national seed production and distribution system toward neonicotinoid-treated corn seeds was equally significant. First approved by the Environmental Protection Agency in 1994, neonicotinoid use began to increase dramatically in 2003. Higher seed prices linked to expanding ethanol production, beetles that spread Stewart's wilt, and effective marketing strategies combined to encourage farmers to protect their corn crops with the chemically treated seeds. By 2011, nearly 80 percent of corn acreage in the United States was planted with this type of seed, and the acreage has likely only grown since.[29] Because local seed distributors were embedded within this broader system of seed production and distribution, farmers who had cooperative agreements with the refuge could not get corn seed from distributors in the region that was not treated with neonicotinoids. As a result, they planted soybeans instead.

The move toward soybean production at the refuge also depended on Canada geese migrations shifting away from the refuge. The consumption of dry soybeans by Canada geese can cause crop impaction, a fatal condition caused by soybeans lodging in a goose's upper digestive tract.[30] When large concentrations of geese feed on especially dry soybeans, mass deaths in the hundreds or thousands can result. In 1953, after nearly a thousand geese died from crop impaction at the refuge, refuge manager Robert Russell wrote about the potential blowback the USFWS could face over the deaths:

> There is considerable evidence indicating that [recent goose] losses are due to the consumption of refuge grown soybeans. This would indeed be a sad state of affairs if we were actually killing birds with a crop produced on the refuge! . . . So far as I know we have never been accused of killing geese by feeding them soybeans. However, it is by no means inconceivable that some day we will be.[31]

To avoid mass deaths and any ensuing consequences, Swan Lake staff began to avoid the production of soybeans on the refuge. It is very unlikely that refuge management strategies would have shifted toward increased soybean production in 2014 if geese were still using the area in significant numbers, because geese could have died en masse, bringing a public relations nightmare and lawsuits.

Local residents were generally upset that corn was not going to be grown on the refuge, and a different understanding of nature and how people ought to relate to it than the one forwarded by the lawsuit plaintiffs informed these reactions. As Chapter 4 details, two ways of conceptualizing how people should relate to nature are biocentrism and utilitarianism.[32] According to biocentrism, humans are merely one species in an interconnected web of life, and disruptions to the web could have catastrophic consequences for both humans and nonhumans. According to utilitarianism, environments are important because they can be useful for people. Instead of being concerned with the health of an ecosystem as a whole, this moral stance posits that environmental harms are appropriate as long as they benefit people and the nonhumans that are most useful to them.

The suit filed against the USFWS was based on a biocentric understanding of conservation. Focusing on the health consequences (non)humans can face because of the use of genetically engineered (GE) crops, the original injunction filed by the Center for Food Safety and fellow plaintiffs notes:

Certain pesticides used on Refuges decrease biodiversity and impact pollinators and wildlife. GE crop use on Refuges also injures Beyond Pesticides members. GE crops increase the use of certain herbicides by encouraging the growth of weeds that are resistant to herbicides. In turn, farmers have to use more, and more toxic, pesticides to stop these cultivated "superweeds." As a result, Beyond Pesticides members are at a greater risk of suffering health effects from pesticide use. Additionally, GE crop cultivation compromises members' enjoyment of Region 3 Refuges because the crops pose risks to wildlife and biodiversity.[33]

According to the plaintiffs, GE crops pose health risks to both nonhumans and humans because of a potential future in which farmers would use an expanding repertoire of dangerous chemicals to combat plants that were increasingly difficult to kill.

Local residents used a utilitarian conceptualization of conservation to understand the lawsuit as well as the new farming policy. They also tended to link this conception of how people ought to relate to environments with a conservative conception of governance that framed federal regulations as overly intrusive. These entangled understandings of conservation and governance enabled frames of risk that were in sharp contrast to those of the plaintiffs in the lawsuit. As a result, the lawsuit and regulations linked to it were considered symptomatic of an overly intrusive government that promoted irrational policies divorced from commonsense, progressive ways of using landscapes.

Local residents who had contracts to grow crops on the refuge were especially concerned that these policies would affect their ability to farm. Tom, who had a contract for 2014, was especially displeased by the situation. In his forties and generally amicable, he was anything but good-humored when he came into the visitor center one morning after the new farming policy had been implemented. Wearing a Pioneer seed cap, plaid shirt, and well-worn jeans, he peppered the refuge manager with questions about why he could not plant corn. Growing more and more frustrated, Tom eventually exclaimed:

> What if we just say we aren't going to farm it this year because you-all have changed the contract? You-all are hurting our livelihood as farmers. You-all have changed the contract. You know, I could say you-all changed the original contract, so legally you-all can't say

anything to us farmers as far as what we can and can't do. It didn't
say anything about not using treated seeds for corn when we bid it.

Any environmental harms that might result from using neonicotinoids
were far less concerning to Tom than a future in which he was not allowed
to manipulate the landscape in a manner that, in his opinion, allowed him
to be the best farmer that he possibly could. The new policy likely undercut
his profits, but more than this, neonicotinoids were squarely in line with
utilitarianism and locally accepted conceptions of agriculture that linked
progress to intensive, industrialized manipulations of the landscape.

Community members more generally often worried about a future in
which there would be fewer animals in the area that liked to eat corn, such
as deer and waterfowl. While I talked with Kurt at the bar one afternoon, he
argued that planting less corn would result in fewer deer:

> It took almost fifty hours before we even saw a deer, deer hunting
> this year! That's terrible! You know what else? This year there isn't
> going to be a deer anywhere near that refuge because they aren't go-
> ing to be able to grow corn on it. They aren't allowing them to have
> treated seed, so they aren't growing corn on the refuge. No corn!
> There won't be a fuckin' deer within twenty miles of that refuge
> without any corn on it. How does that make any sense?

"Yeah," I agreed, before diving into the details of why no corn was going
to be grown on the refuge. "You know why that is, right? There's a lawsuit
against the USFWS for allowing those seeds to be used. I guess the farmers
around here can't get any other kind of seeds."

But ignoring the seed production and distribution system that offered
only neonicotinoid seeds, Kurt zeroed in on the state institutions at play. As
in Chapter 4, where he derides overly educated, urban-based USFWS officials,
Kurt scoffed at those making farming policies as being misguided lawyers
who lacked sufficient firsthand knowledge of the refuge. He exclaimed, "That's
the problem right there. That's just fuckin' un-American. This isn't the land of
the free anymore. Somebody [is] making policies that hasn't ever been here in
their lives and doesn't have a clue about what's going on. That's the problem
in this country. Once the lawyers get ahold of it, it just gets fucked up."

Kurt's exaggerated contention that there would not be a deer within
twenty miles of the refuge also depicted a future in which there would be
fewer desirable animals on and around the refuge. Because of the implicit

assumption that nonhumans were most worthy of consideration for their utility for people, and because deer were prized for their symbolic and material uses, a future with fewer deer was far more concerning than any negative outcomes that might be accrued by other, less useful plants and animals. Accordingly, Kurt emphasized that the new policy was an affront to progress and stemmed from burdensome governmental institutions that repeatedly violated taken-for-granted understandings about how individuals ought to relate to environments and the nonhumans therein.

Public Events

Staff at the regional and federal levels of the USFWS consistently framed members of the public as potential plaintiffs in lawsuits against the organization. Directives coming from these levels repeatedly sought to reduce the likelihood that members of the public would sue the USFWS because of something that had happened at a refuge event. Notable examples, in addition to the new raffle ticket and food policies, were requirements to have pilot cars in front of and behind the tractor conducting hayride-style tours of the refuge and an attempted prohibition of an archery station. As with the implementation of the policy prohibiting neonicotinoids, frictions over space and time between differentially empowered (non)humans informed the meanings and uses of the refuge as they continued to be reworked in response to such policies.

"I just," Chris began, before pausing, obviously frustrated. It was the March 2014 Friends meeting, and the group had just been informed that they needed to carry liability insurance. "It just appears everything in the last six to twelve months has been to get the public off the refuge. Would it be better to do habitat improvement instead of fighting them on it? Do we need to rethink what we're doing? Don't get me wrong, I think First Fridays are great, but now you have only two or three events this year. You have to have insurance. You can't have entertainment. It's just a lot of things. . . . I thought the refuge policy was opening it up for the kids, families, and education. That's what I thought the service wanted."

"They do want that," the refuge manager pleaded.

"But how do we do it? How do we make that happen?" Chris asked. "I'm not pointing the finger at you. I'm just frustrated and don't understand. How can we make that happen?"

"We have to go through these compatibility determination processes," the manager explained, referring to the long trail of paperwork that had to be completed to get public uses of the refuge approved by staff in the regional office. "It's a process. We research these policies, and we send them up; people look at them and suggest all sorts of things. You can see how paperwork can bog you down. That's where we are now. It's frustrating, but that's just how it is."

"I'm not saying we should walk away. I'm just saying it seems like we're beating our heads against the wall and maybe we should reevaluate," Chris responded.

To work within the new regulations, as the refuge manager alluded to, required an extensive amount of coordination between USFWS staff at the refuge and supralocal levels of the organization. Documents called compatibility determinations (CDs) were centrally important to this process. According to USFWS policy, every public use of a refuge nationwide needed an approved CD that addressed the who, what, where, why, and how of public uses in relation to a bevy of policies and laws within and beyond the USFWS. Usually seven to ten single-spaced pages, a determination took from a couple of hours to a full day to write, depending on how complicated the use was and how likely it seemed that regional staff would find it objectionable. Even if revisions to the proposed CD were not requested by regional staff, it usually took months to get approval. If revisions were requested, the time frame was only extended. It took roughly ten months to receive approval for the CD that included the food service standard operating procedure after revisions were requested because the original twenty-nine-step hot-dog cooking procedure was not detailed enough.

But coordinating with complex-, regional-, and federal-level staff was not always necessarily a process of capitulating to what representatives in higher-level offices wanted. At times, refuge staff leveraged their resources and institutional knowledge to resist staff at higher levels. They creatively cited and interpreted policies, called on personal connections in the organization, and even played the different levels of the organization against each other. An example of this is how refuge staff managed to keep hosting an archery station at refuge events.

The refuge manager believed an archery station was a safe and effective way to get children interested in an activity related to outdoor recreation, but staff in the regional office vetoed it because of liability concerns. Then the refuge manager received an email from a federal branch of the USFWS that promoted archery as a means of encouraging outdoor recreation. Armed with this email, he submitted a CD for archery that was approved.

The manager explained his success to the Friends members during one of their monthly meetings when Chris indicated his surprise that the regional office had signed off on archery. "Well, they wouldn't have let us if we wouldn't have gotten an email from [the National Conservation Training Center] promoting archery as a way for the USFWS to promote involvement," he said. "Braden will tell you, we put that into our CD when we wrote it up. I heard our regional office was surprised to see that archery was being promoted by the USFWS."

Alluding to how the organizational arrangement of the USFWS enabled this back and forth from archery being prohibited to being approved, Chris said, "The left hand doesn't know what the right hand is doing half the time, it seems like."

The ability to continue having an archery station at public events depended on frictions among local, regional, and federal levels of the USFWS. Although members of the regional office had considerable influence over what was happening at the refuge, local staff leveraged an email sent from the federal level of the USFWS to do exactly the opposite of what the regional office wanted. And related to the significance of links across different institutions, it was likely not inconsequential that the approved CD included training of staff and volunteers to run the archery station in accordance with National Archery in the Schools Program safety standards. By referring to the program's sterling safety record of no archery-related injuries, refuge staff emphasized that no one was likely to get hurt even though giving kids bows and arrows might not seem the safest thing to do.

Community members were well aware of the frictions involved in getting CDs approved by regional staff, but they were still frustrated by having to work within the institutional structure of the USFWS. This frustration was often increased because frames of risk used by members of the public were starkly different from the frames used by USFWS staff at supralocal levels of the organization. Instead of focusing on the risk of lawsuits, community members often drew on the utilitarian approach to conservation and the neoliberal take on governance to focus attention on the potential for decreased public uses of the refuge. Instituting regulations that could reduce participation in public events was particularly concerning given that these events were how community members had repurposed the refuge in response to the lack of geese.

I interviewed Chris after a monthly Friends meeting, asking what he thought the biggest obstacle facing the Friends group was. Almost instantly, he responded, "Government."

"What do you mean by that?" I asked.

"Just the stipulations that we have to play by," Chris explained. "I think in that room that we just came out of are a lot of folks that are truly interested in getting the general public involved in what's going on, on the refuge. I mean, that's really what we want to do." As Friends members often did, he then talked about a lack of commitment to refuges in rural areas:

> I don't understand if the Fish and Wildlife Service really cares if the general public in Sumner, Missouri, is involved with the refuge or not. And that bothers me. . . . When we started this, I thought that was what we wanted to do, was to bring more people, more interest to the refuge. And I feel like a lot of the steps that we take, we're making it difficult to do. And I don't know if that is on purpose or if that's just the way that government is. I feel that the Fish and Wildlife Service creates roadblocks along the way, and it's hard to handle. . . . It's frustrating. It really frustrates me because we really want to do good things, and it feels like every time we turn around we get hit with something. We're not trying to abuse anything. We're not trying to cheat anything. We're just trying to bring people to the refuge. What I thought we were supposed to do.

Chris's concern that unnecessary regulations were undermining public uses of the refuge was remarkably similar to Greg's comments about the new food policy. While we talked at the bar one afternoon, I informed Greg that I had been drafting the new hot-dog-preparation procedure so that hot dogs could be served at refuge events again. Setting his drink down on the bar and swiveling in his seat to face me to better emphasize his point, he exclaimed, "Hot dogs?" Laughing and shaking his head, he said, "My god! That's the problem with this country. Now you see! You can't get a damn thing done. There's a million problems like that. You need an attorney just to get anything done. Then, once you solve that one, you'll have another three million to solve after that just like it! Hot dogs! They oughta put that in the paper!" Letting out an especially loud "Ha!" he concluded, "You gotta laugh, or you would cry about something like that! Hell, you can eat the damn things raw!"

Like other local residents, Chris and Greg held that increasingly restrictive regulations were unacceptable because they increased the likelihood that fewer members of the public would use the refuge. That these policies were meant to reduce risk of lawsuits for the USFWS was largely irrelevant because they used frames of risk that backgrounded this possibility as unimportant. As with the corn policy, they were concerned whether members of the public would be able to use the refuge given its increasingly restrictive regulations. Even if lawsuits were a threat, this was portrayed as being more a consequence of lawyers and government officials run amok than a reflection of legitimate concerns being expressed through proper legal channels.

The Duality of Multilevel Institutions: Constraining and Enabling Adaptations

Conflicts between local residents and conservation officials working off-site regularly afflict natural resource management strategies.[34] Hands-on experiences of the refuge informed how the public perceived and worked with the USFWS.[35] As regulations were put in place over the year and a half I worked in Sumner, members of the public increasingly considered that working with the USFWS was a risk in itself.[36] The organizational arrangement of the USFWS was centrally important to unease in residents and influenced how they worked with the USFWS as tensions grew over new regulations.

Ross was a farmer in his fifties who had a cooperative agreement to farm on the refuge. Following the implementation of the new farming program, Ross applied for approval to use a bevy of pesticides that he never intended to use. By getting advance approval, he hoped to avoid a situation in which a new regulation prevented him from using a pesticide that targeted an organism that could potentially attack the crops he had planted. His actions were undoubtedly informed by the backdrop of increasing regulations that facilitated the imagining of a possible future in which further, unforeseen regulations were likely, but the institutional arrangement of the USFWS was equally important.

While in the visitor center one afternoon, he was informed it would be preferable if he stopped applying for pesticide approval unless he actually planned to use them. Raising his hands in despair, Ross said, "Well, they've got us scared that something will come up and we won't be able to do anything!" Ross's anxiety was linked to the structure of the USFWS ("they"). He was not necessarily concerned refuge staff would undermine his ability to farm. What was especially concerning to Ross was that bureaucrats in distant places could formulate and implement policies that affected the refuge with little to no warning.

Friends members expressed similar understandings of an uncertain future that stemmed from the institutional structure of the USFWS. Like Ross, they had transformed how they worked with refuge staff as a result. By 2015, a theme I heard from Friends members during their monthly meetings was needing assurance that the rules guiding public uses would not be changed without notice. At their February 2015 meeting, Don and the refuge manager had the following exchange about the food service standard operating procedure that had been submitted to regional staff for approval. Don wanted assurance that the group's plan for a fish fry that coming July would not be ruined by rejection of the proposed procedure.

"Before we go too far on this, I want to see something in writing," Don said.

"Well, I'm supposed to get them," the manager assured him.

"I've heard this 'supposed to,' but you understand what I'm saying?" Don wearily asked.

Similarly, at their July 2015 meeting, Don inquired about whether the new agreement the group had entered into with the USFWS had gotten final approval from staff in the regional office. "Did that Friends agreement get signed?" he asked.

"Well, I sent it in," the refuge manager assured him and the group. "You signed it, and I signed it. We both signed it, and it's good."

"Can we quote you on that?" Diane asked, testing the manager over just how sure he was.

"Yes, you can quote me on that until the cows come home," he quipped, to the amusement of the group.

Importantly, refuge staff members were not purposefully encouraging uncertainty among members of the public.[37] Because of the USFWS's institutional arrangement, Swan Lake staff were often unsure what officials at other levels of the bureaucracy were thinking and doing. Almost daily, refuge staff members expressed frustration at their inability to know whether officials working off-site were going to implement new policies. Even when it was clear that a particular policy was going to be put in place, there was often considerable confusion regarding how officials up the USFWS chain of command wanted the policy to be interpreted.

A particularly telling example was when refuge staff were informed they needed an adult to supervise the 2015 Youth Conservation Corps (YCC) crew. At first, this was not overly concerning because one of the crewmembers was eighteen. Then staff were informed this would not be good enough.

"You want to run the YCC crew this summer?" Pete asked me, as we talked with Larry, Ray, and Russ inside the visitor center one afternoon.

"Ha! I don't think so," I responded, thinking about how little I had enjoyed clearing brush in the boiling heat and humidity the previous summer.

"They have to have immediate, adult supervision, and the adult has to be twenty-one," he explained.

"I thought you-all clarified that wasn't actually the case?" I thought this issue had been cleared up the week before.

"It can't even be the [Student Conservation Association] intern because of liability," Pete said.

"What?" I asked, surprised.

"Yeah, so you need to do it this summer," Pete explained.

Swan Lake staff members often referred to such regulations as handcuffs, but on numerous other occasions they compared trying to promote public uses of the refuge to "walking through a minefield." This spoke directly to the significance of their inability to know what USFWS higher-ups were thinking and doing. Seemingly at any moment they could accidentally make a misstep and get blown up by an unseen regulation. The confusion and uncertainty that diminished community members' trust in the USFWS was not bred from ill will of state officials but was largely a byproduct of Swan Lake's position at the end of a long chain of command that stretched from Washington, D.C., to Sumner, Missouri.

The organizational arrangement of the USFWS bred confusion and uncertainty. How institutions are arranged influences responses to risks and, subsequently, processes of adaptation. Scholars studying adaptations generally agree that relatively inflexible bureaucratic procedures and policies can undermine adaptations by making it more difficult for individuals, organizations, and communities to respond to shifting environmental conditions.[38] But at Swan Lake responses to shifting goose migrations were often undermined by the flexibility to change regulations at the federal, regional, and complex levels of the USFWS. In turn, this generated uncertainty and conflict at Swan Lake while constraining the ability of refuge staff and members of the public to work together to adapt to the lack of geese. It was actually a combination of relative flexibility and inflexibility at the different levels of the USFWS that inhibited adaptations at Swan Lake.

I do not wish to imply that multilevel institutions inherently undermine adaptations, though. Rather, multilevel institutions *simultaneously* constrain and enable adaptations at localized levels. There is a duality to how institutions inform adaptations,[39] and how institutions inform adaptations is contingent on how they are organized.

Numerous scholars agree that multilevel governmental institutions can facilitate adaptations to climate change.[40] They argue that officials at national and regional levels of institutions should focus on providing policy objectives, funding, and support for adaptations, and officials at more localized levels of institutions should be given the flexibility to design and implement policies. In contrast to the national and regional levels, this is the level at which the perceptions, preferences, and site-specific knowledges possessed by state and nonstate actors can be more readily acknowledged and used.[41] It is only by linking institutions across regions, while allowing adequate maneuverability at localized levels, that the resources of larger institutions and the in-depth knowledges of a location can both be leveraged to maximize responses to socioenvironmental challenges. My analysis supports these arguments.

The number of refuge events and visitors decreased, at least in part, because increasing regulations impeded community members' ability to adapt to the lack of geese using Swan Lake. Nevertheless, the USFWS still enabled community members to repurpose the refuge so that it could continue to be used by members of the public in spite of a lack of geese. After all, the refuge would not have been a suitable place for large numbers of people to gather for activities related to environmental education if the USFWS had not provided funding and labor to constantly maintain roads, a visitor center, picnic tables, restroom facilities, and waste disposal. It would be relatively easy to see decreasing usage numbers and conclude that adaptations at the refuge would have been better off without the USFWS, but this would overlook the ways that adaptations to shifting goose migrations completely depended on the funding and labor provided by the USFWS.

Without doubt, the multilevel institutional arrangement of the USFWS inhibited adaptations in some respects, but equally certain is that this arrangement facilitated adaptations in other respects. Future considerations of how institutions inform adaptations should address how they simultaneously facilitate and constrain adaptations. Failing to account for this duality, and how the organizational arrangement of institutions informs it, obscures the simultaneous benefits *and* drawbacks presented by institutions such as the USFWS.

Conclusion: Risks, Institutions, and (Non)Human Entanglements

The meanings and uses of the refuge had been remade so that the connections between community members and the refuge could be sustained.[42]

The refuge had primarily been used to research, hunt, and observe geese when they were congregating in large numbers there. By the time I began fieldwork in 2013, public uses of the refuge hinged largely on events with environmental education components. Over the next year and a half, the meanings and uses of the refuge continued to be refashioned through conflicts that emerged in response to new policies coming from the USFWS.

Divergent frames of risk that focused attention on different harms that could happen in the future were centrally important to these conflicts. USFWS staff at the complex, regional, and federal levels of the organization tended to focus on the risk of lawsuits, while members of the public tended to focus on the risk of less public use of the refuge. Far from being calculating, rational actors, individuals defined and responded to risks in ways that were fundamentally emotional and informed by deeply seated beliefs about everyday activities such as fish fries and broader topics such as progress, governance, and conservation. That is, conflicts were fueled by divergent understandings of how humans ought to relate to each other and to environments. To understand responses to risks, the cultural assumptions guiding peoples' profoundly emotional ways of being in the world must be considered. Anything less obscures how people actually understand and respond to possible negative outcomes.

Adaptations at the refuge were being undermined by USFWS staff members who were concerned about future lawsuits. Two points are notable here. First, responses to climate change will be informed by risks that are seemingly unrelated to climate change. Consequently, it is inappropriate to separate responses to climate-related risks from responses to all the other risks individuals and communities face. Second, power informs how individuals and communities respond to risks. Frictions between differentially empowered things, beings, and institutions informed responses to a multitude of possible negative outcomes at Swan Lake. Officials at the upper levels of the USFWS influenced how the refuge was repurposed, but they could not control this process. Refuge staff, members of the public, and institutions beyond the USFWS such as the national seed production and distribution industry also informed the rearrangement of the refuge. Beyond humans, changing goose migrations, neonicotinoids, the material infrastructure of the refuge, and microorganisms also affected how the refuge was repurposed.

Given that (non)human entanglements inform (re)arrangements of communities,[43] adaptations in other contexts will also emerge through (non)human interactions that are both particular to a given community and embedded in broader networks of things, beings, and institutions. The particularities of (non)human interconnections at the refuge enabled adaptations, but this will not always be the case. Some contexts will actually be made uninhabitable because of shifting (non)human entanglements. While the refuge provides some hope that adaptations can occur in other communities, not all contexts will have social and ecological entanglements that facilitate adaptations. Policy makers and those working in conservation and land management agencies would be well advised to account for the significance of (non)human interdependencies because they influence whether individuals and groups can successfully rearrange and sustain their ways of life and communities.

In Chapter 6, I explore how members of the public and refuge staff connected local residents with the refuge in spite of the conflicts covered in this chapter. Continuing the discussion of anticipations of risks introduced at the beginning of this chapter, Chapter 6 problematizes the argument that adaptations to climate change would be enhanced if individuals focused more directly on the distant future. Contrary to the belief that focusing on the relatively immediate future undermines adaptations to climate change, responses to shifting climatological conditions can be enhanced by concern for the immediate future.

Working through Risky Frictions

Cooperating to Adapt to an Uncertain Future

Even as tensions mounted over increasing regulations, members of the Friends of Swan Lake continued to work closely with Swan Lake National Wildlife Refuge (NWR) staff to promote public uses of the refuge. Why go to all the trouble to continue working together? It would have been far easier and much less frustrating for everyone involved if the cooperative push to increase public uses of the refuge was abandoned. The Friends were carrying out a tremendous amount of unpaid volunteer work, and refuge staff created more work for themselves by promoting public uses of the refuge. Getting a public use approved was time consuming and regularly compared to walking through a minefield, and more members of the public using the refuge meant more maintenance work for staff.

How did members of the public and refuge staff manage to continue working together? Higher-ups in the U.S. Fish and Wildlife Service (USFWS) considered members of the public to be litigation risks, and local residents increasingly considered working with the USFWS to be a risk in itself. According to Ulrich Beck's theorizing, these groups were not expected to continue working together, because people seek to avoid and marginalize individuals and groups defined as risky.[1] It is not immediately clear why refuge staff and individuals living in the surrounding area continued working cooperatively under such circumstances, but they did over the twenty months I was at the refuge.

In this chapter I focus on how members of the Friends group and refuge staff worked to connect their community with the refuge even as new policies engendered conflicts based on contradictory understandings of the future. The considerable degree of trust and respect that imbued the interpersonal relationships of the Friends and refuge staff shaped their responses to the new regulations, as did emotional attachments to the refuge itself. The mundane intricacies of interpersonal interactions also enabled the Friends and refuge staff to work through mounting tensions. In short, residents' cooperative efforts to rearrange and sustain their ways of life and community were enabled by their abilities to navigate entangled interpersonal relationships and interactions infused with emotions.

Having a better understanding of how the public and state officials work together to respond to socioecological disruptions is especially important because adaptations often depend on, or at least are enhanced by, cooperative partnerships between members of these groups.[2] Others have rightly noted that cooperative efforts to adapt to climate change often involve the ability to reconcile conflicting norms and values,[3] but more specifically, the ability to ease tensions that emerge because of contradictory anticipations of the future will be especially important for cooperative relationships between the public and state institutions. Accordingly, I also continue problematizing the relation between anticipations of risks and adaptations. In Chapter 5, we see that adaptations at the refuge were being undermined by USFWS officials' actions to avoid lawsuits in the relatively distant future. In this chapter, I argue that, as long as we continue to focus on whether individuals care about the long-term effects of climate change, we will miss how ways of life and communities are actually rearranged and sustained because of concern for risks in the immediate future.

Friendships, Networks, and Adaptations

During the August 2014 First Friday event I was assigned the role of runner. If staff members or volunteers operating the various stations needed anything, I went to get it. While making a stop at the visitor center for a quick respite from the heat and humidity, I talked with Becky, Mary Anne, and Diane. All over seventy and lifetime residents of Sumner, they routinely baked and handed out a smorgasbord of cookies at refuge events. After chatting with the women and eating a few cookies, I slipped down the hall and into my office to grab a drink. Still well within earshot of their table, I overheard them talking with a man attending the event.

"Where's the hot dogs? I always look forward to having a hot dog while I'm here," he said.

"There's a lot of people disappointed there aren't any hot dogs. It's just too bad," Becky replied, clearly annoyed about the new food service policy that prevented serving hot dogs.

"Why don't you say more [to the USFWS higher-ups] or just do what you want and serve hot dogs?" the man asked.

"We don't want the refuge manager to lose his job," Becky explained.

"Yeah, he's done a lot for this refuge, and we don't want to lose him," Mary Anne agreed, emphasizing his commitment to promoting community involvement at the refuge and local residents' commitment to the manager.

"If we didn't have him, we'd be . . . ," Diane began, before trailing off, evidently daunted by the thought of a future without the manager.

Disdain toward the USFWS was growing because of increasing regulations, but community members usually distinguished refuge staff from the USFWS. And this distinction was crucially important to how the refuge was being redefined in response to the new regulations. Becky, Mary Anne, and Diane's decision to comply with the new food policy was informed by the friendships they had formed with the refuge manager. They had grown to appreciate his commitment to community involvement over the prior seven years, and they did not want him to lose his job because they fought or disobeyed the new regulations. Consequently, they worked within this and other policies they disagreed with while trying to connect members of their community with the refuge.

Friends members were not the only ones whose efforts to repurpose the refuge were complicated by interpersonal relationships. Although not conforming to the ideal-type bureaucracy envisaged by Max Weber, in which bureaucrats neatly carry out their duties without any influence whatsoever from interpersonal relationships and attachments,[4] Swan Lake staff had built friendships with local residents that also informed how the refuge was being repurposed. These personal ties facilitated a willingness to put in the extra effort necessary to continue having public events at the refuge amid increasingly restrictive regulations coming from the upper levels of the USFWS.

Sitting at the welcome desk in the visitor center, I watched as two refuge staff members discussed the difficulties involved in trying to get approval from USFWS staff in the regional office for hayride-style, educational tours at public events.

"They want all kinds of things," the first said. "What time will the tractor rides be? What area of the refuge? Whether it's near any nesting habitat.

You know, you get to the point where you just don't even want to mess with it."

"I thought you were already to that point?" the second asked, referring to the mounting difficulties staff had experienced over the preceding months whenever they had tried to get public uses of Swan Lake approved.

"Yeah, I am," the first staff member admitted. "But the reason we're doing the limited amount we are is because the Friends group is so interested in seeing it happen. They put their time and energy into the refuge, and I really appreciate that."

The first staff member was clearly irked by having to do more work so that tours and other activities could happen at First Fridays, but he was willing to do it because of his relationships with Friends members. It seems unlikely he would have been doing this tedious paperwork if he had not grown to appreciate their support of the refuge. Even I felt this sense of reciprocal obligation to both Swan Lake staff and local residents as I spent more time with them. As a result, though I may not have always been happy about it, I was willing to do the paperwork required for refuge events no matter how maddening it often was.

That feelings of mutual obligation existed between community members and Swan Lake staff is not entirely surprising. Interpersonal relationships have complicated the work of conservation officials for at least the last century.[5] Scholars studying adaptations to climate change, however, have rarely acknowledged the significance of the interpersonal relationships state officials can develop with members of the public. Instead of acknowledging the complexities of bureaucrats and the emotion-infused relationships that they can form with the public, previous works often reduce state agencies to black boxes of homogeneous, emotionless bureaucrats.[6] Members of the public can differentiate state officials from the institutions for which they work, and representatives of state institutions have varying senses of obligation to the individuals with whom they work.

Relationships between refuge staff and residents of Sumner that were imbued with mutual respect, obligation, and trust were especially important at Swan Lake NWR because they enabled state officials and the public to work together while regulations were being put in place that both found objectionable.[7] It seems less likely that they would have continued working together as new regulations were instituted if this shared respect, obligation, and trust had not existed. At a minimum, and as Diane, Becky, Mary Anne, and the refuge staff member's comments reveal, how they were working together would have been transformed if these relationships were not in place.

Interpersonal relationships also complicated adaptations at the refuge because Friends members and refuge staff consistently drew on their interpersonal networks to provide the funds, supplies, and labor necessary to facilitate public uses of Swan Lake.[8] Regarding the funds the Friends used to support events, the group received yearly membership fees, small donations, and proceeds from gift shop sales, but donations of more than $100 came from individuals with long-standing personal ties to board members. In April 2014, for example, the Friends received a $2,500 donation from the son of a board member. This was a considerable amount of money for the group and increased their funds by roughly a third. Friends members also consistently used their networks to access supplies and labor to support refuge events. For example, AGRIServices of Brunswick, Missouri, a major agricultural goods supplier and shipper in the region, provided the food and beverages for the August 2014 First Friday event and the labor required to hand them out because one of the men on the Friends board was also one of the heads of AGRIServices.

Swan Lake staff leveraged their own interpersonal networks to facilitate refuge events. The refuge manager routinely contacted USFWS staff at the biological services office and Big Muddy NWR in Columbia, Missouri, to organize and operate interactive exhibits on reptiles and pollinators. Refuge staff members and I also regularly coordinated with staff from the Missouri Department of Conservation to obtain volunteers and supplies like canoes and archery equipment to offer more diverse activities. We also coordinated with community members who organized exhibits on topics that ranged from bees to gardening to trapping. I cannot know whether the refuge would have been redefined as a place for community involvement without these contributions, but this reorganization would have undoubtedly been carried out differently without staff members' ability to leverage their interpersonal networks that extended far beyond the refuge and even the USFWS.

Previous studies of adaptations to socioecological processes draw attention to the importance of interpersonal networks.[9] Granting more control and flexibility to the local levels of an institution such as the USFWS enables officials to tap into community networks.[10] Interpersonal ties among the public are not the only networks that can enable adaptations, though. Representatives of state institutions have networks that extend into the public and other state institutions, and these networks can also aid adaptations. Consequently, an added benefit of devolving control to more localized levels of institutions is that representatives of institutions can more effectively use their networks. The following example, in which a newly instituted regulation undermined how refuge staff members drew on interpersonal networks to help redefine the refuge as a place for community involvement, supports this point.

Starting in 2009, the refuge manager had cooperated with the local Ducks Unlimited chapter to host an annual field day during which children in the community were invited to the refuge to learn about wetlands and duck hunting. According to community members, the biggest draws were the duck and goose calling contests and the BB gun and clay pigeon shooting stations.[11] The Swan Lake Sportsman's Club provided attendees with a free lunch.

Refuge staff's interpersonal networks were integrally important to the event. In addition to leveraging their networks to provide supplies and volunteers, one of the chief reasons the event was established was because the refuge manager had worked with Mike, one of the leaders in the local Ducks Unlimited chapter, to make it happen. Mike was somewhat notorious for having a particular disdain for organizational rules and authority, but he was also committed to promoting children's involvement in hunting and fishing. According to refuge records, hundreds of children and adults attended annually.

Although both the refuge manager and Mike wanted to host the wildly successful field day at Swan Lake, starting in 2014 regulations prohibited the use of firearms (including BB guns) and the distribution of cooked food at refuge events. Consequently, the field day was moved to Fountain Grove Conservation Area. A fifteen-minute drive from Swan Lake, Fountain Grove had far fewer regulations concerning public events because it was operated by the Missouri Department of Conservation and not the USFWS. Neither the use of firearms nor the distribution of cooked food items was prohibited.

Losing this annual event is a clear example of increasing regulations undermining efforts to leverage interpersonal networks to redefine the refuge as a place for community involvement. Ben made this especially clear during the July 2014 Friends meeting. While the group was discussing losing the event to Fountain Grove, he turned to the refuge manager and said, "You might oughta remind your regional office how big of a deal that was and that we lost it. All those kids coming out here every year. That was a big deal." Ben's point could not have been clearer. Refuge staff and other community members had leveraged their networks to promote community involvement in the past, but regulations coming from supralocal levels of the

USFWS had undermined their ability to use their contacts to continue promoting public uses of the refuge.

Networks did not inform processes of adaptation at the refuge independent of the differences and inequalities that I introduce in Chapters 1 through 3. As the above examples show, how individuals used their interpersonal networks to secure funds and supplies to support public events at Swan Lake corresponded with how community members used networks to repurpose and sustain the Wild Goose Festival. In both cases, residents used gendered strategies to tap into networks to secure resources for adaptations.

Similar to donations to the Goose Festival, large donations to the Friends tended to come from men in the community. Similar to the women on the Wild Goose Festival Planning Committee working to refashion the Goose Festival, women on the Friends board used practices traditionally associated with femininity to supply resources for public events at Swan Lake. One of the women on the board had pieced and donated a quilt to raffle as an annual fundraiser until new regulations stopped the practice, and only the women on the Friends board baked, donated, and distributed cookies at public events. The following conversation that unfolded at a Friends meeting illustrates these gendered dynamics of using networks.

"Are we having cookies and punch? I'm not making them all this time," Mary Anne informed the group as they tried to determine who would provide refreshments at an upcoming event.

"Does Sprague's make cookies?" Chris asked, referring to a catering company in the area.

Don, who liked to tease the women on the board, deadpanned, "Walmart does."

"They're not homemade!" Mary Anne retorted.

"I was just trying to save you work!" Chris said.

"I can do it, but I'm not doing forty dozen again! I'll do ten dozen, but that's it," Mary Anne said, seemingly annoyed that Chris and Don had implied she did not want to bake.

"My wife will make some, but they're not homemade," Don explained.

"*Yes* they are," Mary Anne contradicted him.

"That putting water in a mix isn't homemade," Diane clarified, drawing a clear line in the sand on what was and was not a homemade cookie.

"Well, I make mine from scratch!" Mary Anne said.

"I know *you* do," Diane assured her.

"Well, my wife will make however many cookies you want," Don noted indifferently.

"I'll make some," Sheryl said. In her sixties, Sheryl had been involved with the Friends since the group's inception, and she regularly volunteered to do tasks for the group.

"How many do you want to make?" Mary Anne asked.

"There's no limit on that! I'll suffer through it!" Roscoe said, to the amusement of the group. Also in his sixties, Roscoe was Sheryl's husband. Always quick to crack a joke during meetings, he had no problem with Sheryl baking cookies that he would sample before the event.

"I'll make ten dozen," Sheryl said.

The men in the group were quick to volunteer women to do the time-consuming work of baking cookies. Though the Friends could have easily purchased cookies, this would have undercut the rural femininities of the women in the group given the close links between using skills associated with the domestic sphere, civic engagement, and femininities in Sumner. At least partially because of these understandings of how to be proper women and men, the women in the group, not the men, always ended up being the ones who baked tens of dozens of cookies to hand out at events.[12]

Further, as I discuss in Chapters 1 through 3, heterosexuality intersected with gender to inform how individuals in Sumner rearranged their lives and community. Notably, in this respect, Don and Roscoe did not volunteer random women to bake cookies for the group. They volunteered their wives. Their suggestions were gendered, but they were also informed by an understanding of families in which heterosexual men and women are assumed to provide ideal sexual partners for each other because of their supposedly complementary, gendered skill sets.[13]

Interpersonal relationships provided two key ways through which Friends members and refuge staff continued to try to connect Swan Lake NWR with the surrounding community in spite of increasingly restrictive regulations. Relationships that included feelings of mutual obligation, trust, and respect between members of the Friends and refuge staff contributed to their willingness and ability to cooperate amid growing tensions. Even though regulations undermined the use of interpersonal networks to continue organizing events, these networks still enabled staff and local residents to access resources needed to continue connecting community members with the refuge in a more limited respect. Interpersonal relationships that involve shared senses of respect and mutual obligation are a strong influence in how the public and state officials work cooperatively to adapt to climate change amid conflicts over a multitude of risks.

Place Attachment, Belonging, and Adaptations

Interpersonal relationships infused with mutual respect and obligation strongly influenced how the public and the USFWS continued to cooperate as new regulations were instituted, but emotional connections to the refuge itself were also significant. What authors from across the social sciences refer to as place attachment is an especially useful concept here. Place attachment is usually conceptualized as an emotional connection to a particular place,[14] but it is also something that can be claimed during interactions.[15] In addition to being an internal feeling toward a particular place, place attachment is something individuals can display to others. Feelings and claims of place attachment provided local residents and refuge staff with a desire to and means of cooperating to promote public uses of Swan Lake.

Community members constantly described the refuge as a place that was particularly important to them. Especially for residents who were old enough to remember when goose numbers were high, pride informed why they wished to maintain a connection with the refuge.

I asked Don during our interview why he became involved with the Friends. He said, "Because this refuge is so important to me. I grew up beside it, you know? I've been on it all my life. . . . Swan Lake is a part of who we are. You can't imagine how many times in my lifetime [I've heard], 'Oh, where are you from?' You meet people, you know? And I'll say, 'Oh, a little town called Sumner.' They say, 'Sumner . . . Sumner . . .' and I'll say, 'Well, yeah you've probably never heard of it, but it's by Swan Lake,' and they'll go, 'Oh! My husband used to come up and hunt at Swan Lake all the time!' I've had that happen to me, I swear, five hundred times in my lifetime."

We laughed, and I agreed, "No, it's true! People know, and it's like, it's because someone hunted here or someone they know hunted here."

"Exactly. So I guess it's a part of—and that's what I tried to express to those people from the regional office—it's . . . our refuge. Because, you know, it's a part of who we are to the people that live here," Don said.

Don's wish to maintain a connection with the refuge was motivated by a desire to maintain a connection with a space he felt was noteworthy. The refuge was a place with a storied history, and to be associated with it made many local residents feel worthy of respect.

In interviews and everyday conversations, individuals also frequently justified their efforts to maintain a connection with Swan Lake NWR by mentioning the interpersonal memories it evoked. Sheryl and Roscoe made this clear during our interview. They had lived near and used the refuge their entire lives. While we sat around the kitchen table in the refuge bunkhouse after a community event, I asked why it was important for them to become involved with the Friends.

Sheryl said, "I think it was just to make that connection. You did that years ago with your family. It was kind of a family thing that we'd come over and see all the geese. You know, in the fall that was always one of our outings. We'd used to go buy watermelons, and on a Sunday afternoon one of [our stops] was Swan Lake to go see the geese that would come in." Talking about more recent memories, Sheryl continued, "We brought our grandson with us and encouraged our daughter to bring her boys over a few times. It was a just a connection that we wanted to reconnect."

Roscoe then recalled one of his particularly memorable hunts in a refuge hunting blind. Pointing out the window at an agricultural field behind the bunkhouse, he recounted, "We had a good day just right out here. . . . Yeah, there were three of us down there, and one of them was a fiddle player from Bosworth [Missouri]. And here come a guy that worked on the refuge. Have you ever heard of the name Buzz Collins?"

"Nuh-uh," I replied, shaking my head.

"You ask Don or some of the older guys about Buzz. He was retired out of the military, and he got a job working here at the refuge. Well, here he comes out to the blind. He had a [telephone] call for Johnny Bruce, our fiddle player, that somebody wanted him to play at the dance for the festival! Yeah, that was somethin'," Roscoe said, chuckling and shaking his head.

Like Sheryl and Roscoe's recollections, stories about Swan Lake rarely were about doing anything alone at the refuge. I heard accounts of sneaking off on the refuge to smoke cigarettes with other kids, scouring a dry Swan Lake lakebed for arrowheads with friends, riding bikes down to the refuge just to pass the time, and countless stories of hunting and fishing with friends and family. Desiring to connect with the refuge was about more than feelings of attachment to a material landscape. Interpersonal memories associated with the refuge informed community members' desires to maintain a connection with it. By maintaining a connection with the refuge, people felt a sense of connection to their friends and family.[16]

Attachment to place is more than just an internal desire to maintain a connection with a place, as it is usually conceptualized in considerations of socioenvironmental topics[17] or more general analyses of place attachment.[18] Place attachment is something that people can claim and display to others during interactions.[19] Instead of just being an internal, emotional feeling, in other words, place attachment can be claimed when individuals indicate that a place is important to them. The ability to claim place attachment was especially important for adaptations in Sumner because it allowed individuals to construct and belong to a community that was capable of working cooperatively to adapt to shifting goose migration patterns.[20]

Those living and working in Sumner made claims to place attachment in three ways. First, they recalled their idyllic memories of Swan Lake's past. Second, they made claims about what was happening or should be happening at the refuge in the present. Third, they expressed a desire to keep themselves and their community connected to Swan Lake in the future. Through these common claims of attachment, they continually rearticulated and instilled in themselves a relatively coherent understanding of the refuge as having a sort of utopian past, imperfect present, and significant future.

Many classic works in sociology have found that feelings of togetherness are created through claims to a common past and the sense that a group of people have a shared history and destiny.[21] By making these claims of attachment to the refuge, local residents constructed a sense of community with both a common past and a common future. Greg's and Kurt's comments during the Sportsman's Club meeting in Chapter 5, for example, were filled with almost constant references to a communal "we" having a past, present, and future relationship with the refuge. Fred and Jan also alluded to this sense of a common present and future while we discussed a habitat management plan that was proposed but never implemented in 2010. The plan was a misguided management strategy, they contended, and they also framed it as a threat to the continued well-being of the surrounding community.

"This refuge is such a big deal around here for the communities and the small towns," Fred said. "Anything they do that doesn't improve it hurts somebody around here. Just letting it go, yeah, it makes the government—the government doesn't much care. They've got a natural [landscape]."

"What'd they want to do?" Jan asked. "Bring it back to a hundred years ago?"

"A hundred years ago—prairies and stuff like that," Fred explained. "It's an easy way of saying, 'We don't have any more money, so we're just going to let it go back to the wilderness.' Well, that's the farmer in me and all the neighbors around here. We want to see it get better. You don't want to go back to what it was. That would just be terrible. You know, basically it would just be a watershed for a flood . . . , which I guess we would survive if that happened."

"Oh, we would," Jan agreed. "We've got along without the geese."

While Fred and Jan agreed they could make do no matter what happened, Fred's comments made evident that those living around the refuge were a community with a shared future. Drawing on the conceptual links between agricultural production and progress, Fred noted that reducing the amount of land cultivated on Swan Lake NWR threatened the surrounding communities, which shared a destiny because they lived and worked near Swan Lake.

Greg also believed that refuge management practices were degrading the future of the community. I asked for his thoughts on how the refuge was being managed during our interview.

> You know, it's not the refuge manager's fault. His hands are tied, right? It's just government proxy, you know? And we could talk about this for hours and hours and hours, but they're just letting Swan Lake go to nothing. Weeds and junk. Nothing that's good for ducks. Nothing. And they were gonna do the same thing to Silver Lake. Without a good, decent depth of water the birds won't stay. What do you think that does to everybody that's grown up here? You take away our economy. You take away our refuge. I mean, granted, if you want to go see a couple blue herons, that's all right, but I can show you those in my backyard!

The familiar themes of progress and tension between the biocentric and utilitarian approaches to conservation are apparent, but especially significant in Greg's comments is how he constructed a sense of a shared past and future through a discussion of the refuge. Though the past was idyllic, current management practices threatened the future of those living in the surrounding area. According to Greg, refuge management strategies threatened "everybody" who had grown up in Sumner because the strategies could discourage ducks from using the area.

Professing attachments to the refuge also enabled individuals to belong to the community. To be clear, belonging to a community is never ultimately accomplished, never to be problematic again. Belonging is continually reproduced and potentially troubled through interactions among people, other beings, and things,[22] and relating to a place in socially acceptable manners is a key way individuals can position themselves as belonging to a community.[23] One of the safest ways to accomplish belonging in Sumner was to display attachments to the refuge by nostalgically reflecting on its history, complaining about current management practices, or expressing how important the refuge was to the future of the community.

That I had experienced this past enabled me to build rapport with people in the area. On numerous occasions community members also told me they appreciated my willingness to volunteer at the refuge and work on tasks related to visitor services so that Swan Lake could continue to be a place for community involvement. Following the final Friends meeting I attended, Don approached me to shake my hand. He said, "Young man, we sure do hate to see you go. We really do appreciate everything you've done around here."

Challenging any of these three common claims of place attachment marked one as out of synch with others. All three recurred in conversations at the bar and in community group meetings, and I never personally witnessed anyone disputing these standard claims of place attachment. If someone did, residents were miffed, as Fred and Jan's interview makes clear.

Referring to a woman who had worked at the refuge in the past, Jan said, "One of the gals that came down here—it's been several years ago—she kind of befriended my daughter and a friend of hers, and they were gonna go out one Saturday night. And I can't even think of her name, but she showed up at the house, and we were talking about the geese, and I said something about how many geese there were, and I said, 'Have you seen the pictures?' And she goes, 'Ohhhh, I've heard those stories.' And Fred goes, 'Well, they're not stories. They're real.' And she goes, 'Mhmm, I've heard those stories.' Very condescending."

"You know Doug?" Fred asked me. "He calls it a fable."

"Yeah! That's what he called it," Jan agreed, before rescuing Doug's belonging to the community to some degree. "I mean, Doug hunts, you know, more than anybody."

In Jan's story about the former USFWS employee, proper claims of place attachment were integral to accomplishing belonging. Jan could not remember her name, and it was clear the woman never really belonged to the community, because she questioned residents' portrayals of their past. Fred, Jan, and other community members' comments about Doug were similar. I never heard Doug question accounts of the glory days, but he was somewhat notorious in the community for doing so. People mentioned that he had questioned how great the past really was, and the implication was that he was not quite a full member of the community because of this.

"You know what Doug calls these stories? He calls them fables," Tim said to me after a Friends meeting while telling me about how many geese there used to be.

"Fables?" I asked.

"Yeah, you know, like they're not true or just stories. Like maybe there weren't that many geese. And you know, it kind of rubs some people the wrong way too," he concluded.

Beyond facilitating a sense that a community existed, claims of attachment to the refuge allowed individuals to police the boundaries of who belonged to their community. Anyone who violated these standard claims, as Doug did, was in danger of not being considered a full member of the community.

This ability to police the boundaries of belonging through claims of place attachment was particularly important for how the public and Swan Lake staff worked together. In everyday conversations and interviews, community members routinely said that current staff members did not really know the history of the refuge or how it should be managed because they had not grown up in the area. "They don't want locals down there," Rick said while we sat at the bar one afternoon. Similar to other men in the community who routinely criticized USFWS officials for relying on their formal educations to guide management practices, he said, "They want someone who knows the book and how the book says the water flows. Not how the water actually flows. They want someone to follow orders from upstairs. From someone who's never been here, you know? That's why a lot of people are pissed off and don't want nothing to do with it. It just doesn't seem like they want locals down there."

That refuge staff members did not live on the refuge or in Sumner as staff members had done in the past was especially significant to many community members. Shortly after saying the USFWS did not want locals working on the refuge, Rick detailed why he thought it important for staff to live on the refuge: "The manager ought to live on the refuge. That's how they used to be. They would be part of this community. They'd be all in. They'd be around at night. Not necessarily patrol at night, but hands-on, you know? Now it's wide open up there at night." Like Rick and his comments that managers used to be "part of this community," many people indicated that refuge staff had less belonging in the community because they did not live on the refuge or in Sumner. They were not really members of the community, in other words, because they were not attached to place.

Refuge staff members were well aware of how residents felt about them neither being from Sumner nor living on the refuge. Larry, for example, confided to me that he hoped community members might cut staff members some slack because I was living on the refuge at least a few days out of the week. Nevertheless, while staff lacked long-term attachments to the refuge, and while many residents questioned current management strategies, claims of place attachment enabled staff to work more effectively with the public in one important way.

By acknowledging how significant the refuge was to the community and actively working to connect surrounding residents with Swan Lake, staff tenuously belonged to the community. According to many community members, the one redeeming quality of refuge staff was their effort to facilitate public uses of Swan Lake. That they continued to promote community involvement in the face of roadblocks put in place by the upper levels of the USFWS was especially significant to individuals living in the area. Kurt, while talking with me at Foster's one afternoon, laid out how the refuge was being mismanaged, but eventually he said, "I'll say that at least the refuge manager does try to get people involved down there. I understand he's got his hands tied on what he can do, but at least he's trying to get people down there."

Not inconsequentially, members of the public recognized staff members' efforts to involve the community at the refuge. This enabled refuge staff to distinguish themselves from the broader organization for which they worked. And it allowed refuge staff members to tenuously belong to the community. In turn, this enabled them to work through conflicts related to policies meant to avoid future risks. Becky, Mary Anne, and Diane's concern for the refuge manager and their willingness to serve approved food items rather than fight the new food regulations, for instance, was at least partially predicated on their belief that the refuge manager was a member of their community who was committed to maintaining links between the refuge and local residents.

Attachments to place not only contributed to desires to adapt so that people could maintain a connection with the refuge but also promoted a sense of solidarity and, subsequently, collective action by those who were considered part of the community. In some cases, claims of attachment to place even led to cooperative efforts between refuge staff and the public in spite of increasingly restrictive regulations coming from supralocal levels of the USFWS.

Place attachment has received relatively little attention in the academic literature and in policy debates surrounding adaptations even though scholars generally agree it influences responses to climate change[24] and other socioecological processes.[25] Policy makers and researchers need to consider the importance of attachment to place,[26] but it must be understood as more than just an internal feeling or desire. Attachments to place can also be claimed, enacted, and unevenly realized in interactions. Claims of attachment can and do facilitate unequal belongings, but by making such claims, members of the public and state officials can also construct and belong to groups capable of working together to facilitate adaptations. In some cases, attachments to place can even provide the desires and means that the public and state institutions need to work together in spite of conflicts that emerge over the future and its risks.

Interpersonal Interactions: Conversations, Jokes, and Adaptations

The final piece to understanding how local residents continued to work with refuge staff is interpersonal interactions. More than simply being a vehicle, or means, for cooperating amid conflicts, the complexities of interpersonal interactions transformed responses to new regulations. In particular, the norms of group conversation as well as humor influenced how Friends members and refuge staff cooperated to adapt. I address each in turn.

The issue of mounting regulations came to a head during the February 2015 Friends meeting. At the beginning of the meeting, the refuge manager passed out a set of documents to the nine Friends members who were seated at a group of tables in the visitor center. One of the documents detailed waterfowl and deer counts, another listed the number of event attendees over the previous five years, and the final document was the proposed event schedule for 2015. After discussing the waterfowl and deer estimates, the conversation turned to the 2015 schedule and the number of event attendees. The discussion that ensued is worth considering at length because it illustrates how the norms of group conversation mediated how the Friends and refuge staff responded to frictions over increasing regulations.

Looking at the table listing the annual refuge events and attendees from 2010 to 2014, Don wanted to know how to improve the numbers. He asked, "Then, the event participants—going from 3,812 to 856—what can we and can we not do this year?"

"My concern is with the First Fridays; when you limit the stuff we can do, and we do the same thing, people quit coming," the manager responded, referring to new regulations that had restricted the kinds of activities that could be included in public events.

"Yeah," "Uh-huh," Cindy and Diane agreed in unison.

"You have to have variety," the manager said, "And if you get a reputation of doing the same thing—that's the challenge right now. What we thought about doing is to do an event in July on a Saturday afternoon and try to do a lot of what we do on a First Friday."

"Try to make a big event?" Ben asked.

"Yeah, try to make a nice event, and kind of not get into the repetitive thing," the manager said.

"We're not going to do *any* First Fridays?" Don asked.

"So what is our—what is our goal?" Chris asked, seemingly upset by the plan to abandon First Friday events.

"You guys usually pay for all the [main presentations]," the manager noted, referring to how one of the Friends' key goals was to provide financial support for refuge events.

"But there's really just two [events planned for this year]," Chris explained, referring to the summer event and the annual Eighth Grade Environmental Education Day.

"And I know they don't care [about visitor numbers]," Don began, invoking the "they" of the federal and regional levels of the USFWS. He held up the table listing the declining numbers for annual refuge events and attendees. "But this—what you've given us here! Look at this. This is the reason why we're here!"

"Yeah, that says it all," Frank agreed somberly.

"I'm surprised they don't take part of our membership fees!" Mary Anne said, invoking the familiar specter of bureaucratic overreach by upper-level USFWS officials.

"Don't say that too loud!" Chris said, only half joking. A burst of indignant laughter came from the group. He continued, "I'm seeing that you-all only need $1,500 dollars for the Eighth Grade Day and then this July event. We have enough money to keep going for seven or eight years without doing anything."

"So you're saying why do anything?" Ben asked.

"Exactly. Why does this group come here six or seven times a year for a couple hours? What're we trying to accomplish? What's our mission? It doesn't look like anything right now," Chris said.

As the Friends members murmured their agreement, the manager tried to answer Chris's question, "You need to do three things, I think. Focus down on the visitor services. Then try to address some infrastructure issues at the refuge. So maybe visitor services in a different aspect, so people can do different things when they come here. Then the third thing is habitat stuff. There's going to be an opportunity for that."

"If that's our goal, we need to reevaluate how we raise money and what we're doing," Chris said. "Up to this point we haven't really done any habitat."

"I thought our main goal was to get more people aware of our refuge through the events, and it's pretty apparent they don't want us to do that," Don said, alluding to how moving away from a focus on visitor services would represent a dramatic shift for the group and again invoking the "they" of off-site USFWS officials.

Expanding on Don's thought, Frank looked at the table in his hand and said, "To me, what that paper proves is that we were successful and that the handcuffs are what hurt us," referring to the decline in numbers after the new regulations were instituted.

Not ready to move away from promoting visitor services, Darren asked, "What do you think about doing more education? Wetland tours wasn't something?"

"Yeah," the refuge manager and Mike agreed.

Before other Friends members could take up Darren's proposal, Chris again questioned the purpose of the group, "I keep coming back to what's our goal? What's our mission?"

"I think we'll have to lean more towards habitat and doing that to promote membership," Don said, answering Chris and moving the group away from Darren's suggestion to zero in on education-related events.

The tension in the room was uncomfortable at this point. I could not help but fidget in my seat as the Friends were seemingly about to transition from facilitating public uses of the refuge. This had been their primary objective since the group's inception, but now members were openly questioning their purpose as well as proposing alternative avenues for their efforts because of the increasingly restrictive regulations implemented by the USFWS. After discussing refuge infrastructure issues that the Friends might be able to help with, however, Chris turned the conversation back to visitor services.

"So we're not worried about events?" Chris asked.

"Well, I wouldn't say that," the refuge manager answered.

"It sounds like it," Chris disagreed. "It sounds like you're saying two things in the same breath."

"What do you think is a realistic number at an event this year?" Ben asked.

"It just depends on the weather," the manager explained.

"Well, I think we need a concerted effort to have more than last year," Frank said.

"Yeah," Diane and Cindy agreed.

"How many do we get at Eighth Grade Days?" Ben asked.

"Three or four hundred," the manager said.

"I'm just thinking more than 856," Ben said, referring to how many people had attended events in 2014. "Can we get enough at the Saturday event?"

"It just depends on the weather. It's just, if we keep doing the same thing, you'll get a reputation. Maybe things will change," the manager said.

"Start doing hot dogs again," Don said, recalling how free food had encouraged people to attend events.

"I'm thinking more education, getting those kids here. Teachers are always looking for fieldtrips," Darren said, reiterating his idea of fieldtrips to the refuge.

Instead of being shrugged off with a "yeah" as it had been the first time he mentioned the idea, this time Darren's suggestion was seriously considered as the manager and the Friends discussed its pros and cons. Members of the group eventually concluded it would be the best way forward, despite having some complications.

"I hate to agree with Darren," Don began, before pausing for humorous effect. As the Friends members and the refuge manager started laughing, he continued, "But this sounds like a good idea."

"My thinking is we educate and go off from there," Frank agreed. "Get more kids here and bring on the parents, and I think it all flows together. We get frustrated when someone in some other state says we can't do this or that, and we're like, what!"

"Good point," Don agreed. "With everyone's input, I was wondering [what our goals should be]. [The higher-ups in the USFWS] don't want us to have events, and evidently they're more focused on education, so maybe we've got more of a focus of where we're going. So maybe we'll shoot for getting kids here."

"That was the goal before," Mary Anne said, referring to how the Friends had already been promoting fieldtrips.

"Just a different angle on it. More focused on it," Don said, as the Friends members agreed with yeahs, uh-huhs, and yeps. "I mean, I feel better about where we're going."

Even with Mary Anne voicing her concerns, the mood in the room was far more upbeat than earlier in the meeting when members of the group were openly questioning their purpose and whether they would continue promoting public uses of Swan Lake. They were frustrated by the sharp decline in visitor numbers in 2014 and the low number of events planned for 2015, but they were now more hopeful about the future of visitor services at Swan Lake after agreeing to promote more fieldtrips to the refuge.

The significance of Chris's "So we're not worried about events?" for this eventual outcome cannot be overstated. When group decision-making processes are carried out through interpersonal interactions, they are mediated by the norms of conversation. Conversations are never just a series of unlinked statements made at random. They tend to follow a set of norms, or conversational rules,[27] that involve everything from taking turns at talking to addressing whatever the immediately preceding speaker has stated. Conversations are "sequences of action"[28] that follow trajectories of linked statements in which previous statements affect subsequent statements in other words. Group conversation does more than just generate a decision; it influences the decisions a group makes.[29]

The strategy of promoting field trips to the refuge was clearly mediated by the process of group conversation. Because speakers in group conversations tend to refer to and address the most immediately preceding speaker,[30] it is possible the topic of visitor services would not have been discussed at length again during the meeting if Chris had not asked his question. Yet because Chris reintroduced visitor services, other members of the group could more easily express their desire to continue supporting these activities because they were responding to what an immediately preceding speaker had said. This conversational trajectory eventually provided an avenue for Darren to repeat his proposal of getting more school groups to the refuge. He had suggested a renewed emphasis on education much earlier in the meeting, but his suggestion was largely ignored after being vaguely answered by the refuge manager and Mike. Only after Darren brought it up a second time, when the group had returned to the subject of visitor services, was his suggestion seriously considered and eventually agreed to by the group. The structures of group conversation mediated the outcomes that emerged from this meeting.

Don's joke about hating to agree with Darren in the February meeting is an example of how Friends meetings often involved a great deal of humor and laughter despite tensions over regulations. This may seem somewhat inconsequential, but humor is serious business. Joking around is regularly used to sustain interactions because it can diffuse tensions[31] and facilitate group cohesion.[32] Humor enabled Friends members and refuge staff to work through conflicts over regulations. By joking around, they blew off steam, built group solidarity, and continued cooperative efforts to repurpose the refuge in spite of escalating conflicts.

One of Don's jokes during the March 2014 Friends meeting is illustrative. Tempers began to rise after the group was informed that they would likely need to get liability insurance if they wished to continue serving food at events.

"Do you have to have insurance for [Youth in the Outdoors Day]? They have shooting and all that, you know." Cindy said, implying it did not make much sense to require insurance to serve food if previous events that involved children shooting firearms were not required to.

"Nope. Just have to have it for the food," the refuge manager informed everyone.

Looking up from my computer to gauge the Friends members' reactions, it was easy to see they did not approve of the new policy. Many looked dismayed, others angry. Before anyone else could voice an objection, Don sarcastically suggested that the refuge manager solve the problem by misleading his superiors.

Looking at the refuge manager as if he were deadly serious, Don feigned incredulity and asked, "Well, why did you put it in [the compatibility determination] that we were serving food?"

Don's suggestion subtly reprimanded the refuge manager for enforcing an unpopular policy, but it was also a strategic use of humor. Tempers could have easily escalated to the point that the meeting fell apart, but Don's joke helped avoid that possibility. After a good laugh at his lighthearted suggestion, Friends members and the refuge manager calmly discussed how they could promote public events at Swan Lake if they had to get insurance.

Refuge staff also joked with Friends members in ways that enabled continued cooperation. The following conversation from a Friends meeting ensued after Chris asked whether the refuge might receive approval to serve hot dogs at an upcoming event.

"We're not gonna. It'll just have to be prepackaged," the refuge manager said.

"So will the Lunchables [prepackaged food trays] be ready?" Chris asked, in an aggrieved tone.

"Just give them Skittles. Get them all hopped up on those," the refuge manager joked, diffusing the quickly mounting tension in the room.

As the Friends members laughed, Roscoe added fuel to fire, loudly suggesting, "Give them cold hot dogs still in the package!"

After a roar of laughter, Becky tried to steer the conversation back on track. "How about lunchmeat sandwiches?"

"Nah, we can't do that. There's preparation," the manager said.

"Just give them a sack of meat!" Chris said, lampooning the regulations forbidding any sort of food preparation. Again, the group laughed before tensions could boil over.

The manager's joke about Skittles allowed him to navigate the frictions that emerged from being caught between the public and an unpopular regulation. By joking about the regulation, he facilitated a tenuous sense of belonging in the community. He was even able to generate somewhat positive reactions from Friends members while enforcing a regulation they strongly opposed.

Suggesting that interpersonal interactions enabled local residents and refuge staff to work together may seem obvious, but these interactions were more than just a means to an end. The norms of group conversation mediated how Friends and refuge staff worked together, and humor enabled them to work more effectively through frictions over regulations. Taken together, interpersonal interactions were centrally important to their ability to work together in spite of conflicts over the future.

Researchers have generally ignored how interpersonal interactions influence whether and how ways of life and communities are sustained in response to climate change.[33] The chapter addressing adaptations in the report produced by the American Sociological Association's task force on climate change, for example, discusses an impressive array of factors that inform adaptations.[34] Everything from individuals' perceptions of climate change to the institutional arrangement of world trade are considered, but noticeably absent from the discussion is a consideration of how the complexities of interactions between human beings influence adaptations. This is a troubling oversight. Far from being an ephemeral concern, interactions allow individuals and groups to coordinate courses of action, and the structures of interaction mediate adaptations.

Given the long tradition in sociology of studying the significance of interpersonal interactions,[35] sociologists seem uniquely positioned to continue exploring the relation between interactions and adaptations. Importantly, in this respect, future considerations of interactions and adaptations must not depoliticize interpersonal interactions by divorcing them from the power-infused contexts in which they take place.[36] I emphasize this point and tie it into my ongoing consideration of how inequalities informed and were informed by adaptations by considering how gender informed interactions during Friends meetings.

Even a cursory reading of the excerpts above illustrates that men tended to dominate Friends meetings. Men changed topics, challenged others, and made jokes during meetings far more often than the women in the group, who were often relegated to interjecting supporting "yeahs" and "uh-huhs." This corresponds to findings from a long tradition of research that conversational processes and gendered inequalities are linked. Pamela Fishman's analysis is particularly applicable because she shows that women are generally responsible for the "yeahs" and "uh-huhs" that keep conversations going, while men tend to control what topics are addressed during interactions.[37]

But men in Sumner did not always control meetings at which both women and men were present. Women tended to lead city council meetings even though there were men on the council. Unlike at Friends meetings, at council meetings the women were the ones who proposed solutions, challenged other members on interpretations of rules, and generally made sure the city government continued to function. One of the women who rarely spoke during Friends meetings was one of the most vocal city council members. Instead of sitting quietly as she did during Friends meetings, she routinely raised new issues and corrected others on their understandings of the rules governing the council. Looking at why women and men tended to control city council and Friends meetings, respectively, clarifies the significance of gender for these interactions.

As noted in Chapter 2, rural men are expected to be authorities on topics such as conservation, agriculture, hunting, and fishing.[38] Given the expectation that men should be the ones who are especially knowledgeable about these activities, it is understandable why they led meetings that focused on a national wildlife refuge. In contrast, and as I discuss in Chapter 3, rural women are often expected to be in charge of caring for their community.[39] Consequently, they led city council meetings that focused on the general reproduction of their community. In both cases, men and women tended to take charge of topics they were expected to be authorities on according to their genders.[40] Conversations during Friends and city council meetings and the decisions that emerged from them were informed by the norms of group conversations and the links between gender, communities, and the environment. When considering how adaptations are informed by interpersonal interactions, it is absolutely necessary to consider how power and inequalities influence interactions. Not doing so successfully depoliticizes interactions, adaptations, and climate change.

Protentions, Interactions, and Adaptations

Adaptations to climate change are enabled by individuals' concern for the immediate future. To be clear, I am not suggesting that adaptations would not be facilitated by either more concern over the long-term effects of climate change or a reconceptualization of climate change as posing risks to the immediate future. Instead, I contend that a focus on the immediate future is necessary for cooperative efforts to adapt, especially when those trying to work together to rearrange their lives in response to climate change are juggling multiple, contradictory understandings of the future and its risks.

Over the last century, sociologists have maintained that individuals concern themselves with the immediate future while they are interacting. A basic assumption made by symbolic interactionists is that individuals act according to how they anticipate others will react to them.[41] Not only do individuals think about the immediate future; it is particularly important to them. As Erving Goffman famously illustrated, simply managing to get through an interaction is usually important to those who are interacting.[42] More recently, Iddo Tavory and Nina Eliasoph have expanded on the significance of anticipations through their distinction between protentions and trajectories.[43] This distinction accounts for the different kinds of anticipations people use to interact and coordinate cooperative courses of action. Protentions involve anticipations of the immediate future of interactions, and trajectories are arcs of anticipation that extend into the following hours, days, weeks, months, or even years. For example, a protention is Friends members' and refuge staff's adherence to the norms of group conversation, and a trajectory is their concern for how the implementation of new regulations would affect public uses of the refuge over the coming months.

Protentions and trajectories are both crucially important to cooperation. To interact, individuals must anticipate the immediate future so they can then make plans to cooperate. By concerning themselves with the immediate future of interactions, in other words, they can coordinate more long-term, cooperative trajectories of action.

Protentions undoubtedly informed adaptations at Swan Lake. No matter how contentious the issues were, Friends members and refuge staff always communicated in ways that indicated their concern for the immediate future of their interactions. I never witnessed anyone raise their voice, no one ever cussed during meetings, and nobody ever got up and walked out. Instead, Friends members and refuge staff listened to and addressed each other in ways that helped ensure their interactions would not fall apart. By following the norms of group conversation and using humor as an interactional device, Friends members and refuge staff generated cooperative strategies to try to connect the public with the refuge.

Don pointed this out during our interview. I asked for his thoughts on a new hunting program at the refuge, and he said, "The refuge manager's philosophy is the public should have a place to hunt, so we argue politely about it." Don's invocation of politeness described how Friends members and refuge staff tended to discuss contentious issues. There were undoubtedly disagreements, but staff and the Friends concerned themselves with both the more distant future of the refuge and the more immediate future of their interactions in discussions. By doing so, they generated viable strategies to continue working together to connect local residents with the refuge in spite of a lack of geese, more regulations, and increasing tensions.

Concern for the immediate future is *necessary* for processes of adaptation. Others' contention that individuals' concern for the immediate future is undermining adaptations to climate change ignores how protentions enable cooperative efforts to adapt. In a world where individuals and groups are actively competing to define what risks are significant and where conflicts over which risks reflect legitimate concerns are inevitable, the significance of protentions should not be understated. They allow individuals to smooth frictions that emerge because of divergent understandings of the future and its risks.

Knowing that there are protentions does not mean conflicts over risks will always be resolved through interactions. Far from it. What protentions do illustrate is that instead of acting as a barrier to adaptations, concern for the immediate future creates the potential for collective responses to climate change. Policy makers and researchers need to more fully appreciate and consider the significance of anticipations of the immediate future and the interpersonal interactions they enable. At the very least, we should discard the assumption that people do not adapt to climate change because they focus on the immediate future.

Conclusion: The Messy Interface between the Public and State

The public and USFWS conceptualized each other as risks, but cooperative efforts to redefine the refuge in response to a lack of geese did not fall apart. Relationships and interactions between members of the public, Swan Lake staff, and the refuge itself facilitated continued efforts to repurpose the refuge. Combined with Chapter 5, these findings illustrate that entangled (non)humans, culturally contingent meanings, emotions, multiple institutions, and interpersonal relationships and interactions complicate responses to risks. Put simply, individuals do not respond to a single risk as though they are disentangled from their relationships with a range of (non)human beings, things, and institutions. Responses to risks emerge as individuals and groups who are embedded in complex webs of entangled (non)humans rely on culturally contingent meanings and assumptions to try to respond to a multitude of both short- and long-term risks.

Even members of state institutions are not immune to the push and pull of culture, networks, attachments to place, and the structures of group conversation. Efforts to repurpose the refuge were largely contingent on refuge staff members' belonging, at least tenuously, to the local community. One of the reasons that local residents continued working with refuge staff was that they regularly distinguished staff from their broader institution. Refuge staff in turn were committed to working with community members because they had developed feelings of obligation toward local residents after working with them for years. At the very least, how the public and state officials worked cooperatively would have been different if refuge staff had not been at least tenuous members of the local community.

Given how important the refuge staff's position within the community was for how the refuge was being repurposed, future considerations of adaptations need to acknowledge the messy interface between state institutions and the public. This messiness is crucially important to whether and how the public and representatives of institutions work with each other to respond to climate change. Instead of reducing institutions to black boxes of homogeneous bureaucrats, analysts and policy makers need to consider how bureaucrats operating within local contexts can be liminal members of the communities in which they work. This liminal position can be crucially important to whether and how they work cooperatively with individuals and groups outside state institutions to rearrange and sustain their communities in response to climate change.

These findings correspond with findings from numerous works that the ability to construct and belong to a community can be crucially important to adaptations to shifting socioecological conditions.[44] Joined with my analysis in Chapter 3 on the importance of social heterogeneity for adaptations to socioecological processes,[45] this points to a complex tension between feelings of solidarity, social heterogeneity, and adaptations. Heterogeneity can present avenues for adaptations, but feelings of togetherness can also be centrally important to collective efforts to capitalize on those opportunities. At the refuge, local residents and refuge staff drew on networks that were infused with feelings of mutual obligation, respect, trust, and belonging to work together to encourage public uses of the refuge that were not tied to goose hunting. If either this sense of community or a group of new, potential users had not been present, it seems far less likely that the refuge would have been repurposed to cater to families. By building, maintaining, and belonging to a community, local residents and refuge staff were able to work together to tap into the complexities of Sumner to adapt to shifting goose migration patterns and increasing regulations.

Conclusion

Adaptations as Entangled, Open-Ended Processes

Throughout this book I emphasize that adaptations are exceedingly complex processes. Efforts to rearrange and sustain ways of life and community in Sumner were informed by a dizzying array of entanglements between social and ecological things, beings, and processes. Allergens that could be in homemade cookies. Assumptions regarding the meaning of progress, conservation, and governance. Corn seeds treated with neonicotinoids. The organizational arrangement of the U.S. Fish and Wildlife Service (USFWS). Swan Lake National Wildlife Refuge infrastructure. An absence of geese. Rural masculinities and femininities complicated by race, class, and sexuality. Ducks that continued to use the refuge. Interpersonal interactions and relationships built on trust. They all intersected to influence how connections between and among people and places were rearranged and sustained.

These entanglements are what made adaptations possible. If they had not been present, and if individuals and groups in Sumner had not been able to creatively navigate and leverage them, the community would not have been rearranged and sustained. My hope is that highlighting the wealth of social and ecological entanglements that informed adaptations in Sumner will afford us a better understanding of how ways of life and communities are rearranged in response to the effects of climate change. At the risk of oversimplifying these intricacies, I summarize the preceding chapters in the following three points. Though presented as distinct points, they bleed into and become entangled with each other in practice.

First, efforts to rearrange and sustain ways of life and communities emerge through entanglements between (non)human beings, things, and institutions. Sumner demonstrates the significance of a range of entanglements, from socially constructed understandings of progress to nonhuman organisms. In Chapter 2, the shift from goose to duck hunting was informed by a mash of intersectional rural masculinities, laws regarding corn, the material landscape of the surrounding area, and the different landscape preferences of geese and ducks. In Chapter 3, the festival was rearranged at least partially because women in the community convinced men to allow the festival committee to use Sumner's limited public infrastructure. Chapter 4 describes how the refuge had been constructed through (non)human interactions. Chapters 5 and 6 cover the process of repurposing the refuge and how that was informed by links between institutions such as the federal courts and the USFWS, beliefs regarding conservation and governance, emotion-infused relations between and among people and places; and nonhumans that ranged from corn seeds to geese.

In all these cases, community members' abilities to reorganize and sustain ways of life and community were informed by entangled (non)human beings, things, and institutions. Future analyses and policies concerning adaptations must consider such entanglements, which are always particular to the social and ecological characteristics of a given community, and how they create avenues for rearranging cultures and communities. Because nonhumans can never be fully controlled by people, these entanglements will complicate and transform how cultures and communities can and will be rearranged. In some cases, adaptations may not be possible because of the (non)human entanglements present in some contexts. Consequently, while I think that Sumner provides a relatively hopeful account of resilience because community members effectively responded to the lack of geese, recognizing that adaptations simply will not be possible in some places because of the social and ecological entanglements that compose them is absolutely crucial.

Second, throughout this book we see that intersecting inequalities inform processes of reorganizing culture and community and that adaptations have the potential to rearrange and even undermine inequalities. Chapters 2 and 3 explore the intersecting inequalities pertaining to race, gender, and class that influenced how individuals in Sumner rearranged their relationships with each other and the surrounding landscape. In

Chapters 5 and 6 we see that the institutional arrangement of the USFWS enabled officials at the complex, regional, and federal levels of the organization to implement policies based on their perceptions of the future and its risks, often despite local residents vehemently disagreeing with these perceptions. Inequalities informed adaptations, but inequalities themselves were also rearranged as community members remade their lives in response to the lack of geese. The shift from goose to duck hunting recounted in Chapter 2 enabled new ways of accomplishing classed masculinities that made it harder for working-class men to achieve masculinities considered worthy of respect. Adaptations did not always intensify inequalities, though. In Chapter 3 a group of women in the community simultaneously undermined and reproduced intersecting inequalities as they reorganized the Wild Goose Festival.

Future considerations of adaptations must take account of how intersecting inequalities both inform and are informed by processes of adaptation. Doing otherwise risks missing the intricate ways that inequalities facilitate and constrain adaptations and how responses to climate change can both intensify and undermine inequalities. Further, either-or, zero-sum approaches to inequalities must be avoided. In Chapter 3, Sumner residents creatively leveraged the messy complexities of inequalities to rearrange their community in manners that both reproduced and undermined intersecting inequalities. Adaptations, in other words, will result in ambivalent, and at times contradictory, rearrangements of inequalities.

Third, efforts to rearrange and sustain ways of life and communities emerge through entanglements between the past, present, and future. Sumner's past, when the title of Wild Goose Capital of the World was more true than not, was crucially important. Chapter 1 notes that this past was part of the reason Foster's was considered especially significant to local residents. Chapter 2 emphasizes men's desires to continue achieving masculinities similar to those enabled by goose hunting. In Chapter 3 community members revived a festival that had become centrally important to Sumner during the goose hunting heyday. The importance of the past is especially evident in Chapters 4, 5, and 6. They discuss efforts to repurpose the refuge, which were influenced by a refuge landscape built over the preceding decades, and community members' attachments to place, which had been carried over from prior experiences on the refuge. Despite the importance of the past, Sumner's residents repeatedly demonstrated their investment in the future. Chapters 5 and 6 show how individuals' and groups' perceptions of the future informed how the refuge was repurposed in response to the lack of geese. Anticipations of risks that could become manifest in the relatively distant future informed adaptations, but equally as important were anticipations of the more immediate future. Understandings of both the past and the future animated the interactions among refuge staff and members of the public as they rearranged the meanings and uses of Swan Lake NWR.

Subsequent considerations of adaptations need to include these temporal dynamics. And the idea that a lack of focus on the distant future is why adaptations do not take place must be discarded. Focusing on the relatively distant future can actually undermine adaptations, and cooperative efforts to adapt would not be possible without concern for the immediate future.

Entanglements will not always present opportunities to adapt, but we can respond to climate change more effectively by acknowledging how the complexities of social and ecological entanglements within particular locations have the potential to create avenues through which ways of life and communities can be reorganized and sustained. This finding provides hope for those seeking to promote resilient communities in an era of climate change even as it clarifies the realities of entanglements, adaptations, and climate change. Even in small, rural communities such as Sumner, where we might not expect to find the social and ecological complexities that present opportunities to adapt, the intricacies of entanglements that underpin such places can still present openings for reorganizing and sustaining ways of life and community. Further, even though the residents in this tiny community did not necessarily realize they were adapting to climate change, they still worked together to navigate and rearrange the social and ecological entanglements of their community. In a political context in which climate change is often used to divide people, this is especially significant. Regardless of whether individuals believe in climate change, it will disrupt their communities. By drawing on and reorganizing the vibrant entanglements that constituted Sumner, residents were able to reorganize and sustain their ways of life and community, even though they did not indicate that they knew that climate change had disrupted their lives.

This hopefulness is tempered because social and ecological entanglements will not always present opportunities for adaptations. In extreme cases, such as when rising sea levels inundate coastal communities, entanglements can seemingly eliminate prospects for adaptations. Even in Sumner, entanglements sometimes undermined adaptations in more mundane manners. The organizational arrangement of the USFWS enabled adaptations to a lack of geese in some respects but in other respects undercut community members' efforts to repurpose the meanings and uses of the refuge. Social and ecological entanglements can present opportunities to adapt, but we must remain aware that the spiraling consequences of climate change present very serious challenges. Entanglements can offer avenues for adaptations, but they can also undermine efforts to reorganize and sustain cultures and communities.

While I was wrapping up fieldwork, the USFWS was implementing a new hunting program at the refuge. For the first time ever, in the fall of 2015, duck hunting would be allowed on the refuge. Intended as a way to increase public uses of the refuge, the new hunting plan was a lightning rod of controversy between some local residents and Swan Lake staff. The majority of residents were not necessarily against the program, but a sizable faction of men in the community opposed the program because they were concerned it could cause ducks to stop using the area. This was a particularly troubling possibility considering how important duck hunting was to the accomplishment of respectable rural masculinities in the community.

The program involved a multiyear bevy of environmental assessments, regulation changes, and sign-offs from various levels of the USFWS. Intersections of race, gender, class, and rurality; interactive (non)humans; perceptions of the past and future; and multiple levels of governance simultaneously mediated how this transition was being implemented and discussed by community members. Men with duck hunting spots near the refuge were concerned that allowing duck hunting on the refuge would ruin duck hunting in the area. To justify these concerns, some drew on the history of the area and argued that hunting on the refuge would cause the ducks to leave just as the geese had. Others drew on a conservative understanding of governance to argue that any new regulation the federal government implemented would invariably lead to negative outcomes. Most commonly, I heard men draw attention to how the complexity of interconnections between humans, ducks, and landscapes across multiple spatial scales made it impossible to predict the consequences of the new program. According to these men, it was best to just leave a good thing alone and not implement the program.

Unfortunately, or perhaps fortunately for the completion of this project, I concluded fieldwork in May 2015, before the new hunting program was implemented. Although I wanted to observe its implementation, I needed the time I was committing to fieldwork to complete my dissertation. I also received a teaching position that required me to be in Columbia every day of the week. I probably would not have concluded fieldwork when I did without this justification for extracting myself, however incompletely, from the relationships I had formed with those living and working in the area.

My inability to observe the consequences of the new hunting program highlights how our analyses of adaptations are necessarily incomplete because adaptations are ongoing, emergent processes. Thus, I answer the question that begins this book—how are cultures and communities reconstructed in response to climate change?—with this: adaptations were incomplete and open-ended in Sumner, and adaptations elsewhere will always be ongoing because our ways of life and communities are constantly being refashioned through evolving entanglements. We must continue exploring these entanglements to learn how to more effectively navigate and leverage their complexities to rearrange and sustain our lives and communities. When conducting such explorations, it will be necessary to consider entanglements between differentially empowered (non)human beings, things, and institutions that exist across space and time. The dynamic entanglements that make up communities will influence adaptations in context-specific manners, but they will always facilitate and constrain whether and how cultures and communities are sustained in response to climate change.

Appendix

A Situated Community Study

Over the previous century sociologists have studied particular communities to develop theories of how communities function more generally.[1] Usually, the primary objective of a community study is to understand how its members organize their lives and relationships with each other. Numerous classic community studies even look at how individuals rearrange their lives and relationships with each other in response to disruptions such as industrialization or an environmental disaster. Researchers often suggest that the best way to do a community study, and get a complete view of it, is to spend as much time getting to know as many different people in a community as possible.[2]

Therefore, I spent large amounts of time at the Swan Lake National Wildlife Refuge, the bar, and with community groups. Whenever anyone suggested I do something with them, I generally did. I attended barbeques, banquets, fish fries, and Christmas parties. If anyone invited me to go fishing or hunting, I was there. If someone wanted me to see their farm, stock their pond, or help out with a community group, I did. And when Darla suggested I try the aptly named "blueberry pie" drink sitting right outside the front door of Foster's, I willingly took a sip.

Even so, my research cannot be interpreted as a complete, all-encompassing account of residents of Sumner rearranging their ways of life and community. Even in a community with just 102 people, it was impossible to arrive at a complete viewpoint of everything that was going on. The concept of situatedness is useful for understanding why.

Since the 1980s, feminist scholars have argued that research is always informed by how researchers are situated, vis-à-vis intersecting inequalities, with their research subjects.[3] As Sandra Harding notes, this is not a drawback; it is simply part of the research process that must be acknowledged.[4] By considering how our own identities inform the generation and interpretation of data, we can produce better research. Recognizing that research is situated necessitates acknowledging that a "god trick"—the researcher getting an all-encompassing, complete view of a community that is unmediated by the researcher's situatedness within the community— is impossible.[5] Instead, our understandings of communities are necessarily partial and informed by who we are, who we interact with, and when we interact with them.

My study is a situated community study. Though I made an effort to get to know many people in a variety of settings in Sumner, my identity as a white, heterosexual man undoubtedly influenced this project. It allowed me to fit in demographically, but that does not mean I freely moved throughout the community unaffected by my identity. I operated in the racialized, classed, and gendered dynamics of Sumner that I introduce in Chapter 1 and then explore throughout this book.

The bar, for example, was informally segregated along intersecting lines of gender and familiarity. Men and women who were familiar with each other sat in integrated groups at the tables in the back of the bar, but there were two other places to sit in the bar. Just to the right of the front door was a large round table where, depending on the day, groups of women or men sat. The other place to sit was at the bar itself. A set of regulars as well as relative outsiders sat here. Women rarely sat at the bar, but when they did they were almost always married to or longtime friends with whomever they were sitting beside. I was trying to fit in, and so I sat at the bar because this was the appropriate place for me given my gender and status as a relative outsider. Being anchored to the bar was concerning at first, but eventually I realized that sitting there enabled a situated form of data generation. By sitting in the appropriate place, I participated in the gendered dynamics of the bar. As I describe in Chapter 1, this helped me understand the bar and the gendered dynamics of the community.

That I was a sociology graduate student from a city in the surrounding region also complicated how I generated data for this project. I generally avoided bringing up my graduate student status because it marked me as out of place. Men liked to give me a hard time about being a "college boy" or "career student," for example. I was also wary of talking about sociology because the primary tenets of the discipline run counter to community members' conceptualization of social processes as being determined by individuals' choices and actions. As Greg said, after I told him I was teaching a course on social inequalities, "Well, how do you teach that? How do you teach something that doesn't exist?"

I did not always try to fit in as best as I could, though. Many of the same men who gave me a hard time about being a student also liked to give me grief about my Kansas City Royals hat. But I wore it religiously because I did not want to give in to their taunts. Besides, the Royals had been perennial cellar dwellers before 2014, so I did not want to miss the first chance I had ever had to show my fandom for a winner. Just as importantly, I also found reactions to my hat to be important for my research. It initiated conversations with strangers, much as a dog[6] or a child would,[7] and responses to it revealed the racialized, gendered, and classed understandings of what it meant to be a rural person worthy of respect. In effect, my hat presented opportunities to explain what it meant to be rural because it was a visible reminder of the biggest city in the region.

Demographic characteristics such as race, gender, and education status do not affect the research process in a static manner. These characteristics have emergent, shifting effects on how research subjects perceive researchers as they become enveloped in the social networks and relations of a site.[8] An especially notable example from my work was that members of the public associated me with the refuge and its staff members because of how much time I spent at Swan Lake. Whenever community members introduced me to another local resident, they often explained my project before saying that I worked at the refuge. This complicated my data in two key ways. First, men in the community sometimes joked that I was an undercover "narc" for the USFWS or the Missouri Department of Conservation because the refuge was associated with game wardens. I believe some were not completely joking and as a result were more cautious about discussing illegal activities regarding fishing and hunting than they otherwise might have been. Second, I felt that some community members softened their remarks to me about Swan Lake staff members because they knew I had personal relationships with the staff.

Community studies have also drawn on the posthumanities to account for how the researcher and others in the community are situated in relation to nonhuman beings and things.[9] When I began my project, I was aware of the significance of (non)human interactions because I had read authors who urged social scientists to pay attention to more than just people.[10] However, I was not planning to do an ethnography that included those interactions. Nevertheless, I quickly realized that an approach that ignored interactions among (non)humans would be inadequate. Seemingly, at every turn, (non)human entanglements transformed how individuals went about their lives and tried to rearrange their community in response to the lack of geese. I made the conscious choice for that reason to not write (non)human interactions out of my account of Sumner.

I spent more than 1,800 hours observing, getting to know, and working with community members, and I formally interviewed twenty-one individuals for this project. I did not interview more for two primary reasons. First, following the work of Barney Glaser and Anselm Strauss, as well as that of Kathy Charmaz,[11] I generated data and did interviews only as long as they contributed new insights. Second, what people say they do and what they actually do during their everyday lives are often quite different.[12] Thus, I purposefully relied heavily on participant observations because this project seeks to understand what individuals were doing to reorganize and sustain their community. Using data from interviews with twenty-one key individuals to supplement an extensive amount of rich, in-depth data from participant observations is a strength of this project. It is squarely in line with established qualitative research strategies, and using data from interviews to complement a wealth of data from participant observations allowed me to analyze and illustrate how individuals were sustaining their community during their everyday, mundane lives. The extensive amount of data from my participant observations also enable me to make significant contributions to a climate change literature that has often relied on survey and interview data.[13]

Interviews were just as situated as participant observations. I chose interviewees through a combination of theoretical and snowball sampling. By theoretical I mean that I chose interview subjects because they were key players in the processes of adaptation on which I eventually focused. Consequently, they could provide valuable insights for ideas and theories I was generating at the time.[14] By snowball I mean I accessed further interviewees through their contacts with chosen interviewees. Saying interviewees were chosen through theoretical and snowball sampling belies the actual complexities involved in arranging interviews. In particular, the primary reason more men than women were interviewed for this project was because I had trouble getting women to agree to be formally interviewed. Men I did not know rarely turned down interview requests, but women I had not gotten to know through community groups routinely declined to be interviewed. In one case, even a woman I knew quite well declined to be interviewed. This was likely related to our different places in the community's gender dichotomy,[15] but more than this, it was related to her understandings of who was an expert on a community steeped in the masculine activity of goose hunting. On numerous occasions, women would tell me to go talk to particular men "who knew all about the geese."

All interviews were semistructured and used responsive interviewing techniques, in which observations from fieldwork informed interview scripts.[16] All interviews included questions regarding the refuge and community, but interviews were also tailored to particular individuals. Interviews with refuge personnel were conducted as I was exiting the field and included questions regarding everyday tasks of working at the refuge. Interviews with residents included questions about personal and community histories. Waterfowl biologists were asked questions that dealt with the everyday work they did at the refuge when goose numbers were high.

The following sets of questions represent the guide I worked from to formally interview participants. I started interviews by asking people the same basic background questions regarding age, occupation, and time spent living or working in the area, but the interviews themselves rarely followed the order of the guide below. Questions and topics tended to lurch from one subject to another as interviewees brought up particular points and I asked them for additional information.

In the first set of questions, I took particular care to get interviewees' perceptions of changes that had occurred or were occurring in their community.

> What was it like growing up or working in the Wild Goose Capital of the World? What was it like when the geese started coming? Did you take pride in that claim to fame? Any favorite stories? Is there still a sense of pride with the title of Goose Capital of the World?
>
> How has the community changed over the time you've lived here? How has the Wild Goose Festival changed?
>
> What was it like when the geese stopped coming? Was it a gradual realization? A focusing event?
>
> Do you have a sense of loss now that the geese are gone? Does it feel as though there's something missing?
>
> What do you see as the community's biggest challenge now and in the future?

Another set of questions concerned the relation between the community and the refuge and residents' perceptions of how the refuge should be managed.

> Has the relation between the refuge and the community changed over the years? How?
>
> Do you think the refuge is an important part of the community? Why or why not?
>
> Are you involved on the refuge at all—for example, in Friends of Swan Lake?
>
> Do you generally agree with how the refuge is being run today?
>
> Would you like to see the refuge opened for duck hunting?

Finally, I always asked interviewees about their understandings of the goose migration shift and whether they hunted geese or ducks.

> Why do you think the geese stopped coming to Swan Lake NWR? Do you think climate change played any part?
>
> Did you ever do any goose hunting?
>
> Did you do any duck hunting?
>
> Do you see any important differences between hunting ducks and geese?

All field notes, interviews, and documents were coded by hand through a process of open-ended coding and memo writing.[17] This allowed me to continually describe, analyze, and interpret the data,[18] and I could organize the large amount of data I was generating, keep incorporating new literature, and refine my questions and observations during fieldwork. Modifying questions and observations through the incorporation of new information and literature was critical to my research process because I had not intended to write about many of the topics addressed in this book. I went into the project with a broad focus and then narrowed it to significant issues.[19]

Historic texts were somewhat unusual compared to data from participant observations, interviews, and contemporary texts. Beyond dramatic changes in political-economic circumstances such as the movement from the Great Depression to World War II to the beginning of neoliberalism under Ronald Reagan, the texts include mundane details of their time. Because some of these texts were over seventy-five years old, it was necessary to be especially cognizant that they were produced in different eras. The contemporary meaning of "nimrod," for example, is very different from that in 1951. Consequently, when refuge manager Robert Russell wrote, "This fall, for the first time, nimrods were not permitted to enter the refuge to retrieve waterfowl dropped within the boundary," he probably was not referring to these hunters as idiots.[20] Because reports are not objective lenses into the actual happenings within institutions but are written with institutional objectives and constraints in mind, it was also important to consider how the changing institutionalized structures and objectives of the USFWS influenced the who, what, where, and how of refuge documents.[21]

Notes

INTRODUCTION

1. Population figures are available from the U.S. Census Bureau's *American FactFinder* database, at https://factfinder.census.gov; see also Missouri Census Data Center 2014.

2. For comparison, New York County, New York, the most densely populated county in the United States, had 69,468 people per square mile in 2010.

3. Median household income in Sumner was $29,531 in 2010–2014. This was less than two-thirds the median income for Missouri households (U.S. Census Bureau 2014b). Unemployment rates for the county where Sumner is located, however, were below statewide averages fifteen of the twenty months I was conducting fieldwork (Missouri Department of Labor and Industrial Relations, n.d.). The portion of individuals in poverty in the county (12 percent) was also below the portion in poverty in Missouri (15.5 percent) during 2014 (U.S. Census Bureau 2014a).

4. See Leap 2017.

5. Figures are available from the U.S. Census Bureau's *American FactFinder* database, at https://factfinder.census.gov.

6. Manke 1976.

7. Nonhuman animals can be the linchpin of human communities (Jerolmack 2007; Trudeau 2006; Grigsby 2012).

8. Residents provided hunters with places to hunt, food and beverages, lodging, and goose-picking services. Upton Henderson (1965) estimates that in 1964 the geese wintering at Swan Lake NWR were responsible for an additional $523,000 in revenue within a twenty-five mile radius around the refuge. When adjusted for inflation, that amounts to $4,020,621 in 2015 (U.S. Bureau of Labor Statistics 2015). If anything, Henderson underestimated the value added to the local economy because he did not

consider land values that increased because of quality hunting opportunities (see Pope, Adams, and Thomas 1984; Bastian 2002; Henderson and Moore 2005).

9. Thornsberry 1969; Nass 1964; DeStefano et al. 1991; Austin 1987; Kahl and Samson 1984; McDougle and Vaught 1968; Donahue and Olson 1969. Howard Thornsberry, a local resident who was a maintenance worker at the refuge during the goose heyday, was a local legend for developing the cannon net—a device that shoots a large net over a baited area to capture geese so that they can be fitted with bands (metal bracelets with serial numbers) to enable tracking (see Dill and Thornsberry 1950).

10. Manke 1976, 2–3.

11. Sheaffer et al. 2004; Raedeke et al. 2006.

12. See Wuthnow (2011) for an in-depth consideration of whether rural communities throughout the midwestern United States should be perceived as withering away.

13. Berkes and Folke 1998; Berkes et al. 2003; Kendrick 2003; D. Davidson 2010; Berkes and Ross 2013; Ashwood et al. 2014.

14. U.S. Department of Housing and Urban Development 2016.

15. Davenport and Robertson 2016.

16. Beck 2009; Urry 2011; Klein 2014; Brulle and Dunlap 2015.

17. For discussions of climate change and the Arctic, see Berkes and Jolly 2001; Ford, Smit, and Wandel 2006; Ford et al. 2008. For climate change and the Global South, see Manuel-Navarrette, Pelling, and Redclift 2011; J. Davidson 2012; Becken, Lama, and Espiner 2013. For climate change and the Global North, see Gorman-Murray 2010; Norgaard 2010; Sakurai et al. 2011.

18. Hulme 2008; Adger et al. 2009; Nelson, West, and Finan 2009; Gorman-Murray 2010; Jantarasami, Lawler, and Thomas 2010; Nielsen and Reenberg 2010; Berrang-Ford, Ford, and Paterson 2011; Adger et al. 2013; Becken, Lama, and Espiner 2013; Carmin et al. 2015.

19. Adger et al. 2009; Dunlap 2010; Berrang-Ford, Ford, and Paterson 2011; Ford, Berrang-Ford, and Paterson 2011; Adger et al. 2011; Mulligan 2014; Zehr 2015.

20. Others also argue that we must take account of both the negative and the positive opportunities presented by climate change (Beck 2009; Nelson, West, and Finan 2009; Kaijser and Kronsell 2014; Klein 2014).

21. Geographers and political-ecologists have written extensively on the topic of community resilience, and I use "resilience" as they do. As opposed to original interpretations of resilience that framed it as the ability to bounce back to a previous equilibrium or ideal state, newer analyses focus on whether communities can absorb or be rearranged in response to socioenvironmental disruptions such as climate change (Cote and Nightingale 2012; Turner 2013; Cretney 2014). If communities can be sustained in the face of disruptions, they are described as resilient. Some have argued that the concept of resilience in effect erases or even intensifies inequalities by romanticizing communities and the inequalities that inform them (e.g., MacKinnon and Derickson 2012), but more recently, authors have emphasized that the concept is not critically flawed in this respect (Cote and Nightingale 2012; Cretney 2014; Ingalls and Stedman 2016; Leap 2018a).

22. Haraway 1985, 1988, 2008; Latour 1993, 2005; Barad 2003; Alaimo and Hekman 2008; J. Bennett 2010.

23. Sanders 2003; Irvine 2004; Robbins 2007; McDonnell 2010; Jerolmack 2007, 2013; Kohn 2013; Moore and Kosut 2013; Ellis 2014; Leap 2014, 2015, 2018b.

24. I use "(non)human" here and throughout the book as shorthand for humans and nonhumans. It is more concise than "humans and nonhumans," but it also draws

attention to how humans and nonhumans are often (non)human hybrids who have come into being through their mutually constitutive interactions (Haraway 1985, 2008). When I use "nonhuman," I am talking specifically about plants, material objects, and nonhuman animals.

25. Catton and Dunlap 1980; Schnaiberg 1980; Freudenburg, Frickel, and Gramling 1995; Foster 1999; York and Mancus 2013; Davidson, Andrews, and Pauly 2014.

26. Slater 2002; Ingold 2008; Ogden 2011; Nading 2014. Bruno Latour (1993, 2005) questions partitioning social and ecological things, beings, and processes because of the intensity and significance of entanglements between them. Nevertheless, I use the language of the social and the ecological throughout this book because it is a straightforward way to talk about these interconnections. Even as we acknowledge interconnections between humans and nonhumans, authors are beginning to emphasize that we must account for differences between them, such as the significance of humans' ability to anticipate far into the future (e.g., Kohn 2013; Jerolmack and Tavory 2014; Leap 2015). Thus, while it is readily apparent that humans and nonhumans do not carry out their lives independent of each other, it is not entirely clear whether we should do away with categories such as social and ecological.

27. Communities emerge through "material-semiotic" interplays of (non)humans (Haraway 2008, 4).

28. See, e.g., Haraway 2008; Ogden 2011; Stuart, Schewe, and Gunderson 2013; Nading 2014; De León 2015.

29. J. Scott 1998; Latour 2005; Tsing 2005, 2015; Gibson-Graham 2006; Haraway 2008; Escobar 2008; Gordon 2008; Wuthnow 2011; Anzaldúa 2012.

30. Cohen and Duckert 2017.

31. Latour (2005, 43–62) describes this as an underdetermined reality, and J. K. Gibson-Graham (2006: xix–xxxvii, 202) refers to this as an ontology of overdetermination, but both find that interconnections between beings and things across space and time create avenues through which lives and communities can be transformed. Anna Lowenhaupt Tsing's (2015) consideration of matsuke mushrooms, for example, illustrates how patchy, or place specific, social and ecological entanglements between people and mushrooms present opportunities to (re)organize lives and communities as they are rendered increasingly precarious by globalized capitalist economic production.

32. Henderson 1965; Vaught and Kirsch 1966.

33. See, e.g., Krumm 1940, 1941, 1942.

34. Animals' statuses as "problems" change over time (Jerolmack 2008). Far from the park and neighborhood nuisances they are often thought to be today, when Canada geese began congregating at Swan Lake they were associated with beauty, grace, and romanticized understandings of nature and peoples' place in it. *Waterfowl Tomorrow*, a book published in 1964 by the U.S. Department of the Interior that sat in my office at the refuge, noted, "Canada geese are the big game of North American waterfowl—the kings, aristocrats, trophy species—to all who hunt them with gun or camera. Wary and keen of eye, the Canadian honker walks proudly, and flies with marvelous grace" (Hansen and Nelson 1964, 109).

35. One landowner with 160 acres adjacent to the refuge refused an offer of $38,000 for his property even though he had purchased the land for just $5,000 in the early 1940s. He had good reason to shun the more than 600 percent profit margin because by 1949 hunters were willing to pay more than $30,000 just to lease hunting spots near the refuge (Dill 1950).

36. Dill 1949, 24.

37. Russell 1955.
38. Russell 1956.
39. Dobbins 1978.
40. Raedeke et al. 2006.
41. Similar shifts in snow goose migration patterns have been observed in the central United States. Waterfowl biologists argue that, like changes in Canada goose migrations, these shifts have been facilitated by rapidly expanding agricultural yields (Jefferies, Rockwell, and Abraham 2003; Abraham, Jefferies, and Alisauskas 2005).
42. Raedeke et al. 2006.
43. For an overview of the social processes affecting corn production, see Sacks and Kucharik 2011; Wright and Wimberly 2013.
44. U.S. Department of Agriculture 2012. See Elizabeth Weise (2013) for a journalist's account of corn cultivation shifting farther north because of lengthening growing seasons.
45. Whereas other regions around the world have seen corn yields depressed by warmer growing seasons, the Midwest is a clear outlier, temperaturewise, and has seen enhanced yields as a result (Twine and Kucharik 2009; Lobell, Schlenker, and Costa-Roberts 2011).
46. Twine and Kucharik 2009; Lobell, Schlenker, and Costa-Roberts 2011; U.S. Department of Agriculture 2012.
47. Pryor et al. 2014; Samenow 2016.
48. NOAA 2018.
49. "Todd" is a pseudonym.
50. Parmesan and Yohe 2003; Robinson et al. 2015.
51. Berkes and Jolly 2001; Pickering 2005; Ford, Smit, and Wandel 2006; Smit and Wandel 2006; Nelson, West, and Finan 2009; Gaard 2011; Adger et al. 2013; IPCC 2013; Melillo, Richmond, and Yohe 2014.
52. Sherman 2009, 3.
53. Khan and Jerolmack 2013; Jerolmack and Khan 2014.
54. Texts help situate individuals' everyday lives within broader social processes (Smith 2005), but the point also applies to socioecological processes. Laura Ogden (2011), for example, draws heavily on texts to situate Florida men's hunting practices within broader processes of socioenvironmental transformation in the Everglades.
55. Norman Denzin (1978, x) calls this "triangulation," because multiple sources of data strengthen analysts' insights by allowing them to cross-check claims. Others contend that we should not expect data sources to corroborate each other and that discrepancies can be invaluable if we interrogate why these discrepancies exist and what they might mean (Tracy 2010; Khan and Jerolmack 2013).
56. Matthew Desmond (2007, 30, 88, 170) characterizes a "country-masculine habitus" as an embodied skill set, knowledge, and way of being in the world that men gain through years of living, working, and recreating in rural communities.
57. In waterfowl hunting, blinds can be a single-person, low-profile boat (a layout boat); large wooden box sitting on the ground in which three to five people can comfortably sit (a box blind); concrete or metal box buried so that its top is level with the ground (a pit blind); or canvas sleeping bag in which a single person lies on his or her back (a layout blind). In all four cases, the blinds are covered with whatever materials allow them to blend in with the surrounding landscape. The refuge had one box blind and several concrete pit blinds that refuge staff and I grassed with prairie cordgrass to make them blend in with the surrounding vegetation.

58. Duneier 1992; Campbell 2000; Macgregor 2010.

59. For considerations of the playful banter often involved in male friendships, see Campbell 2000; Fox 2004; Kaplan 2005; Jerolmack 2013.

60. This is also why Lyn Macgregor (2010) named the rural Wisconsin community she studied.

61. Fine 2007.

62. See Emerson, Fretz, and Shaw 2011.

63. Julie Bettie (2003) provides an excellent discussion on taking notes while observing and on some strategies to make note-taking less disruptive.

64. Hulme 2008; Adger et al. 2011; Urry 2011.

65. York, Rosa, and Dietz 2003; Shandra 2004; Clark and York 2005; Jorgenson 2006; Beck 2009; Jorgenson, Rice, and Clark 2010; Prew 2010; York 2010; Urry 2011; Burke, Shahiduzzaman, and Stern 2015; Liddle 2015; Raleigh, Choi, and Kniveton 2015; Gunderson, Stuart, and Petersen 2018; Grant, Jorgenson, and Longhofer 2018.

66. Lorenzoni and Pidgeon 2006; Byg and Salick 2009; Hamilton and Keim 2009; Gorman-Murray 2010; Jasanoff 2010; Spence et al. 2011; Wolf and Moser 2011; Pidgeon 2012; Leonard et al. 2013; Devine-Wright, Price, and Leviston 2015; Finnis, Sarkar, and Stoddart 2015; Lewandowsky et al. 2015; Shwom et al. 2015.

67. Brechin 2003; Brulle, Carmichael, and Jenkins 2012; Brechin and Bhandri 2011; Jang and Hart 2015; Tranter and Booth 2015. A sprawling literature finds that perceptions of climate change in the United States tend to vary sharply between Democrats and Republicans because of the purposeful politicization of the issue by think tanks, industry officials, and politicians (see Jacques, Dunlap, and Freeman 2008; Dunlap and McCright 2008; Oreskes and Conway 2011; Hamilton 2010; McCright and Dunlap 2011a; McCright and Dunlap 2011b; McCright, Dunlap, and Xiao 2013; Marquart-Pyatt et al. 2014).

68. See, e.g., Berkes and Jolly 2001; Young and Lipton 2006; Tompkins et al. 2010; J. Davidson 2012. To be clear, analyses that document what adaptations have taken place (e.g., Berkes and Jolly 2001; Tompkins et al. 2010) or what might be preventing them (e.g., Marshall et al. 2012) are not considerations of the *process* of how individuals and groups refashion their lives in response to climate change. While important, these kinds of analyses tend to focus on adaptation strategies implemented after adaptation and not before adaptation. Such discussions provide valuable insights into the strategies used to adapt to climate change, but they do not illustrate the mundane intricacies involved in getting from before adaptation to after adaptation.

69. Tompkins and Adger 2004; Smit and Wandell 2006; Adger et al. 2009; Amundsen, Berglund, and Westskog 2010; Nelson, West, and Finan 2009; Jantarasami, Lawler, and Thomas 2010; Petheram et al. 2010; P. McLaughlin 2011; Marshall et al. 2012; Park et al. 2012.

70. Arnell 2010; Dovers and Hezri 2010; Berrang-Ford, Ford, and Paterson 2011; Ford, Berrang-Ford, and Paterson 2011; Biesbroek et al. 2013; Thorn, Thornton, and Helfgott 2015. Kari Marie Norgaard's (2011) work on a Norwegian town being the obvious exception, this is especially true for sociologists (Carmin et al. 2015; Zehr 2015).

71. IPCC 2007, 2013.

72. See Zehr (2015), as well as Carmin et al. (2015, 165), who note, "Adaptation research by sociologists is still in its infancy."

73. Andrew Pickering (2005), Anna Kaijser and Annica Kronsell (2014), and Micah Ingalls and Richard Stedman (2016) also advocate interdisciplinary approaches for this reason.

74. James Ford and colleagues (2010) note this trend. For examples, see Manuel-Navarette, Pelling, and Redclift 2011; Alston and Whittenbury 2012; Artur and Hilhorst 2012; Alston 2014; Perez et al. 2015.

75. See, e.g., Snorek, Renaud, and Kloos 2014.

76. Feminist scholars have noted that individuals can be simultaneously (dis)advantaged because of how they are positioned vis-à-vis multiple dimensions of institutionalized inequalities (Beal 1969; Mohanty 1988; Crenshaw 1989; Collins 2009; Anzaldúa 2012). A white woman in the United States, for example, enjoys privileges because of her race while being disadvantaged by her gender.

77. Individuals can sustain and even improve their communities by operating in and using the complexities of inequalities to reorganize and undermine inequalities (Collins 2009; Anzaldúa 2012).

78. This is a commonly forwarded and accepted argument for why individuals and communities do not adapt to climate change (see Adger et al. 2009; Jasanoff 2010; Dovers and Hezri 2010).

79. See Tompkins and Adger 2004; Young and Lipton 2006; Byg and Salick 2009; Dovers and Hezri 2010; Ford et al. 2010; Gorman-Murray 2010; Petheram et al. 2010; Becken, Lama, and Espiner 2013. Environmental and rural sociologists also argue that partnerships between members of institutions and a community's residents can enable responses to environmental transformations (e.g., Burley et al. 2007; Ashwood et al. 2014).

CHAPTER 1

1. Rural communities are far more complex than they are often represented in popular media and even academic discussions (Cloke and Little 1997; M. Gray 2009; Wuthnow 2011).

2. See Aaron Fox's (2004) work on a rural, working-class bar outside Austin, Texas. See also Cabras and Mount 2017.

3. Rural bars can be key sites in which inequalities between and among men and women are reproduced (Campbell 2000).

4. Sumner was not a unique rural community in this respect. Rural communities are characterized by multiple, intersecting forms of difference and inequality (Cloke and Little 1997). Consequently, and in contrast to a long line of sociological literature (e.g., Durkheim 1933; Simmel 1957; Wirth 1938; see Fischer 1972, 1975 for overviews), rural cannot be equated with homogeneity and simplicity, although rural contexts may be relatively less heterogeneous compared to cities in some respects.

5. A jackolope is a fictitious animal that is half rabbit and half antelope. Taxidermists create jackolope mounts by putting deer or antelope antlers on a rabbit head.

6. Others (Fordham 1993; Morris 2007) also draw attention to what could be described as the gendered politics of volume.

7. See West and Zimmerman 1987; Butler 1990; Deutsch 2007; Risman 2009.

8. This corresponds to Hugh Campbell's (2000) discussion of men in a pub in rural New Zealand who did masculinity by remaining reserved regardless of how much they drank.

9. Feminist scholars have long emphasized the significance of the ideology of separate spheres for the reproduction of gender inequalities (e.g., Hartmann 1979; Hochschild and Machung 1989; Acker 1990; Plumwood 1993; Cha 2010).

10. Hartmann 1979; Hochschild and Machung 1989; Plumwood 1993.

11. Shortall 2002; Little 2003; Heather et al. 2005; Price and Evans 2006; M. Gray 2009; Alston and Whittenbury 2012; Silva 2017.

12. Pascoe 2007; Silva 2017.

13. I was conflicted over whether to include this passage and a later one in which the dialogue uses the "N" word because of the offensiveness of the word and my corresponding lack of desire to reproduce it in print. I considered slightly changing this and the later passage by substituting "black," but this would have obscured the intensity with which racial prejudices were expressed in Sumner. Consequently, I decided to include a censored version as a middle ground that avoids both reproducing the word and obscuring how race was talked about.

14. Elijah Anderson 2015.

15. Edward Said (1978), Amanda Lewis (2004), and Rebecca Scott (2010) also stress that representations of ideal racial identities are constructed through references to marked others (Brekhus 1996, 1998) who are portrayed as deviant and inferior.

16. Said's (1978) discussion of how Europeans made the Orient a trope in constructing what it meant to be European illustrates that representations of spaces and the people therein who were portrayed as different were centrally important to constructing representations of ideal, white Europeans. Similarly, in their study of white nationalists following the farm crisis of the 1980s, Michael Kimmel and Abby Ferber (2000) found that white nationalists associated whiteness with rural men through stylized juxtapositions of white, rural men with black, urban men.

17. Willits, Bealer, and Timbers 1990; Cronon 1991; Gans 1995; Elijah Anderson 2015.

18. White individuals regularly jump through conversational hoops to emphasize the significance of race without appearing prejudiced (Bonilla-Silva 2010; Mueller 2017).

19. Goffman 1959; Foucault 1995; S. Low 2000. William Force (2011) applies this insight to bars.

20. Marks 1991.

21. See Marks 1991; Jacoby 2001; Trudeau 2006; Neo 2012; Kim 2015.

22. An example of the links between whiteness and duck hunting is A&E's *Duck Dynasty*. Leandra Hernandez (2014) determined that a central theme of the show is that duck hunting allows the men on the show to continue accomplishing a white, Southern masculinity even while their lives are being disrupted by the material wealth brought through their family business. Duck hunting, in other words, allows the men to accomplish a particular kind of regional identity infused with whiteness.

23. U.S. Fish and Wildlife Service 2014.

24. See Lipsitz 1998; Bonilla-Silva, Goar, and Embrick 2006; Hughey 2010, 2011; Hagerman 2016; Silva 2017. I intentionally draw attention to racism in (sub)urban areas here to contextualize Sumner, and rural areas more generally, within the racial system that operates across the United States. Beyond empirical accuracy, this is especially important to note in order to avoid the stereotypical portrayal of rural people (and rural residents who are white and working class, in particular) as the primary purveyors of racism in the United States (see Jarosz and Lawson 2002; Hartigan 2003; Eastman and Schrock 2008; R. Scott 2010; Hubbs 2014).

25. Men in white working-class communities sometimes use racialized strategies to gain respect amid shifting political-economic conditions that put their breadwinning status in jeopardy (Fine et al. 1997; Kimmel and Ferber 2000; Eastman and

Schrock 2008; Morris 2008; Sherman 2009; Kimmel 2017). This is not to imply that middle- or upper-class white men in the United States are less concerned with race than their working-class counterparts, but it could help explain why men in Sumner were more apt than women to emphasize and police the boundaries of whiteness.

26. See, e.g., Brandth and Haugen 2005; R. Scott 2010.

27. R. Scott 2010, 170.

28. Omi and Winant 1994; Lipsitz 1998; Lewis 2004.

29. George Lipsitz (2007) describes this as a white spatial imaginary, in which socially constructed and institutionalized ways of relating to landscapes developed by whites facilitate the reproduction of white privileges. Environmental sociologists also note that institutionalized landscape uses are informed by and involved in the reproduction of racial inequalities (see Bullard 1990; Cole and Foster 2001; Park and Pellow 2011; Voyles 2015). Although developed and legitimated by Western societies, these landscape interventions have also drawn from colonized societies (see Shiva 1997; Escobar 2008). I highlight how, in practice, these means of relating to landscapes have been pushed and legitimated worldwide by state-corporate actors from Western states.

30. William Cronon's (1991, 198, 339–340) conceptualization of the "geography of capital" entails landscapes as being socially constructed; capitalist production processes have often transformed landscapes in such all-encompassing manners that they begin to appear natural.

31. See Polanyi 1944. Traci Voyles (2015) examines the racial dynamics of this method of agricultural production through her discussion of how the U.S. federal government treated indigenous peoples and the systems of agricultural production used over the last two centuries.

32. Shiva 1997.

33. Kenney et al. 1989; Barnett 2000.

34. Even the relative lack of black farmers in the United States is a testament to centuries of institutional and interpersonal racism (Benson 2012). Private property is linked to whiteness because of the institutional roadblocks put in place throughout the history of the United States to exclude people of color from owning property (Oliver and Shapiro 2006; R. Scott 2010).

35. Jones 1994; Pigford v. Glickman 1999; National Black Farmers Association 2007; J. Hoffman 2009; Benson 2012; Schneider 2013; Mizelle 2014.

36. Recognizing that farm subsidies facilitate the reproduction of white structural advantages does not mean all whites benefit equally from these programs. As Lipsitz (1998, 2007) notes, however, such political-economic institutions, programs, and policies and culturally legitimated meanings still facilitate the reproduction of racial inequalities by benefiting almost exclusively white individuals and households. That there are differences among whites does not preclude that opportunities and material resources are being channeled to whites and away from people of color (Lewis 2004; Oliver and Shapiro 2006; Hughey 2012).

37. Stevens 1997; Igoe 2004; West 2006; Doane 2012.

38. Cronon 1995; Stevens 1997; Spence 1999; Jacoby 2001; Taylor 2016. According to Karl Jacoby (2001, 92–93), understandings of whiteness were fluid and rearticulated in ways to undercut rural whites' use of Yellowstone as well. He notes that these rural peoples' claims to Yellowstone were delegitimized by framing them as "white Indians" who were not quite white because of how they related to the landscape.

39. See Roderick Neumann's (1998) discussion of Arusha National Park in Tanzania, for example. Conservation officials there label locals who transgress the park

boundaries as poachers or thieves, but locals offer a different interpretation by using the colonial history of the park as a way to question its legitimacy. For analyses of the racial dynamics of conservation in other contexts, see Stevens 1997; Slater 2002; West 2006; Loperena 2016.

40. Kosek 2006.

41. It is easy to explain these racial disparities by noting that the vast majority of those living near the refuge were white, but this overlooks two key points pertaining to institutionalized racism. First, this obscures how centuries of institutional and interpersonal racial discrimination in the United States produce racially segregated landscapes. Second, this overlooks how the construction and use of public parks and wildlife areas has been informed by and aided racial inequalities across the United States. Even in areas with more racially heterogeneous populations, white individuals make up a disproportionately high proportion of those who use wildlife areas and parks (Byrne and Wolch 2009; Byrne 2012).

42. Others (e.g., Thody 2014) have associated particular brands of beer with particular classes of consumers. I also suggest that there was an element of embodied taste for particular beers that was an expression of class habitus (see Bourdieu 1984).

43. Bourdieu 1984.

44. My approach to class is in line with authors who find that class is simultaneously informed by how individuals are positioned in relation to institutionalized political-economic processes concerning the production and distribution of resources that operate on national and global scales *and* the innumerable intricacies of particular places that transform how people perceive, experience, and go about reproducing such political-economic processes (e.g., E. P. Thompson 1966; Bettie 2003; Gibson-Graham 2006; Sherman 2009; R. Scott 2010).

45. There has been some debate about the pros and cons of concentrated agricultural production for rural communities (see Lobao and Meyer 2001; Lyson, Torres, and Welsh 2001), but sociologists have found that class inequalities in such communities are closely linked to consolidation of farms (e.g., Goldschmidt 1978), deindustrialization (e.g., Carr and Kefalas 2009), and economic restructuring (e.g., D. McLaughlin 2002).

46. Weber 1946b, 186–188.

47. Bettie 2003, 45.

48. In Julie Bettie's (2003) argument that class is performative instead of a performance, ways of doing class are always set in relation to the institutionalized processes of producing and distributing capital.

49. Unlike Lyn Macgregor (2010), who argues that class as an institutional position and process did not inform consumer culture in a rural Wisconsin community, Allison Pugh (2009) finds that we often consume to belong to a group. Along with Bettie (2003), she finds that our abilities to act in particular ways are often predicated on whether we have the resources to do so. In line with Pierre Bourdieu (1984), this emphasizes that it is hard to separate habitual behaviors from traditional understandings of class focused on the resources that are accessible through particular positions in labor markets. Pugh's work focuses on consumer culture and my focus is on a different kind of equally cultured and classed consumption.

50. Stuart Marks (1991) and Mary Grigsby (2012) provide detailed analyses of the classed dynamics of the preparation and consumption of wild game and fish.

51. Bourdieu 1984; Mintz 1986.

52. Guthman 2011; Jordan 2015.

53. Marks 1991; Grigsby 2012.

54. Class inequalities are detached from their institutional underpinnings in perception through beliefs and ideologies that stigmatize those in poverty and that frame class inequalities as stemming from differences in personal work ethic (Gans 1995; Bellah et al. 2008; Benson 2012; Santiago 2015).

55. C. Wright Mills (1959) contrasts social issues that affect large swaths of people because of the intersections of the structure and history of society with personal troubles that affect individuals because of their choices and actions. Numerous authors directly relate class inequalities and rural unemployment to economic restructuring in rural communities (e.g., Goldschmidt 1978; D. McLaughlin 2002; Brown and Swanson 2003; Carr and Kefalas 2009; Filteau 2015). That rural residents use social programs to get by is a direct consequence of such processes (Sherman 2009).

56. Whether members of rural communities receive respect and support from their communities is largely contingent on whether they are deemed morally upright, good people (M. Gray 2009; Sherman 2009; Macgregor 2010).

57. M. Gray 2009; Sherman 2009.

58. Jennifer Sherman (2009) and Rebecca Scott (2010) found similar dynamics in the rural communities they studied.

59. Crenshaw 1989; Bettie 2003; McCall 2005; Collins 2009; Choo and Ferree 2010; Carbado 2013.

60. McCall 2005; Choo and Ferree 2010. In Frances Beal's (1969) discussion of double jeopardy, for example, multiple dimensions of inequality simultaneously inform individuals' lives, but she does not consider how these inequalities are transformed through their intersections.

61. Understandings of rurality intersect with race, class, and gender to inform how individuals in rural communities think of themselves and arrange their communities (Cloke and Little 1997). A long tradition of scholarship examines how representations of rural spaces inform rural individuals' arrangement of their lives and communities (e.g., Williams 1973; Falk and Pinhey 1978; Cronon 1991; Murdoch and Pratt 1993; M. Bell 1994). These analyses support a broader cultural turn in the rural studies literature that emphasizes that representations of rurality are equally as important to rural peoples' lives and communities as the material conditions in rural settings (see Halfacree 2006; M. Bell 2007; Leap 2017).

62. An extensive literature finds that understandings of rurality inform how rural men and women do gender. How rural women or men do gender is complicated not just by race and class, then, but also by understandings of what it means to be a good *rural* man or woman (see Brandth 1995, 2006; Little and Austin 1996; Little 1997a, 1997b, 2002; Campbell and Bell 2000; Campbell 2000; Kimmel and Ferber 2000; Shortall 2002; Heather et al. 2005; Connell 2006; Price and Evans 2006; Desmond 2007; Wright and Annes 2014; Leap 2017, 2018a, 2018b).

63. Benson 2012.

64. Kefalas 2003; Sherman 2009.

65. Lipsitz 2007; R. Scott 2010.

66. Use of machinery to manipulate landscapes is closely tied to the accomplishment of masculinities in rural contexts in the United States and in Europe (see Brandth 1995; Peter et al. 2000; Brandth 2006; Brandth and Haugen 2005; R. Scott 2010; Benson 2012; Bell, Hullinger, and Brislen 2015).

67. Little and Austin 1996; Hughes 1997; Little 1997a, 1997b; Heather et al. 2005; Midgley 2006; Leap 2018a.

68. Rural geographers and sociologists have repeatedly found that understandings of rurality inform how individuals living in rural places think of themselves and arrange their communities. See Cloke and Little 1997; Falk and Pinhey 1978; Murdoch and Pratt 1993; M. Bell 1994.

69. For applications, see Halfacree 2006; M. Bell 2007; M. Gray 2009; Sherman 2009; Wuthnow 2011; Leap 2017.

CHAPTER 2

1. Goose and duck calls are comparable to woodwind instruments. They are a wooden or plastic cylinder from three to seven inches long with one or two reeds inside. Blowing on the correct end of a call with the proper air pressure and rhythm makes it emit the sounds and cadences of geese or ducks.

2. Seek 1980.

3. Discussions of masculinity over the last thirty years have implicitly (e.g., Carrigan, Connell, and Lee 1985) or more explicitly (e.g., Connell and Messerschmidt 2005; Sherman 2009; R. Scott 2010) drawn on the concept of intersectionality to show that masculinities are complicated by intersections of gender, race, class, and sexuality. This applies to men with marginalized races, classes, and sexualities as well as men with privileged institutional statuses (Carbado 2013; Leap 2017). A number of studies have illustrated how men draw on and rearrange intersections of race, gender, class, and sexuality to respond to shifting social and ecological conditions that threaten their status as men worthy of respect (see Fine et al. 1997; Kimmel and Ferber 2000; Lamont 2000; Broughton 2008; Eastman and Schrock 2008; Morris 2008; Groes-Green 2009; Sherman 2009; R. Scott 2010; Benson 2012; Filteau 2014, 2015; Bell, Hullinger, and Brislen 2015; Aure and Munkejord 2016).

4. Feminist scholars have called for greater attention to how intersecting inequalities influence adaptations to climate change (Carr and Thompson 2014; Kaijser and Kronsell 2014; Leap 2018a). This corresponds with feminist works on socioecological processes that find that intersecting inequalities inform and are informed by responses to socioecological processes that disrupt communities (e.g., R. Scott 2010; Dominey-Howes, Gorman-Murray, and McKinnon 2014; Voyles 2015).

5. See, e.g., Nielsen and Reenberg 2010; Leap 2018a.

6. See, e.g., Manuel-Navarrete, Pelling, and Redclift 2011; Artur and Hilhorst 2012. Luis Artur and Dorothea Hilhorst (2012) note that class and gender informed responses to flooding in Mozambique, but they do not illustrate how class and gender *intersected*. When scholars have looked at the relation between intersecting inequalities and adaptations, they tended to focus on how these inequalities inform individual or household responses to climate change as opposed to how they affect rearrangements of communities (e.g., Sugden et al. 2014).

7. Edward Carr and Mary Thompson (2014) and Anna Kaijser and Annica Kronsell (2014) also advocate intersectional analyses of adaptations.

8. Nira Yuval-Davis (2006) advocates an intersectional approach to considerations of human rights for this purpose.

9. The WRP was a racialized project because it funneled resources and opportunities to white landowners. Those enrolled in the federal program received direct cash payments. Even white farmers who were not in the WRP enjoyed higher prices for their commodities because the WRP reduced the supply of agricultural commodities

in circulation. By 2010, 2.35 million acres were enrolled in the WRP (Ducks 2010). That's 2.35 million acres that were not being used to grow commodities such as corn and soybeans.

10. For analyses exploring rural masculinities, see Brandth 1995; Campbell and Bell 2000; Campbell 2000; Little 2002; Brandth and Haugen 2005; Brandth 2006; Connell 2006; Desmond 2007; and Leap 2017, 2018b.

11. The USFWS estimates that in 2011 roughly 90 percent of those who hunted were men (U.S. Fish and Wildlife Service 2014). Though women hunt and individuals have complex, varied reasons for hunting (Dizard 2003; Bronner 2004), feminist research finds long-standing links between hunting and masculinity (Adam 1991; Stange 1997; Luke 2004). Whether portraying animals as feminine objects to be controlled (Kheel 2008) or cunning adversaries to be combatted (Bronner 2004), men construct masculinities through hunting by positioning themselves as adventurous, paternalistic providers or protectors (Emel 1995; Anahita and Mix 2006; Leap 2018b). Urban men hunt, but rural men often accomplish rural masculinities by distinguishing themselves from urban men through hunting (Bye 2003; Hogan and Pursell 2008; Leap 2018b).

12. For the links between hunting, fishing, and rural masculinities, see Desmond 2007; Hogan and Pursell 2008; Grigsby 2012; Leap 2018b.

13. Marks 1991; Jacoby 2001; Ogden 2011; E. P. Thompson 2013.

14. Marks 1991, 232.

15. Sociologists, race scholars, and feminists have long argued that race informs how we perceive ourselves and our communities. Studies of double consciousness (Du Bois 1989), studies of colonialism (Fanon 2008), feminist works that tie race into standpoint theory (e.g., Beauboeuf-Lafontant 2009; Collins 2009), and analyses of white habitus (Bonilla-Silva et al. 2006; Hagerman 2016) all find that our (sub)conscious understandings of the world, including how we perceive the environment and our places in it (Kosek 2006; Outka 2008; R. Scott 2010; Mizelle 2014), reflect racialized experiences and standpoints. Similarly, following Marx's (1983) analysis of the relation between the means of production and different classes' views of the world, a number of scholars emphasize there are classed standpoints generally (e.g., Bourdieu 1984) and on environments specifically (e.g., Jacoby 2001; Grigsby 2012).

16. Like Daina Harvey (2015), I draw attention to the significance of waiting, which is often overlooked by ethnographers because it seems that it is not where the action is. But waiting can serve particularly important social purposes.

17. Anahita and Mix 2006; Grigsby 2012.

18. For analyses of the links between masculinity, heterosexuality, and sports, see Pronger 1990; Messner 1992; Eric Anderson 2002, 2008; Grindstaff and West 2006.

19. The parallels between waterfowl hunting and "girl hunt[ing]" (Grazian 2007) are apparent. Because of the association between these activities and heterosexuality, men can spend time with each other without having their heterosexuality questioned.

20. Masculinities complicated by class, sexuality, and race inform adaptations to socioenvironmental transformations (Sherman 2009; R. Scott 2010; Benson 2012).

21. The criteria for achieving respectable masculinities can be reorganized in response to shifting social and ecological conditions (Brandth 1995; Brandth and Haugen 2005; Sherman 2009; Filteau 2014; R. Scott 2010).

22. An Ice Eater pulls water through a vertical tube with a propeller. The machines "eat" ice by pulling relatively warm water up from the bottom of a pond or marsh to the frozen surface, which then melts the ice.

23. Following the Marxist tradition of examining the relation between political-economic institutions and inequalities (e.g., Marx 1983), scholars have repeatedly investigated the numerous ways state institutions facilitate the reproduction of inequalities, including how state institutions enable the reproduction of class and racial/ethnic inequalities through the governance of landscape uses (e.g., Bullard 1990; Peluso 1993; Neumann 1998; Escobar 1999; Zimmerer 2006; Freudenburg et al. 2009; Voß and Bornemann 2011; Downey 2015).

24. Rural men regularly construct masculinities by denigrating urban men (Kimmel and Ferber 2000; Bye 2003; Desmond 2007; Hogan and Pursell 2008; Leap 2017).

25. Following ecofeminist analyses (see Gaard 1993), numerous analysts find that an ability to kill animals can be integrally important to masculinities (Emel 1995; Bronner 2004; Anahita and Mix 2006).

26. This is similar to others' findings that meritocratic understandings of success inform perceptions of class in the United States (Bettie 2003; Bellah et al. 2008; Benson 2012; Santiago 2015). Robert Bellah and colleagues (2008) also find that such understandings of class inform understandings of community.

27. Henderson 1965.

28. Durkheim 1951, 159–160.

29. Others also find that shared ways of relating to landscapes and animals can facilitate interpersonal relationships and a sense of community between people (e.g., Trudeau 2006; Ogden 2011; Grigsby 2012; Jerolmack 2007, 2013).

30. Agricultural concentration in the United States over the last century has had similar community-level consequences. There is some debate about the consequences of increasingly large, industrialized farms for rural communities (Lobao and Meyer 2001), but rural sociologists generally agree that larger farms, with fewer people controlling or accessing landscapes, have facilitated depopulation, increased class divisions, and increased disintegration of social ties between residents in rural communities (Goldschmidt 1978; Tolbert, Lyson, and Irwin 1998; Irwin, Tolbert, and Lyson 1999; Lobao and Stofferahn 2008).

31. Geertz 1972; Durkheim 2001; Trudeau 2006; Ogden 2011; Grigsby 2012; Jerolmack 2007, 2013.

32. For analyses of how the spatial ranges of numerous species are transforming because of climate change, see Parmesan and Yohe 2003; Robinson et al. 2015.

33. For example, shifting moose migration patterns are undermining the sustainability of communities in Alaska (McNeeley 2012), and shifting precipitation patterns are undermining ways of life in rural Australia (Alston and Whittenbury 2012).

34. Carr and Thompson 2014; Kaijser and Kronsell 2014. This is particularly true in analyses of responses to climate change in the Global North (Ford, Berrang-Ford, and Paterson 2011).

35. Intersections of class, caste, and gender have informed individual and household adaptations to climate change in India and Nepal, for example (Sugden et al. 2014). For additional analyses, see Alston and Whittenbury 2012; Thorn, Thornton, and Helfgott 2015; Carmin et al. 2015.

36. Ford et al. 2010; Manuel-Navarrete, Pelling, and Redclift 2011; Turhan, Zografos, and Kallis 2015. In Julie Snorek, Fabrice G. Renaud, and Julia Kloos's (2014) discussion of divergent adaptations, adaptations are portrayed as a zero-sum game in which pastoralists or sedentary farmers are either advantaged or disadvantaged by responses to climate variability in Niger.

37. McCall 2005; Escobar 2008; Gordon 2008; Collins 2009; Anzaldúa 2012.

CHAPTER 3

This chapter is adapted from Braden Leap, "Not a Zero-Sum Game: Inequalities and Resilience in Sumner, Missouri, the Gooseless Goose Capital of the World," *Gender, Place and Culture* 25, no. 2 (2018): 288–308. doi:10.1080/0966369X.2018.1428536. Reprinted with permission from Taylor and Francis (www.tandfonline.com).

    1. Annual festivals facilitate the reproduction of social cohesion and inequalities in communities (Fortier 1999; Bennett 2009).

    2. This was not just a story the residents of Sumner were "telling themselves about themselves" (Geertz 1972, 26). They were actively (re)writing the culture of their community through the festival each year.

    3. As individuals go about their lives they simultaneously subvert and reproduce gender inequalities because they must simultaneously contend with the institutional inertia pushing them toward reproducing inequalities even as they try to trouble or undo these inequalities (Butler 1990; Deutsch 2007; Risman 2009; Brandth and Haugen 2010).

    4. Women in rural communities draw on their rural femininities to facilitate the reproduction of their households and communities during times of economic or ecological disruption (Shortall 2002; Heather et al. 2005; Price and Evans 2006; Brandth and Haugen 2010; Alston and Whittenbury 2012). Often, rural women undertake more work in response to these disruptions at least partially so that they can support the men in their households and communities (Heather et al. 2005; Sherman 2009; Alston and Whittenbury 2012). This regularly facilitates the reproduction of patriarchal privileges, but this added work can simultaneously challenge gendered inequalities (Brandth and Haugen 2010). For how women reproduced gender inequalities by picking up the slack when men's ways of doing rural masculinities were put in jeopardy by economic restructuring, see Shortall 2002 and Price and Evans 2006.

    5. The complexities of intersecting inequalities present opportunities for individuals to rearrange their communities more justly and equitably (Mohanty 2003; Escobar 2008; Collins 2009; Anzaldúa 2012). This corresponds to poststructuralists and posthumanists (e.g., Butler 1990; Barad 2003; Gibson-Graham 2006) who note that systems of inequality are so incredibly complex that there are always openings through which mundane actions and interactions can subvert these institutionalized inequalities.

    6. See, e.g., Snorek, Renaud, and Kloos 2014; Ingalls and Stedman 2016.

    7. Mohanty 1988; Crenshaw 1989; Bettie 2003; Gordon 2008; Collins 2009; Carbado 2013.

    8. I draw from Ann Swidler's (1986) conceptualization of culture as a toolkit. Instead of conceptualizing culture as norms and values, Swidler frames culture as a toolkit of available practices, or strategies of action, that people can use to achieve culturally legitimated ends. Weston Eaton (2016) also draws on this understanding of culture to explore responses to socioenvironmental transformations, but unlike Eaton I draw on feminist scholars to draw attention to the gendered dynamics of the tools available to people.

    9. Theophano 2002; Martyris 2015; Tipton-Martin 2015.

    10. Following a tradition of feminist scholarship focusing on rural women in the United Kingdom (e.g., Little and Austin 1996; Hughes 1997; Little 1997a, 1997b), Jane Midgley (2006) finds that women sustain their community by using knowledge and skills associated with the traditional feminine activity of managing household budgets. Jennifer Sherman's (2009) findings are similar: women in a rural community in the

northwestern United States used flexible gender strategies to navigate the public-private divide to sustain their households as men's employment opportunities vanished.

11. Perkins 2012.

12. This is similar to others' findings on gender and civic activism. See, e.g., Bell and Braun 2010; Dolhinow 2010; S. Bell 2013, 2016.

13. Similar gendered dynamics of community work were found in a rural English community (Little 1997b).

14. Similar statements and reactions have been reported from other rural women (Heather et al. 2005; Price and Evans 2006).

15. Little 1997b.

16. Indoor work is often associated with rural femininities, whereas outdoor work is associated with rural masculinities (Cánoves et al. 2004; Pini 2004; Brandth and Haugen 2005; Brandth and Haugen 2010).

17. Rural women are often positioned as the behind-the-scenes caretakers for their communities through conceptual links between femininities, rurality, and civic engagement (Little and Austin 1996; Little 1997a, 1997b; Hughes 1997; Heather et al. 2005).

18. Rural women who step up during times of crisis to reproduce their communities or households feel that their contributions go largely unacknowledged because this work is feminized and then devalued (Heather et al. 2005; Alston and Whittenbury 2012), much in the way that women's reproductive work is generally devalued (Hartmann 1979; Hochschild and Machung 1989).

19. Krauss 1993; Naples 1998a, 1998b.

20. See Sherman 2009; Dolhinow 2010; Alston and Whittenbury 2012; S. Bell 2016; Larkins 2018.

21. Durkheim 1933; Cronon 1991; M. Bell 1994.

22. Price and Evans 2006.

23. An analysis of LGBTQ activists in rural Appalachia also finds that rural communities are metaphorically framed as families and that these metaphors were integrally important to how these communities were organized and reproduced (M. Gray 2009).

24. Sally Shortall (2002, 172) characterizes this work as an "add women and stir" approach that perpetuates the reproduction of patriarchal privileges, but other researchers believe that this work facilitates a convoluted mix of reproducing and undermining patriarchal privileges (Milroy and Wismer 1994; Little 1997a, 1997b; Heather et al. 2005; Midgley 2006).

25. For an analysis of the significance of gatekeepers and access to infrastructure in rural communities, see M. Gray 2009.

26. See, e.g., Rose 1993; Brekhus 2003; M. Gray 2009.

27. Gibson-Graham 2006; Gordon 2008; Collins 2009; Anzaldúa 2012.

28. Heather et al. 2005; Brandth and Haugen 2010; Alston and Whittenbury 2012.

29. Adger 2003; Hornborg 2009; Fabinyi, Evans, and Foale 2014; Snorek, Renaud, and Kloos 2014; Ingalls and Stedman 2016.

30. Morris 2008; Groes-Green 2009; R. Scott 2010)

31. Others (e.g., Desmond 2007; Morris 2008; R. Scott 2010), also find that men from different classes draw on the resources and opportunities they have available to them to construct respectable masculinities.

32. See, e.g., Turner 2013; Ingalls and Stedman 2016.

33. See, e.g., Hornborg 2009; Snorek, Renaud, and Kloos 2014.

34. Feminist scholars have promoted this view over the last thirty years (e.g., Mohanty 1988; McCall 2005; Gordon 2008; Collins 2009).

35. Social heterogeneity can undermine adaptations in cases in which a lack of trust or conflicts between groups undermine collective responses to socioenvironmental challenges (see Singleton and Taylor 1992; Pretty and Ward 2001; Dietz, Ostrom, and Stern 2003; Pretty 2003; Bryan 2004).

36. Berkes, Colding, and Folke 2003; Low et al. 2003; Berkes and Ross 2013.

37. Berkes and Folke 1998.

38. Davidson 2010.

39. Kendrick 2003; Ashwood et al. 2014; Fabinyi, Evans, and Foale 2014; Buday 2017.

40. Katz 2008, 16.

41. Gibson-Graham 2006; Escobar 2008; Anzaldúa 2012.

CHAPTER 4

1. Haraway 2008, 3–4; see also 205–246.

2. Desmond 2007, 30.

3. This number is derived from Krumm 1938, 1939, 1940, 1941, 1942.

4. Heitmeyer et al. 2011.

5. My use of "wild" matches Jamie Lorimer's (2015) use of the term.

6. The production of fine art is a collective process involving vast networks of humans (Becker 1982), but Ray highlighted how manipulating the refuge landscape could be considered a work of art whose production and consumption was a collective process in the Latourian (1993, 2005) sense. It involved an array of human influences on and far beyond the refuge, but it also involved a vast network of entangled (non)humans.

7. This corresponds to the model of conservation championed in the West and then exported worldwide over the last century. According to this model, state officials are expected to intensively manipulate landscapes to benefit nonhumans defined as important (see Stevens 1997; Neumann 1998; J. Scott 1998; Jacoby 2001; West 2006).

8. See Nash 1967; Cronon 1995. Conservation agencies have actively manipulated landscapes and the (non)humans using them in this paradoxical conception of wilderness (Cronon 1995; Neumann 1998; Jacoby 2001).

9. The socially constructed, cultural underpinnings of landscape practices (e.g., Fine 1997; Agrawal 2005; Trudeau 2006) are often tied to understandings of progress (e.g., J. Scott 1998; Benson 2012).

10. Many point to Locke's *Second Treatise on Government*, published in 1689, as being especially important to linking understandings of progress to labor that transforms landscapes. According to Locke, labor improves and removes landscapes from nature, which is supposedly beneficial for individuals as well as society as a whole. For discussions on the meanings and inequalities associated with class, race, and gender and how they inform discursive links between landscape manipulations and progress, see Gaard 1993; Shiva 1997; J. Scott 1998; Peter et al. 2000; Bellah et al. 2008; Kheel 2008; R. Scott 2010; Benson 2012; Bell, Hullinger, and Brislen 2015; Voyles 2015.

11. Others also note that vegetation considered out of place is often taken as a sign of disorder and decay (e.g., J. Scott 1998; Benson 2012).

12. Greider and Garkovich 1994; Fine 1997; Gieryn 2000; S. Low 2000; Agrawal 2005.

13. A complex is a handful of refuges in the same general geographic vicinity that are lumped together to create another level of bureaucracy between the regional and

refuge levels of the USFWS. Swan Lake's complex also includes Big Muddy NWR in Columbia, Missouri, and Loess Bluffs NWR in Mound City, Missouri.

14. It is common for employees in multilevel, multiregional organizations to chafe at regulations, because standardized processes impede flexibility in meeting challenges in particular contexts (Fine 2007).

15. For overviews of neoliberalism and its pervasive effects on how communities and societies are organized, see Peck and Tickell 2002; Hackworth 2007; David Harvey 2007; Fujiwara 2008; Somers 2008.

16. In the first half of the twentieth century, Karl Polanyi (1944) argued that such approaches to governance would destroy nature. Though some analyses of neoliberal approaches to conservation show they can benefit particular nonhumans (Castree 2008; Leap 2014), sociologists, geographers, and political-ecologists generally agree that neoliberal approaches to conservation facilitate environmental destruction as well as the intensification of social inequalities (McCarthy and Prudham 2004; Prudham 2004; Robertson 2004; Bakker 2005; Gould, Pellow, and Schnaiberg 2008; Brockington and Duffy 2010; Fletcher 2010; Duffy and Moore 2010; Rutherford 2011; Munster and Munster 2012; Duffy 2013; Schwartz 2013). In short, and not surprisingly, individuals' pursuit of their own economic interests does not usually produce ecologically desirable or sustainable outcomes.

17. See Peter et al. 2000.

18. The rural Wisconsinites Katherine Cramer (2016) talked with described governmental institutions in strikingly similar terms.

19. The goals and practices of conservation are inherently cultural (Peluso 1993; Cronon 1995; Stevens 1997; Neumann 1998; J. Scott 1998; Jacoby 2001; Slater 2002; West 2006).

20. Farrell 2015.

21. Farrell 2015.

22. For in-depth discussions on otter restoration in Missouri, see Goedeke 2005; Goedeke and Rikoon 2008.

23. Bourdieu 1984; Butler 1990; Hays 2000; Bettie 2003; Collins 2009.

24. From the enclosure of the English countryside in the 1700s to the establishment of conservation areas across the globe throughout the 1900s, state governments, corporations, and nongovernmental organizations have repeatedly reproduced and intensified inequalities by delegitimizing localized ways of knowing landscapes. See Polanyi 1944; Schnaiberg 1980; Taussig 1987; Peluso 1993; Kuletz 1998; Neumann 1998; J. Scott 1998; Brosius 1999; LaDuke 1999; Jacoby 2001; Slater 2002; Ribot and Peluso 2003; Agrawal 2005; Trudeau 2006; West 2006; R. Scott 2010; Ogden 2011; Voyles 2015; Kojola 2018.

25. See Hallett and Ventresca 2006; Hallet and Meanwell 2016.

26. This corresponds with earlier work by interactionists (e.g., Blumer 1969; Hall 1972; Fine 1984).

27. Sociologists have shown the cultural underpinnings of institutional practices (Meyer and Rowan 1977; Powell and DiMaggio 1991).

28. This corresponds with Peter Hall's work on meta-power (Hall 1997, 2003; Hall and McGinty 1997), which finds that outcomes produced through institutions such as the USFWS emerge from interpersonal interactions that are informed by previous decisions made within those institutions and the organizational arrangements of those institutions.

CHAPTER 5

1. Beck 2009.

2. My use of frames draws from scholars focused on mundane interactions (e.g., Goffman 1974; Brewster and Bell 2010) and works inserting culture, power, and conflict into frame analyses (e.g., Snow and Benford 1988, 1992; Johnston and Noakes 2005; Kim 2015; Selfa, Iaroi, and Burnham 2015; Lewin 2017). Starting with the insight that "frames define parts of our perceptual environment as irrelevant, thus separating that which we attend in a focused manner from all the out-of-frame experience that we leave 'in the background' and 'ignore'" (Zerubavel 1991, 12), I find that frames employed in everyday interactions at the refuge were informed by unequal power relations among (non)humans.

3. For other explorations of conflicts over landscape uses that were grounded in divergent orientations to relating to environments, see Peluso 1993; LaDuke 1999; R. Scott 2010; Farrell 2015; Voyles 2015.

4. See, e.g., Van Liere and Dunlap 1981; Freudenburg 1993; Klineberg, McKeever, and Rothenback 1998; Marshall 2004; Desmond 2007; Konisky, Milyo, and Richardson 2008; Weszkalnys 2014; Hochschild 2016; Price and Peterson 2016.

5. Krogman 1996; Elliot, Gray, and Lewicki 2003; Barbara Gray 2004; Shriver and Peaden 2009; Tierney 2014; Selfa, Iaroi, and Burnham 2015; Lapegna 2016; Auyero, Hernandez, and Stitt 2017.

6. See Grothmann and Patt 2005; Beck 2009; Truelove, Carrico, and Thabrew 2015.

7. "A recurring perceived barrier to adaptation across much climate policy literature, although one rarely matched to policy and institutional responses, is the dominancy of short-term over long-term factors in decision making. Climate adaptation, with impacts decades away, is perceived to be outweighed by nearer term imperatives. This raises the perennial question in many policy sectors: how to incorporate the long term in decision making?" (Dovers and Hezri 2010, 219; see also Adger et al. 2009; Jasanoff 2010).

8. For example, differentially empowered residents of a Nairobi slum had to juggle multiple risks while adapting to climate change (Thorn, Thornton, and Helfgott 2015).

9. Other studies, although not concentrating on climate change, find that perceptions of and responses to a multitude of risks are transformed by the power-infused relations between individuals and groups (Auyero and Swistun 2009; Bates 2016; Auyero, Hernandez, and Stitt 2017; Lewin 2017).

10. Multilevel bureaucracies can undermine responses to socioenvironmental disruptions because of red tape and gatekeepers who set up roadblocks (Sobel and Leeson 2006).

11. See Tompkins and Adger 2004; Young and Lipton 2006; Amundsen, Berglund, and Westskog 2010; Dovers and Hezri 2010; Dumaru 2010; Ford et al. 2010. Illustrating the details in how multilevel institutions complicate adaptations is particularly important because while there are theoretical (e.g., Tompkins and Adger 2004; Amundsen, Berglund, and Westskog 2010; Park et al. 2012) and survey- and interview-based (e.g., Jantarasami, Lawler, and Thomas 2010; Tompkins et al. 2010) analyses, further analysis on how these processes play out in everyday practice is needed (Amundsen, Berglund, and Westskog 2010; Dovers and Hezri 2010).

12. Over 11,500 individuals hunted geese on the refuge in 1979, for example (Seek 1980).

13. See Dill and Thornsberry 1950; Thornsberry 1969; Nass 1964; DeStefano et al. 1991; Austin 1987; Kahl and Samson 1984; McDougle and Vaught 1968; Donahue and Olson 1969.

14. I use Terence McDonnell's (2010) concept of affordance, in which the materiality of objects and settings informs how people interpret them. As he illustrates, the meanings of objects emerge through the interplay of the materiality of objects, their settings, and the individuals interpreting them. When red AIDS-awareness ribbons became bleached by the sun, for example, they afforded different meanings than their original red forms. Corresponding with other analyses of how spaces come to have meanings (e.g., Erikson 1976; Freudenburg, Frickel, and Gramling 1995; M. Bell 1997; Stedman 2003; Tsing 2005; Smith and Bugni 2006; Wright 2014; Leap 2015), this stresses the importance of considering how the materiality of spaces constrain and enable particular understandings and uses of those spaces.

15. Leap 2014.

16. Brandenburg and Carroll 1995; Cheng, Kruger, and Daniels 2003; Herda-Rapp and Goedeke 2005; Burley et al. 2007; Brehm, Eisenhauer, and Stedman 2013.

17. Douglas and Wildavsky 1982; Glassner 1999; Beck 2009.

18. Fine 2007; Desmond 2007.

19. See S. Bell 2016; Lewin 2017.

20. Fine 2007; Beck 2009.

21. Kuletz 1998, 7.

22. See R. Scott 2010, 2017; Lewin 2017.

23. Scholars have shown that marginalized groups are much more likely to be exposed to hazards (e.g., Bullard 1990; Di Chiro 2003; Mizelle 2014; Voyles 2015) and that these increased levels of exposure are directly tied to how risks are understood and produced (e.g., Freudenburg et al. 2009; Rebotier 2012).

24. Beck 2009.

25. Tsing 2005.

26. Like many other refuges, Swan Lake National Wildlife Refuge had a cooperative farming program that accepted bids for the right to farm areas of the refuge. Beyond generating revenue for the USFWS, farming programs can provide food sources for nonhumans such as waterfowl.

27. Center for Food Safety et al. v. Jewell et al. 2013.

28. Center for Food Safety et al. v. Jewell et al. 2015.

29. For an overview of expanding neonicotinoid use, see Douglas and Tooker 2015.

30. Durant 1956; Jarvis 1976.

31. Russell 1953, 7–8.

32. Farrell 2015.

33. Center for Food Safety et al. v. Jewell et al. 2013, 7–8.

34. See, e.g., Peluso 1993; Slater 2002; Kosek 2006; West 2006; Burley et al. 2007.

35. Matthew Desmond (2007) and Gary Fine (2007) also argue that understandings of and responses to risks are influenced when personal and collective memories are leveraged to legitimate divergent understandings of the future and its risks.

36. Emma Tompkins, Roger Few, and Katrina Brown (2008) and L. Petheram and colleagues (2010) explore similar processes of growing distrust of natural resource managers.

37. This is in sharp contrast to Javier Auyero and Debora Swistun's (2009) findings that state and corporate officials were purposefully promoting confusion and ambiguity about the future to discourage environmental activism.

38. Shannon McNeeley (2012), for example, draws on others (Smithers and Smit 1997; Tompkins and Adger 2004; Thomas and Twyman 2005) in a discussion of the relative inflexibility of Alaskan hunting regulations and how that has undermined sustainable adaptations in Alaskan communities. She finds that the institutionalized processes of determining hunting dates makes it impossible to modify the dates so that a hunting season corresponds to weather-induced moose migration.

39. I draw on Anthony Giddens's (1984) discussion of the duality of structure here. Rejecting previous discussions that pitted agency against social structures, Giddens argues that social structures simultaneously enable and constrain agency.

40. See, e.g., Young and Lipton 2006; Dumaru 2010; Ford et al. 2010.

41. Tompkins and Adger 2004; Young and Lipton 2006; Tompkins, Few, and Brown 2008; Byg and Salick 2009; Dumaru 2010; Ford et al. 2010; Petheram et al. 2010; McNeeley 2012; Leonard et al. 2013; Thorn, Thornton, and Helfgott 2015. These analyses correspond with other findings that effective responses to shifting socioecological processes can be enabled when local knowledges are linked with broader expertise and resources provided by multilevel institutions (e.g., Stevens 1997; Low et al. 2003; Bryan 2004; Berkes 2009; Ashwood et al. 2014; D. Thompson 2016). Of course, while institutional authority centralized at the level of the nation-state has led to some disastrous socioenvironmental outcomes (Dietz, Ostrom, and Stern 2003), devolving control to local levels or practicing what conservation scholars call comanagement guarantees neither more equitable outcomes nor effective conservation practices (see Coggins 1999; D. Hoffman 2009).

42. Others (e.g., Adger et al. 2011) also emphasize that adaptations to climate change will be contingent on rearranging the meanings and uses of spaces.

43. The (non)human interactions through which communities are constructed are both extremely mundane and embedded in broader social and ecological entanglements (Tsing 2005; Haraway 2008; R. Scott 2010; Ogden 2011; Jerolmack 2013; Voyles 2015).

CHAPTER 6

1. Beck 2009.

2. Young and Lipton 2006; Byg and Salick 2009; Dovers and Hezri 2010; Ford et al. 2010; Gorman-Murray 2010; Petheram et al. 2010; Becken, Lama, and Espiner 2013; Thorn, Thornton, and Helfgott 2015.

3. See Young and Lipton 2006; Adger et al. 2009; and Thorn, Thornton, and Helfgott 2015. This corresponds with the insight that social conflicts inform (in)effective responses to environmental challenges (see Dietz, Ostrom, and Stern 2003; Bryan 2004).

4. Weber 1946a.

5. Interpersonal relationships between resource management officials and members of the public transform natural resource management strategies that rely on cooperative work between members of these groups (e.g., Kruse et al. 1998; Pretty and Ward 2001; Pretty 2003; Agrawal 2005; D. Hoffman 2009). Even when management styles and strategies are not explicitly based on what is referred to as the comanagement model, personal relationships between government officials and members of the public complicate conservation work (e.g., Jacoby 2001; Ogden 2011).

6. See Tompkins and Adger 2004; Petheram et al. 2010; Artur and Hilhorst 2012; Sugden et al. 2014; Turhan, Zografos, and Kallis 2015.

7. Situating her work in social movement literature, Shannon Bell (2016) connects interpersonal, trusting relationships within communities to the ability to respond collectively to socioecological disruptions to communities.

8. Classic sociological works (e.g., Fischer 1972, 1975, 1995; Granovetter 1973) and more recent case studies (e.g., Bebbington 1999; Lauer 2005; M. Gray 2009) find that individuals rely on interpersonal networks to access resources.

9. See Acheson 1988; Sugden et al. 2014; Banerjee and Steinberg 2015; Thorn, Thornton, and Helfgott 2015; S. Bell 2016; Auyero, Hernandez, and Stitt 2017; Buday 2017.

10. Tompkins and Adger 2004.

11. Clay pigeons are saucer-sized disks that are tough enough to be launched into the air by hand or through the use of a mechanical thrower but fragile enough to be broken when hit with a pellet from a shotgun shell.

12. Rural women routinely draw on links between femininity and domestic care work to guide their civic activism (see, e.g., Little and Austin 1996; Hughes 1997; Little 1997a, 1997b; Midgley 2006; Leap 2018a).

13. Feminist scholars refer to this as the ideology of separate spheres, which posits that men have particular skills and dispositions that make them better suited for the public spheres of business and politics and women have dispositions and skills that make them better suited for the domestic sphere of caretaking (see Hartmann 1979; Hochschild and Machung 1989; Acker 1990).

14. See Hidalgo and Hernandez 2001; Manzo and Devine-Wright 2014.

15. See Di Masso, Dixon, and Durrheim 2014. Arturo Escobar (2001, 2008) and J. K. Gibson-Graham (2006) provide in-depth considerations of the profound significance of everyday processes of constructing and claiming attachments to place.

16. This corresponds with other analyses of place attachment (Hidalgo and Hernandez 2001; Kosek 2006; Wuthnow 2011; Grigsby 2012).

17. See Burley et al. 2007; Mishra, Mazumdar, and Suar 2010; Marshall et al. 2012.

18. See Hidalgo and Hernandez 2001; Hernandez et al. 2007; Chesire, Meurk, and Woods 2013; Manzo and Devine-Wright 2014.

19. This follows Jennifer Cross's (2015) call for a greater focus on the interactive processes involved in place attachment and Adrés Di Masso, John Dixon, and Kevin Durrheim's (2014) conceptualization of place attachment.

20. The ability to construct and belong to a community can be crucially important to responses to shifting socioenvironmental conditions (e.g., Acheson 1988; Singleton and Taylor 1992; Ostrom 1992; Bryan 2004; S. Bell 2016).

21. Rememberings of the past are not necessarily accurate, but they lead to senses of togetherness (Davis 1979; B. Anderson 1983; Hobsbawm and Ranger 1983; Halbwachs 1992; Walton 2001). Selective rememberings of the past can allow members of communities to work together to cope with economic and ecological change in the present (K. Bennett 2009; Sherman 2009; Banerjee and Steinberg 2015; Beel et al. 2017). Rememberings, however, can also suppress collective responses to socioecological disruptions (Messer, Shriver, and Adams 2015).

22. Delanty 2003; Jerolmack 2007; Wright 2014.

23. Trudeau 2006.

24. Adger et al. 2011; Marshall et al. 2012.

25. Burley et al. 2007; Mishra, Mazumdar, and Suar 2010; Farrell 2015.

26. Adger et al. 2011; Marshall et al. 2012; Devine-Wright, Price, and Leviston 2015.

27. Conversations follow particular patterns that are centrally important to both conversations and how we organize our lives and communities through conversations (Sacks, Schegloff, and Jefferson 1974; Schegloff 1988, 1992; Holstein and Gubrium 2000). Nina Eliasoph and Paul Lichterman (2003) complicate earlier conversation analysts' findings by noting that conversational norms are specific to particular groups whose group styles are informed by the cultures of groups, communities, and broader societies. In other words, while some aspects of conversations are somewhat standard regardless of context, particular groups also have their own expectations for how conversations should unfold.

28. Holstein and Gubrium 2000, 127.

29. David Gibson put this succinctly in his analysis of John F. Kennedy's eventual decision to quarantine Cuba during the Cuban missile crisis: "The perception of a correct answer, of a way forward, is an interactional outcome, something achieved through conversation and subject to its rules and vicissitudes rather than merely discovered by means of it" (2011, 406).

30. Sacks, Schegloff, and Jefferson 1974; Schegloff 1988; Gibson 2011.

31. Goffman 1959; Fine 1988; Francis 1994.

32. Robinson and Smith-Lovin 2001; Fine and De Soucey 2005; Fine and Corte 2017.

33. Norgaard 2011 is the exception here.

34. Carmin et al. 2015.

35. See, e.g., Mead 1934; Goffman 1959.

36. Brulle and Dunlap 2015.

37. Fishman 1978. Also see West and Zimmerman 1977; Kollock, Blumstein, and Schwartz 1985; Johnson 1994; Robinson and Smith-Lovin 2001.

38. Feminist researchers find links between masculinity, conservation, farming, hunting, and fishing in the United States (Gaard 1993; Anahita and Mix 2006; Kheel 2008), especially in rural communities (Bronner 2004; Grigsy 2012; Bell, Hullinger, and Brislen 2015).

39. Little and Austin 1996; Hughes 1997; Little 1997a, 1997b.

40. Complicating Fishman's (1978) analysis, Cathryn Johnson (1994) finds that women tend to control mixed-gender discussions when they are in positions of authority, such as when a woman manages male employees.

41. Mead 1934; Jerolmack and Tavory 2014.

42. Goffman 1959, 1983. Goffman's concept of "the interaction order," or face-to-face interactions predicated on a "veneer of consensus" (Goffman 1959, 9), emphasizes the weight individuals give to the immediate future of interactions. While the veneer can be shattered in an endless number of ways, Goffman argues that individuals go to great lengths to sustain interactions *for the sake of the interactions themselves*. Also see Rawls 1987.

43. Tavory and Eliasoph 2013.

44. Earlier research often focused on how communities regulate the use of common-pool resources such as fisheries (e.g., Acheson 1988; Singleton and Taylor 1992; Ostrom 1992; Bryan 2004). Scholars have also increasingly noted that group solidarity is crucially important to responses to industrial pollution (e.g., Shriver et al. 2000; Wulfhorst 2000; Messer, Shriver, and Adams 2015; S. Bell 2016).

45. Berkes et al. 2003; Low et al. 2003; Berkes and Ross 2013; Ashwood et al. 2014; Buday 2017.

APPENDIX

1. See, e.g., Du Bois 1899; Lynd and Lynd 1929; Blumenthal 1932; Wirth 1938; Erikson 1976; M. Bell 1994; Elijah Anderson 1999; Macgregor 2010.

2. Gans 1962; Macgregor 2010.

3. See, e.g., Haraway 1988; Bettie 2003; Harding 2004.

4. Harding 2004.

5. Haraway 1988, 581.

6. See Sanders 2003; Macgregor 2010.

7. See Grazian 2015.

8. Bettie 2003; Desmond 2007.

9. See, e.g., Ogden 2011; Nading 2014.

10. See, e.g., Catton and Dunlap 1980; Latour 1993; Sanders 2003; Jerolmack 2007.

11. Glaser and Strauss 1967; Charmaz 2003.

12. Khan and Jerolmack 2013; Jerolmack and Khan 2014.

13. Helene Amundsen, Frode Berglund, and Hege Westskog (2010) and Stephen Dovers and Adnan Hezri (2010) call for more observation-based work on climate change adaptations.

14. This corresponds with Barney Glaser and Anselm Strauss's (1967) understanding of theoretical sampling.

15. Jennifer Sherman (2009) saw similar dynamics when trying to arrange interviews in a community underpinned by the ideology of separate spheres.

16. Rubin and Rubin 2012.

17. This is a standard method of analyzing qualitative data. See Emerson, Fretz, and Shaw 2011 for an overview.

18. Wolcott 1994.

19. Approaching data generation and analysis in an open, flexible manner is standard ethnographic practice. For a discussion of how this works in real time, see Cerwonka and Malkki 2007. For more theoretical considerations, see Glaser and Strauss 1967 and Gubrium and Holstein 2013.

20. Russell 1952, 17.

21. Garfinkel 1967; Lynch 2009.

References

Abraham, Kenneth F., Robert L. Jefferies, and Ray T. Alisauskas. 2005. "The Dynamics of Landscape Change and Snow Geese in Mid-continent North America." *Global Change Biology* 11:841–855.

Acheson, James M. 1988. *The Lobster Gangs of Maine*. Hanover, NH: University Press of New England.

Acker, Joan. 1990. "Hierarchies, Jobs, Bodies: A Theory of Gendered Organizations." *Gender and Society* 4 (2): 139–158.

Adam, Carol J. 1991. *The Sexual Politics of Meat: A Feminist-Vegetarian Critical Theory*. New York: Continuum.

Adger, W. Neil. 2003. "Social Capital, Collective Action, and Adaptation to Climate Change." *Economic Geography* 79 (4): 387–404.

Adger, W. Neil, Jon Barnett, Katrina Brown, Nadine Marshall, and Karen O'Brien. 2013. "Cultural Dimensions of Climate Change Impacts and Adaptation." *Nature Climate Change* 3:112–117.

Adger, W. Neil, Jon Barnett, F. S. Chapin III, and Heidi Ellemor. 2011. "This Must Be the Place: Underrepresentation of Identity and Meaning in Climate Change Decision-Making." *Global Environmental Politics* 11 (2): 1–24.

Adger, W. Neil, Suraje Dessai, Marisa Goulden, Mike Hulme, Irene Lorenzoni, Donald R. Nelson, Lars Otto Naess, Johanna Wolf, and Anita Wreford. 2009. "Are There Social Limits to Adaptation to Climate Change?" *Climatic Change* 93:335–354.

Agrawal, Arun. 2005. "Environmentality: Community, Intimate Government, and the Making of Environmental Subjects in Kumaon, India." *Current Anthropology* 46 (2): 161–190.

Alaimo, Stacy, and Susan Hekman. 2008. "Introduction: Emerging Models of Materiality in Feminist Theory." In *Material Feminisms*, edited by Stacy Alaimo and Susan Hekman, 1–19. Bloomington: Indiana University Press.

Alston, Margaret. 2014. "Gender Mainstreaming and Climate Change." *Women's Studies International Forum* 47:287–294.

Alston, Margaret, and Kerri Whittenbury. 2012. "Does Climate Crisis in Australia's Food Bowl Create a Basis for Change in Agricultural Gender Relations?" *Agriculture and Human Values* 30 (1): 115–128.

Amundsen, Helene, Frode Berglund, and Hege Westskog. 2010. "Overcoming Barriers to Climate Change Adaptation—a Question of Multilevel Governance?" *Environment and Planning C* 28 (2): 276–289.

Anahita, Sine, and Tamara L. Mix. 2006. "Retrofitting Frontier Masculinity for Alaska's War against Wolves." *Gender and Society* 20 (3): 332–353.

Anderson, Benedict. 1983. *Imagined Communities: Reflections on the Origins and Spread of Nationalism.* New York: Verso.

Anderson, Elijah. 1999. *Code of the Street: Decency, Violence, and the Moral Life of the Inner City.* New York: W. W. Norton.

———. 2015. "'The White Space.'" *Sociology of Race and Ethnicity* 1 (1): 10–21.

Anderson, Eric. 2002. "Openly Gay Athletes: Contesting Hegemonic Masculinity in a Homophobic Environment." *Gender and Society* 16 (6): 860–877.

———. 2008. "'Being Masculine Is Not about Who You Sleep With . . . ': Heterosexual Athletes Contesting Masculinity and the One-Time Rule of Homosexuality." *Sex Roles* 58:104–115.

Anzaldúa, Gloria. 2012. *Borderlands/La Frontera: The New Mestiza.* 4th ed. San Francisco: Aunt Lute Books.

Arnell, Nigel W. 2010. "Adapting to Climate Change: An Evolving Research Programme." *Climatic Change* 100:107–111.

Artur, Luis, and Dorothea Hilhorst. 2012. "Everyday Realities of Climate Change Adaptation in Mozambique." *Global Environmental Change* 22:529–536.

Ashwood, Loka, Noelle Harden, Michael M. Bell, and William Bland. 2014. "Linked and Situated: Grounded Knowledge." *Rural Sociology* 79 (4): 427–452.

Aure, Marit, and Mai Camilla Munkejord. 2016. "Creating a Man for the Future: A Narrative Analysis of Male In-Migrants and Their Constructions of Masculinities in a Rural Context." *Sociologia Ruralis* 56 (4): 531–551.

Austin, Jane E. 1987. "Wintering Ecology of Canada Geese in Missouri." Ph.D. diss., University of Missouri, Columbia.

Auyero, Javier, Maricarmen Hernandez, and Mary Ellen Stitt. 2017. "Grassroots Activism in the Belly of the Beast: A Relational Account of the Campaign against Urban Fracking in Texas." *Social Problems,* October 26. Available at https://doi.org/10.1093/socpro/spx035.

Auyero, Javier, and Debora Alejandra Swistun. 2009. *Flammable: Environmental Suffering in an Argentine Shantytown.* New York: Oxford University Press.

Bakker, Karen. 2005. "Neoliberalizing Nature? Market Environmentalism in Water Supply in England and Wales." *Annals of the Association of American Geographers* 95 (3): 542–565.

Banerjee, Damayanti, and Sheila L. Steinberg. 2015. "Exploring Spatial and Cultural Discourses in Environmental Justice Movements: A Study of Two Communities." *Journal of Rural Studies* 39:41–50.

Barad, Karen. 2003. "Posthumanist Performativity: Toward an Understanding of How Matter Comes to Matter." *Signs* 28 (3): 801–831.

Barnett, Barry J. 2000. "The U.S. Farm Financial Crisis of the 1980s." *Agricultural History* 74 (2): 366–380.

Bastian, Chris T. 2002. "Environmental Amenities and Agricultural Land Values: A Hedonic Model Using Geographic Information Systems Data." *Ecological Economics* 40 (3): 337–349.

Bates, Diane C. 2016. *Superstorm Sandy: The Inevitable Destruction and Reconstruction of the Jersey Shore*. New Brunswick, NJ: Rutgers University Press.

Beal, Frances. 1969. "Double Jeopardy: To Be Black and Female." In *Black Woman's Manifesto*, 19–34. New York: Third World Women's Alliance.

Beauboeuf-Lafontant, Tamara. 2009. *Behind the Mask of the Strong Black Woman*. Philadelphia: Temple University Press.

Bebbington, Anthony. 1999. "Capitals and Capabilities: A Framework for Analyzing Peasant Viability, Rural Livelihoods and Poverty." *World Development* 27 (12): 2021–2044.

Beck, Ulrich. 2009. *World at Risk*. Translated by Ciaran Cronin. Malden, MA: Polity.

Becken, Susanne, Ana Kumari Lama, and Stephen Espiner. 2013. "The Cultural Context of Climate Change Impacts: Perceptions among Community Members in the Annapurna Conservation Area, Nepal." *Environmental Development* 8:22–37.

Becker, Howard. 1982. *Art Worlds*. Berkeley: University of California Press.

Beel, David E., Claire D. Wallace, Gemma Webster, Hai Nguyen, Elizabeth Tait, Marsaili Macleod, and Chris Mellish. 2017. "Cultural Resilience: The Production of Rural Community Heritage, Digital Archives, and the Role of Volunteers." *Journal of Rural Studies* 54:459–468.

Bell, Michael Mayerfeld. 1994. *Childerly: Nature and Morality in a Country Village*. Chicago: University of Chicago Press.

———. 1997. "The Ghosts of Place." *Theory and Society* 26 (6): 813–836.

———. 2007. "The Two-ness of Rural Life and the Ends of Rural Scholarship." *Journal of Rural Studies* 23:402–415.

Bell, Shannon Elizabeth. 2013. *Our Roots Run Deep as Ironweed: Appalachian Women and the Fight for Environmental Justice*. Urbana: University of Illinois Press.

———. 2016. *Fighting King Coal: The Challenges of Micromobilization in Central Appalachia*. Cambridge, MA: MIT Press.

Bell, Shannon Elizabeth, and Yvonne A. Braun. 2010. "Coal, Identity, and the Gendering of Environmental Justice Activism in Central Appalachia." *Gender and Society* 24 (6): 794–813.

Bell, Shannon Elizabeth, Alicia Hullinger, and Lilian Brislen. 2015. "Manipulated Masculinities: Agribusiness, Deskilling, and the Rise of the Business-Farmer in the United States." *Rural Sociology* 80 (3): 285–313.

Bellah, Robert N., Richard Madsen, William M. Sullivan, Ann Swidler, and Steven M. Tipton. 2008. *Habits of the Heart: Individualism and Commitment in American Life*. 3rd ed. Berkeley: University of California Press.

Bennett, Jane. 2010. *Vibrant Matter: A Political Ecology of Things*. Durham, NC: Duke University Press.

Bennett, Katy. 2009. "Telling Tales: Nostalgia, Collective Identity and an Ex-Mining Village." In *Emotion, Place and Culture*, edited by Mick Smith, Joyce Davidson, Laura Cameron, and Liz Bondi, 187–205. Burlington, VT: Ashgate.

Benson, Peter. 2012. *Tobacco Capitalism: Growers, Migrant Workers, and the Changing Face of a Global Industry*. Princeton, NJ: Princeton University Press.

Berkes, Fikret. 2009. "Evolution of Co-management: Role of Knowledge Generation, Bridging Organizations and Social Learning." *Journal of Environmental Management* 90 (5): 1692–1702.

Berkes, Fikret, Johan Colding, and Carl Folke. 2003. *Navigating Social-Ecological Systems: Building Resilience for Complexity and Change.* New York: Cambridge University Press.

Berkes, Fikret, and Carl Folke. 1998. *Linking Social and Ecological Systems: Management Practices and Social Mechanisms for Building Resilience.* New York: Cambridge University Press.

Berkes, Fikret, and Dyanna Jolly. 2001. "Adapting to Climate Change: Social-Ecological Resilience in a Canadian Western Arctic Community." *Conservation Ecology* 5 (2). Available at https://www.ecologyandsociety.org/vol5/iss2/art18.

Berkes, Fikret, and Helen Ross. 2013. "Community Resilience: Toward an Integrated Approach." *Society and Natural Resources* 26:5–20.

Berrang-Ford, Lea, James D. Ford, and Jaclyn Paterson. 2011. "Are We Adapting to Climate Change?" *Global Environmental Change* 21:25–33.

Bettie, Julie. 2003. *Women without Class: Girls, Race, and Identity.* Chicago: University of Chicago Press.

Biesbroek, G. Robbert, Judith E. M. Klostermann, Catrien J.A.M. Termeer, and Pavel Kabat. 2013. "On the Nature of Barriers to Climate Change Adaptation." *Regional Environmental Change* 13:1119–1129.

Blumenthal, Albert. 1932. *Small-Town Stuff.* Chicago: University of Chicago Press.

Blumer, Herbert. 1969. *Symbolic Interactionism: Perspective and Method.* Berkeley: University of California Press.

Bonilla-Silva, Eduardo. 2010. *Racism without Racists: Color-Blind Racism and Racial Inequality in Contemporary America.* 3rd ed. Lanham, MD: Rowman and Littlefield.

Bonilla-Silva, Eduardo, Carla Goar, and David G. Embrick. 2006. "When Whites Flock Together: The Social Psychology of White Habitus." *Critical Sociology* 32 (2–3): 229–253.

Bourdieu, Pierre. 1984. *Distinction: A Social Critique of the Judgement of Taste.* Translated by Richard Nice. Cambridge, MA: Harvard University Press.

Brandenburg, Andrea M., and Matthew S. Carroll. 1995. "Your Place or Mine? The Effect of Place Creation on Environmental Values and Landscape Meanings." *Society and Natural Resources* 8:381–398.

Brandth, Berit. 1995. "Rural Masculinity in Transition: Gender Images in Tractor Advertisements." *Journal of Rural Studies* 11 (2): 123–133.

———. 2006. "Agricultural Body-Building: Incorporations of Gender, Body and Work." *Journal of Rural Studies* 22:17–27.

Brandth, Berit, and Marit S. Haugen. 2005. "Doing Rural Masculinity—from Logging to Outfield Tourism." *Journal of Gender Studies* 14 (1): 13–22.

———. 2010. "Doing Farm Tourism: The Intertwining Practices of Gender and Work." *Signs* 35 (2): 425–446.

Brechin, Steven R. 2003. "Comparative Public Opinion and Knowledge on Global Climate Change and the Kyoto Protocol: The US versus the World?" *International Journal of Sociology and Social Policy* 23 (10): 106–134.

Brechin, Steven R., and Medani Bhandari. 2011. "Perceptions of Climate Change Worldwide." *WIREs Climate Change* 2 (6): 871–885.

Brehm, Joan M., Brian W. Eisenhauer, and Richard C. Stedman. 2013. "Environmental Concern: Examining the Role of Place Meaning and Place Attachment." *Society and Natural Resources* 26 (5): 522–538.

Brekhus, Wayne. 1996. "Social Marking and the Mental Coloring of Identity: Sexual Identity Construction and Maintenance in the United States." *Sociological Forum* 11 (3): 497–522.

———. 1998. "A Sociology of the Unmarked: Redirecting Our Focus." *Sociological Theory* 16 (1): 34–51.

———. 2003. *Peacocks, Chameleons, Centaurs: Gay Suburbia and the Grammar of Social Identity.* Chicago: University of Chicago Press.

Brewster, Bradley H., and Michael Mayerfeld Bell. 2010. "The Environmental Goffman: Toward an Environmental Sociology of Everyday Life." *Society and Natural Resources* 23:45–57.

Brockington, Dan, and Rosaleen Duffy. 2010. "Capitalism and Conservation: The Production and Reproduction of Biodiversity Conservation." *Antipode* 42 (3): 469–484.

Bronner, Simon J. 2004. "'This Is Why We Hunt': Social-Psychological Meanings of the Traditions and Rituals of Deer Camp." *Western Folklore* 63 (1–2): 11–50.

Brosius, J. Peter. 1999. "Green Dots, Pink Hearts: Displacing Politics from the Malaysian Rain Forest." *American Anthropologist* 101 (1): 36–57.

Broughton, Chad. 2008. "Migration as Engendered Practice: Mexican Men, Masculinity, and Northward Migration." *Gender and Society* 22 (5): 568–589.

Brown, David L., and Louis E. Swanson. 2003. *Challenges for Rural America in the Twenty-First Century.* University Park: Pennsylvania State University Press.

Brulle, Robert J., Jason Carmichael, and J. Craig Jenkins. 2012. "Shifting Public Opinion on Climate Change: An Empirical Assessment of Factors Influencing Concern over Climate Change in the U.S., 2002–2010." *Climatic Change* 114:169–188.

Brulle, Robert J., and Riley E. Dunlap. 2015. "Sociology and Global Climate Change: Introduction." In *Climate Change and Society: Sociological Perspectives*, edited by Riley E. Dunlap and Robert J. Brulle, 1–31. New York: Oxford University Press.

Bryan, Todd A. 2004. "Tragedy Averted: The Promise of Collaboration." *Society and Natural Resources* 17:881–896.

Buday, Amanda. 2017. "The Home Rule Advantage: Motives and Outcomes of Local Anti-fracking Mobilization." *Social Currents* 4 (6): 575–593.

Bullard, Robert D. 1990. *Dumping in Dixie: Race, Class, and Environmental Quality.* Boulder, CO: Westview Press.

Burke, Paul J., Md Shahiduzzaman, and David I. Stern. 2015. "Carbon Dioxide Emissions in the Short Run: The Rate and Sources of Economic Growth Matter." *Global Environmental Change* 33:109–121.

Burley, David, Pam Jenkins, Shirley Laska, and Traber Davis. 2007. "Place Attachment and Environmental Change in Coastal Louisiana." *Organization and Environment* 20 (3): 347–366.

Butler, Judith. 1990. *Gender Trouble: Feminism and the Subversion of Identity.* New York: Routledge.

Bye, Linda Marie. 2003. "Masculinity and Rurality at Play in Stories about Hunting." *Norwegian Journal of Geography* 57 (3): 143–153.

Byg, Anja, and Jan Salick. 2009. "Local Perspectives on a Global Phenomenon—Climate Change in Eastern Tibetan Villages." *Global Environmental Change* 19:156–166.

Byrne, Jason. 2012. "When Green Is White: The Cultural Politics of Race, Nature and Social Exclusion in a Los Angeles Urban National Park." *Geoforum* 43 (3): 595–611.

Byrne, Jason, and Jennifer Wolch. 2009. "Nature, Race, and Parks: Past Research and Future Directions for Geographic Research." *Progress in Human Geography* 33 (6): 743–765.

Cabras, Ignazio, and Matthew P. Mount. 2017. "How Third Places Foster and Shape Community Cohesion, Economic Development and Social Capital: The Case of Pubs in Rural Ireland." *Journal of Rural Studies* 55:71–82.

Campbell, Hugh. 2000. "The Glass Phallus: Pub(lic) Masculinity and Drinking in Rural New Zealand." *Rural Sociology* 65 (4): 562–581.

Campbell, Hugh, and Michael Mayerfeld Bell. 2000. "The Question of Rural Masculinities." *Rural Sociology* 65 (4): 532–546.

Cánoves, Gemma, Montserrat Villarino, Gerda K. Priestley, and Asunción Blanco. 2004. "Rural Tourism in Spain: An Analysis of Recent Evolution." *Geoforum* 35 (6): 755–769.

Carbado, Devon W. 2013. "Colorblind Intersectionality." *Signs* 38 (4): 811–845.

Carmin, JoAnn, Kathleen Tierney, Eric Chu, Lori M. Hunter, J. Timmons Roberts, and Linda Shi. 2015. "Adaptation to Climate Change." In *Climate Change and Society: Sociological Perspectives*, edited by Riley E. Dunlap and Robert J. Brulle, 164–198. New York: Oxford University Press.

Carr, Edward R., and Mary C. Thompson. 2014. "Gender and Climate Change Adaptation in Agrarian Settings: Current Thinking, New Directions, and Research Frontiers." *Geography Compass* 8 (3): 182–197.

Carr, Patrick, and Maria Kefalas. 2009. *Hollowing Out the Middle: The Rural Brain Drain and What It Means for America*. Boston: Beacon Press.

Carrigan, Tim, Bob Connell, and John Lee. 1985. "Toward a New Sociology of Masculinity." *Theory and Society* 14 (5): 551–604.

Castree, Noel. 2008. "Neoliberalising Nature II: Processes, Outcomes and Effects." *Environment and Planning A* 41 (8): 153–173.

Catton, William R., Jr., and Riley E. Dunlap. 1980. "A New Ecological Paradigm for Post-exuberant Sociology." *American Behavioral Scientist* 24 (1): 15–47.

Center for Food Safety et al. v. Jewell et al. 2013. No. 4:2013cv03987 (Cal. N.D. Ct., August 27).

Center for Food Safety et al. v. Jewell et al. 2015. No. 14-360 (CKK) (D.D.C., March 16).

Cerwonka, Allaine, and Liisa H. Malkki. 2007. *Improvising Theory: Process and Temporality in Ethnographic Fieldwork*. Chicago: University of Chicago Press.

Cha, Youngjoo. 2010. "Reinforcing Separate Spheres: The Effect of Spousal Overwork on Men's and Women's Employment in Dual-Earner Households." *American Sociological Review* 75 (2): 303–329.

Charmaz, Kathy. 2003. "Grounded Theory: Objectivist and Constructivist Methods." In *Strategies of Qualitative Inquiry*, 2nd ed., edited by Norman K. Denzin and Yvonna S. Lincoln, 249–291. Thousand Oaks, CA: Sage.

Cheng, Antony S., Linda E Kruger, and Steven E. Daniels. 2003. "'Place' as an Integrating Concept in Natural Resource Politics: Propositions for a Social Science Research Agenda." *Society and Natural Resources* 16:87–104.

Chesire, Lynda, Carla Meurk, and Michael Woods. 2013. "Decoupling Farm, Farming and Place: Recombinant Attachments of Globally Engaged Family Farmers." *Journal of Rural Studies* 30:64–74.

Choo, Hae Yeon, and Myra Marx Ferree. 2010. "Practicing Intersectionality in Sociological Research: A Critical Analysis of Inclusions, Interactions, and Institutions in the Study of Inequalities." *Sociological Theory* 28 (2): 129–149.

Clark, Brett, and Richard York. 2005. "Carbon Metabolism: Global Capitalism, Climate Change, and the Biospheric Rift." *Theory and Society* 34:391–428.

Cloke, Paul, and Jo Little. 1997. *Contested Countryside Cultures: Otherness, Marginalisation, and Rurality*. New York: Routledge.

Coggins, George C. 1999. "Regulating Federal Natural Resources: A Summary Case against Devolved Collaboration." *Ecology Law Quarterly* 25 (4): 602–610.

Cohen, Jeffrey Jerome, and Lowell Duckert. 2017. *Veer Ecology: A Companion for Environmental Thinking*. Minneapolis: University of Minnesota Press.

Cole, Luke W., and Sheila R. Foster. 2001. *From the Ground Up: Environmental Racism and the Rise of the Environmental Justice Movement*. New York: New York University Press.

Collins, Patricia Hill. 2009. *Black Feminist Thought*. 2nd ed. New York: Routledge.

Connell, R. W., and James W. Messerschmidt. 2005. "Hegemonic Masculinity: Rethinking the Concept." *Gender and Society* 19:829–859.

Connell, Raewyn. 2006. "Country/City Men." In *Country Boys: Masculinity and Rural Life*, edited by Hugh Campbell, Michael Mayerfeld Bell, and Margaret Finney, 255–267. University Park: Pennsylvania State University Press.

Cote, Muriel, and Andrea J. Nightingale. 2012. "Resilience Thinking Meets Social Theory: Situating Social Change in Socio-ecological Systems (SES) Research." *Progress in Human Geography* 36 (4): 475–489.

Cramer, Katherine. 2016. *The Politics of Resentment: Rural Consciousness in Wisconsin and the Rise of Scott Walker*. Chicago: University of Chicago Press.

Crenshaw, Kimberle. 1989. "Demarginalizing the Intersection of Race and Sex: A Black Feminist Critique of Antidiscrimination Doctrine, Feminist Theory, and Antiracist Politics." *University of Chicago Legal Forum* 140:139–167.

Cretney, Raven. 2014. "Resilience for Whom? Emerging Critical Geographies of Socio-ecological Resilience." *Geography Compass* 8 (9): 627–640.

Cronon, William. 1991. *Nature's Metropolis: Chicago and the Great West*. New York: W. W. Norton.

———. 1995. "The Trouble with Wilderness; or, Getting Back to the Wrong Nature." In *Uncommon Ground: Rethinking the Human Place in Nature*, 69–90. New York: W. W. Norton.

Cross, Jennifer Eileen. 2015. "Processes of Place Attachment: An Interactional Framework." *Symbolic Interaction* 4 (38): 493–520.

Davenport, Coral, and Campbell Robertson. 2016. "Resettling the First American 'Climate Refugees.'" *New York Times*, May 3. Available at http://www.nytimes.com/2016/05/03/us/resettling-the-first-american-climate-refugees.html.

Davidson, Debra J. 2010. "The Applicability of the Concept of Resilience to Social Systems: Some Sources of Optimism and Nagging Doubts." *Society and Natural Resources* 23:1135–1149.

Davidson, Debra J., Jeffrey Andrews, and Daniel Pauly. 2014. "The Effort Factor: Evaluating the Increasing Marginal Impact of Resource Extraction over Time." *Global Environmental Change* 25:63–68.

Davidson, Joanna. 2012. "Of Rice and Men: Climate Change, Religion, and Personhood among the Diola of Guinea-Bissau." *Journal for the Study of Religion, Nature and Culture* 6 (3): 363–381.

Davis, Fred. 1979. *Yearning for Yesterday: A Sociology of Nostalgia*. New York: Free Press.

Delanty, Gerard. 2003. *Community*. New York: Routledge.

De León, Jason. 2015. *The Land of Open Graves: Living and Dying on the Migrant Trail.* Berkeley: University of California Press.

Denzin, Norman K. 1978. *The Research Act: A Theoretical Introduction to Sociological Methods.* New York: McGraw-Hill.

Desmond, Matthew. 2007. *On the Fireline: Living and Dying with the Wildland Firefighters.* Chicago: University of Chicago Press.

DeStefano, Stephen, Christopher J. Brand, Donald H. Rusch, Daniel L. Finley, and Murray M. Gillespie. 1991. "Lead Exposure in Canada Geese of the Eastern Prairie Population." *Wildlife Society Bulletin* 19:23–32.

Deutsch, Francine M. 2007. "Undoing Gender." *Gender and Society* 21 (1): 106–127.

Devine-Wright, Patrick, Jennifer Price, and Zoe Leviston. 2015. "My Country or My Planet? Exploring the Influence of Multiple Place Attachments and Ideological Beliefs upon Climate Change Attitudes and Opinions." *Global Environmental Change* 30:68–79.

Di Chiro, Giovanna. 2003. "Beyond Ecoliberal 'Common Futures': Environmental Justice, Toxic Touring, and a Transcommunal Politics of Place." In *Race, Nature, and the Politics of Difference*, edited by Donald S. Moore, Anand Pandian, and Jake Kosek, 204–232. Durham, NC: Duke University Press.

Dietz, Thomas, Elinor Ostrom, and Paul C. Stern. 2003. "The Struggle to Govern the Commons." *Science* 302:1907–1912.

Dill, Herbert H. 1949. *Annual Report: Swan Lake National Wildlife Refuge, September 1, 1948–December 31, 1948.* Sumner, MO: U.S. Fish and Wildlife Service.

———. 1950. *Annual Report: Swan Lake National Wildlife Refuge, September 1, 1949–December 31, 1949.* Sumner, MO: U.S. Fish and Wildlife Service.

Dill, Herbert H., and William H. Thornsberry. 1950. "A Cannon-Projected Net Trap for Capturing Waterfowl." *Journal of Wildlife Management* 14 (2): 132–137.

Di Masso, Adrés, John Dixon, and Kevin Durrheim. 2014. "Place Attachment as Discursive Practice." In *Place Attachment: Advances in Theory, Methods and Applications*, edited by Lynne C. Manzo and Patrick Devine-Wright, 75–86. New York: Routledge.

Dizard, Jan E. 2003. *Mortal Stakes: Hunters and Hunting in Contemporary America.* Amherst: University of Massachusetts Press.

Doane, Molly. 2012. *Stealing Shining Rivers: Agrarian Conflict, Market Logic, and Conservation in a Mexican Forest.* Tucson: University of Arizona Press.

Dobbins, Robert. 1978. *Report of Operations: Swan Lake Wildlife Management Area.* Sumner, MO: Missouri Department of Conservation.

Dolhinow, Rebecca. 2010. *A Jumble of Needs: Women's Activism and Neoliberalism in the Colonias of the Southwest.* Minneapolis: University of Minnesota Press.

Dominey-Howes, Dale, Andrew Gorman-Murray, and Scott McKinnon. 2014. "Queering Disasters: On the Need to Account for LGBTI Experiences in Natural Disaster Contexts." *Gender, Place and Culture* 21 (7): 905–918.

Donahue, J. M., and L. D. Olson. 1969. "Survey of Wild Ducks and Geese for *Pasteurella* spp." *Journal of Wildlife Diseases* 5 (3): 201–205.

Douglas, Margaret R., and John F. Tooker. 2015. "Large-Scale Deployment of Seed Treatments Has Driven Rapid Increase in Use of Neonicotinoid Insecticides and Preemptive Pest Management in U.S. Field Crops." *Environmental Science and Technology* 49:5088–5097.

Douglas, Mary, and Aaron Wildavsky. 1982. *Risk and Culture: An Essay on the Selection of Technological and Environmental Dangers.* Berkeley: University of California Press.

Dovers, Stephen R., and Adnan A. Hezri. 2010. "Institutions and Policy Processes: The Means to the Ends of Adaptation." *WIREs Climate Change* 1:212–231.

Downey, Liam. 2015. *Inequality, Democracy, and the Environment*. New York: New York University Press.

Du Bois, W.E.B. 1899. *The Philadelphia Negro: A Social Study*. Philadelphia: University of Pennsylvania Press.

———. 1989. *The Souls of Black Folk*. New York: Penguin Group.

Ducks Unlimited. 2010. "Record Year for Wetlands Reserve Program: This Farm Bill Conservation Program Is More Popular than Ever." Available at http://www.ducks .org/conservation/public-policy/farm-bill/record-year-for-wetlands-reserve -program.

Duffy, Rosaleen. 2013. "The International Political Economy of Tourism and the Neo-liberalisation of Nature: Challenges Posed by Selling Close Interactions with Animals." *Review of International Political Economy* 20 (3): 605–626.

Duffy, Rosaleen, and Lorraine Moore. 2010. "Neoliberalising Nature? Elephant-Back Tourism in Thailand and Botswana." *Antipode* 42 (3): 742–766.

Dumaru, Patrina. 2010. "Community-Based Adaptation: Enhancing Community Adaptive Capacity in Druadrua Island, Fiji." *WIREs Climate Change* 1:751–763.

Duneier, Mitchell. 1992. *Slim's Table: Race, Respectability, and Masculinity*. Chicago: Chicago University Press.

Dunlap, Riley E. 2010. "Climate Change and Rural Sociology: Broadening the Research Agenda." *Rural Sociology* 75 (1): 17–27.

Dunlap, Riley E., and Aaron M. McCright. 2008. "A Widening Gap: Republican and Democratic Views on Climate Change." *Environment: Science and Policy for Sustainable Development* 50 (5): 26–35.

Durant, A. J. 1956. "Impaction and Pressure Necrosis in Canada Geese Due to Eating Dry Hulled Soybeans." *Journal of Wildlife Management* 20 (4): 399–404.

Durkheim, Emile. 1933. *The Division of Labor in Society*. New York: Free Press.

———. 1951. *Suicide: A Study in Sociology*. Translated by John A. Spaulding and George Simpson. New York: Free Press.

———. 2001. *The Elementary Forms of Religious Life*. Translated by Carol Cosman. Oxford: Oxford University Press.

Eastman, Jason T., and Douglas P. Schrock. 2008. "Southern Rock Musicians' Construction of White Trash." *Race, Gender, and Class* 15 (1–2): 205–219.

Eaton, Weston M. 2016. "What's the Problem? How 'Industrial Culture' Shapes Community Responses to Proposed Bioenergy Development in Northern Michigan." *Journal of Rural Studies* 45:76–87.

Eliasoph, Nina, and Paul Lichterman. 2003. "Culture in Interaction." *American Journal of Sociology* 108 (4): 735–794.

Elliot, Michael, Barbara Gray, and Roy Lewicki. 2003. "Lessons Learned about the Framing of Intractable Environmental Conflicts." In *Making Sense of Intractable Environmental Conflicts: Concepts and Cases*, edited by Roy J. Lewicki, Barbara Gray, and Michael Elliot, 409–436. Washington, DC: Island Press.

Ellis, Colter. 2014. "Boundary Labor and the Production of Emotionless Commodities: The Case of Beef Production." *Sociological Quarterly* 55 (1): 92–118.

Emel, Jody. 1995. "Are You Man Enough, Big and Bad Enough? An Ecofeminist Analysis of Wolf Eradication in the United States." *Society and Space: Environment and Planning D* 13:707–734.

Emerson, Robert M., Rachel I. Fretz, and Linda L. Shaw. 2011. *Writing Ethnographic Fieldnotes*. 2nd ed. Chicago: University of Chicago Press.

Erikson, Kai T. 1976. *Everything in Its Path: Destruction of Community in the Buffalo Creek Flood*. New York: Simon and Schuster.

Escobar, Arturo. 1999. "After Nature: Steps to an Antiessentialist Political Ecology." *Current Anthropology* 40 (1): 1–30.

———. 2001. "Culture Sits in Places: Reflections on Globalism and Subaltern Strategies of Localization." *Political Geography* 20:139–174.

———. 2008. *Territories of Difference: Place, Movements, Life, Redes*. Durham, NC: Duke University Press.

Fabinyi, Michael, Louisa Evans, and Simon J. Foale. 2014. "Social-Ecological Systems, Social Diversity, and Power: Insights from Anthropology and Political Ecology." *Ecology and Society* 19 (4): 28.

Falk, William W., and Thomas K. Pinhey. 1978. "Making Sense of the Concept Rural and Doing Rural Sociology." *Rural Sociology* 43 (4): 547–558.

Fanon, Frantz. 2008. *Black Skin, White Masks*. Translated by Richard Philcox. New York: Grove Press.

Farrell, Justin. 2015. *The Battle for Yellowstone: Morality and the Sacred Roots of Environmental Conflict*. Princeton, NJ: Princeton University Press.

Filteau, Matthew R. 2014. "Who Are Those Guys? Constructing the Oilfield's New Dominant Masculinity." *Men and Masculinities* 17 (4): 396–416.

———. 2015. "A Localized Masculine Crisis: Local Men's Subordination with the Marcellus Shale Region's Masculine Structure." *Rural Sociology* 80 (4): 431–455.

Fine, Gary Alan. 1984. "Negotiated Orders and Organizational Cultures." *Annual Review of Sociology* 10:239–262.

———. 1988. "Dying for a Laugh: Negotiating Risk and Creating Personas in the Humor of Mushroom Collectors." *Western Folklore* 47 (3): 177–194.

———. 1997. "Naturework and the Taming of the Wild: The Problem of 'Overpick' in the Culture of Mushroomers." *Social Problems* 44 (1): 68–88.

———. 2007. *Authors of the Storm: Meteorologists and the Culture of Prediction*. Chicago: University of Chicago Press.

———. 2010. "The Sociology of the Local: Action and Its Publics." *Sociological Theory* 28 (4): 355–376.

Fine, Gary Alan, and Ugo Corte. 2017. "Group Pleasures: Collaborative Commitments, Shared Narrative, and the Sociology of Fun." *Sociological Theory* 35 (1): 64–86.

Fine, Gary Alan, and Michaela De Soucey. 2005. "Joking Cultures: Humor Themes as Social Regulation in Group Life." *Humor* 18 (1): 1–22.

Fine, Michelle, Lois Weis, Judi Addelston, and Julia Marusza. 1997. "(In)Secure Times: Constructing White Working-Class Masculinities in the Late 20th Century." *Gender and Society* 11 (1): 52–68.

Finnis, Joel, Atanu Sarkar, and Mark C. J. Stoddart. 2015. "Bridging Science and Community Knowledge? The Complicating Role of Natural Variability in Perceptions of Climate Change." *Global Environmental Change* 32:1–10.

Fischer, Claude S. 1972. "'Urbanism as a Way of Life': A Review and an Agenda." *Sociological Methods and Research* 1 (2): 187–242.

———. 1975. "Toward a Subcultural Theory of Urbanism." *American Journal of Sociology* 80 (6): 1319–1341.

———. 1995. "Centennial Essay: The Subcultural Theory of Urbanism; A Twentieth-Year Assessment." *American Journal of Sociology* 101 (3): 543–577.

Fishman, Pamela M. 1978. "Interaction: The Work Women Do." *Social Problems* 25 (4): 397–406.

Fletcher, Robert. 2010. "Neoliberal Environmentality: Towards a Poststructuralist Political Ecology of the Conservation Debate." *Conservation and Society* 8 (3): 171–181.

Force, William Ryan. 2011. "Cultural Auspices and Masculinities in Home Territory Bars." Ph.D. diss., Department of Sociology, University of Missouri, Columbia.

Ford, James D., Lea Berrang-Ford, and Jaclyn Paterson. 2011. "A Systematic Review of Observed Climate Change Adaptation in Developed Nations." *Climatic Change* 106:327–336.

Ford, James D., Tristan Pearce, Frank Duerden, Chris Furgal, and Barry Smit. 2010. "Climate Change Policy Responses for Canada's Inuit Population: The Importance of and Opportunities for Adaptation." *Global Environmental Change* 20:177–191.

Ford, James D., Barry Smit, and Johanna Wandel. 2006. "Vulnerability to Climate Change in the Arctic: A Case Study from Arctic Bay, Canada." *Global Environmental Change* 16:145–160.

Ford, James D., Barry Smit, Johanna Wandel, Mishak Allurut, Kik Shappa, Harry Ittusarjuat, and Kevin Qrunnut. 2008. "Climate Change in the Arctic: Current and Future Vulnerability in Two Inuit Communities in Canada." *Geographical Journal* 174 (1): 45–62.

Fordham, Signithia. 1993. "'Those Loud Black Girls': (Black) Women, Silence, and Gender 'Passing' in the Academy." *Anthropology and Education* 24 (1): 3–32.

Fortier, Anne-Marie. 1999. "Re-membering Places and the Performance of Belonging(s)." *Theory, Culture and Society* 16 (2): 41–64.

Foster, John Bellamy. 1999. "Marx's Theory of Metabolic Rift: Classical Foundations for Environmental Sociology." *American Journal of Sociology* 105 (2): 366–405.

Foucault, Michel. 1995. *Discipline and Punish: The Birth of the Prison.* Translated by Alan Sheridan. New York: Vintage Books.

Fox, Aaron A. 2004. *Real Country: Music and Language in Working-Class Culture.* Durham, NC: Duke University Press.

Francis, Linda E. 1994. "Laughter, the Best Mediation: Humor as Emotion Management in Interaction." *Symbolic Interaction* 17 (2): 147–163.

Freudenburg, William R. 1993. "Risk and Recreancy: Weber, the Division of Labor, and the Rationality of Risk Perceptions." *Social Forces* 71 (4): 909–932.

Freudenburg, William R., Scott Frickel, and Robert Gramling. 1995. "Beyond the Nature/Society Divide: Learning to Think about a Mountain." *Sociological Forum* 10 (3): 361–392.

Freudenburg, William R., Robert Gramling, Shirley Laska, and Kai T. Erikson. 2009. *Catastrophe in the Making: The Engineering of Katrina and the Disasters of Tomorrow.* Washington, DC: Island Press.

Fujiwara, Lynn. 2008. *Mothers without Citizenship: Asian Immigrant Families and the Consequences of Welfare Reform.* Minneapolis: University of Minnesota Press.

Gaard, Greta. 1993. *Ecofeminism: Women, Animals, Nature.* Philadelphia: Temple University Press.

———. 2011. "Ecofeminism Revisited: Rejecting Essentialism and Re-placing Species in a Material Feminist Environmentalism." *Feminist Formations* 23 (2): 26–53.

Gans, Herbert J. 1962. *Urban Villagers.* New York: Free Press of Glencoe.

———. 1995. *The War against the Poor: The Underclass and Antipoverty Policy.* New York: Basic Books.

Garfinkel, Harold. 1967. *Studies in Ethnomethodology.* Englewood Cliffs, NJ: Prentice Hall.

Geertz, Clifford. 1972. "Deep Play: Notes on the Balinese Cock Fight." *Daedalus* 101 (1): 1–37.

Gibson, David. R. 2011. "Avoiding Catastrophe: The Interactional Production of Possibility during the Cuban Missile Crisis." *American Journal of Sociology* 117 (2): 361–419.

Gibson-Graham, J. K. 2006. *A Postcapitalist Politics.* Minneapolis: University of Minnesota Press.

Giddens, Anthony. 1984. *The Constitution of Society.* Berkeley: University of California Press.

Gieryn, Thomas F. 2000. "A Space for Place in Sociology." *Annual Review of Sociology* 26:463–496.

Glaser, Barney G., and Anselm L. Strauss. 1967. *The Discovery of Grounded Theory: Strategies for Qualitative Research.* New Brunswick, NJ: Aldine Transaction.

Glassner, Barry. 1999. *The Culture of Fear.* New York: Basic Books.

Goedeke, T. L., and S. Rikoon. 2008. "Scientific Controversy, Dynamism of Networks, and the Implications of Power in Ecological Restoration." *Social Studies of Science* 38 (1): 111–132.

Goedeke, Theresa L. 2005. "Devils, Angels, or Animals: The Social Construction of Otters in Conflict over Management." In *Mad and Wildlife: Looking at Social Conflict over Wildlife*, edited by Ann Herda-Rapp and Theresa L. Goedeke, 25–50. Leiden, Netherlands: Brill Academic.

Goffman, Erving. 1959. *The Presentation of Self in Everyday Life.* New York: Anchor Books.

———. 1974. *Frame Analysis: An Essay on the Organization of Experience.* Boston: Northeastern University Press.

———. 1983. "The Interaction Order: American Sociological Association, 1982 Presidential Address." *American Sociological Review* 48 (1): 1–17.

Goldschmidt, Walter. 1978. "Large-Scale Farming and the Rural Social Structure." *Rural Sociology* 43 (3): 362–366.

Gordon, Avery F. 2008. *Ghostly Matters: Haunting and the Sociological Imagination.* 2nd ed. Minneapolis: University of Minnesota Press.

Gorman-Murray, Andrew. 2010. "An Australian Feeling for Snow: Towards Understanding Cultural and Emotional Dimensions of Climate Change." *Cultural Studies Review* 16 (1): 60–81.

Gould, Kenneth A., David N. Pellow, and Allan Schnaiberg. 2008. *The Treadmill of Production: Injustice and Unsustainability in the Global Economy.* Boulder, CO: Paradigm.

Granovetter, Mark S. 1973. "The Strength of Weak Ties." *American Journal of Sociology* 78 (6): 1360–1380.

Grant, Don, Andrew K. Jorgenson, and Wesley Longhofer. 2018. "Pathways to Carbon Pollution: The Interactive Effects of Global, Political, and Organizational Factors on Power Plants' CO_2 Emissions." *Sociological Science* 5:58–92.

Gray, Barbara. 2004. "Strong Opposition: Frame-Based Resistance to Collaboration." *Community and Applied Social Psychology* 14 (3): 166–176.

Gray, Mary L. 2009. *Out in the Country: Youth, Media, and Queer Visibility in Rural America.* New York: New York University Press.

Grazian, David. 2007. "The Girl Hunt: Urban Nightlife and the Performance of Masculinity as Collective Activity." *Symbolic Interaction* 30 (2): 221–243.

———. 2015. *American Zoo: A Sociological Safari*. Princeton, NJ: Princeton University Press.

Greider, Thomas, and Lorraine Garkovich. 1994. "Landscapes: The Social Construction of Nature and the Environment." *Rural Sociology* 59 (1): 1–24.

Grigsby, Mary. 2012. *Noodlers in Missouri: Fishing for Identity in a Rural Subculture*. Kirksville, MO: Truman State University Press.

Grindstaff, Laura, and Emily West. 2006. "Cheerleading and the Gendered Politics of Sport." *Social Problems* 53 (4): 500–518.

Groes-Green, Christian. 2009. "Hegemonic and Subordinated Masculinities: Class, Violence and Sexual Performance among Young Mozambican Men." *Nordic Journal of African Studies* 18 (4): 286–304.

Grothmann, Torsten, and Anthony Patt. 2005. "Adaptive Capacity and Human Cognition: The Process of Individual Adaptation to Climate Change." *Global Environmental Change* 15:199–213.

Gubrium, Jaber F., and James A. Holstein. 2013. "Analytic Inspiration in Ethnographic Fieldwork." In *The SAGE Handbook of Qualitative Data Analysis*, edited by Uwe Flick, 35–48. Thousand Oaks, CA: Sage.

Gunderson, Ryan, Diana Stuart, and Brian Petersen. 2018. "Ideological Obstacles to Effective Climate Policy: The Greening of Markets, Technology, and Growth." *Capital and Class* 42 (1): 133–160.

Guthman, Julie. 2011. *Weighing In: Obesity, Food Justice, and the Limits of Capitalism*. Berkeley: University of California Press.

Hackworth, Jason. 2007. *The Neoliberal City: Governance, Ideology, and Development in American Urbanism*. Ithaca, NY: Cornell University Press.

Hagerman, Margaret Ann. 2016. "Reproducing and Reworking Colorblind Racial Ideology: Acknowledging Children's Agency in the White Habitus." *Sociology of Race and Ethnicity* 2 (1): 58–71.

Halbwachs, Maurice. 1992. *On Collective Memory*. Translated by Lewis A. Coser. Chicago: University of Chicago Press.

Halfacree, Keith. 2006. "Rural Space: Constructing a Three-fold Architecture." In *Handbook of Rural Studies*, edited by Paul Cloke, Terry Marsden, and Patrick Mooney, 44–62. London: Sage.

Hall, Peter M. 1972. "A Symbolic Interactionist Analysis of Politics." *Sociological Inquiry* 42 (3–4): 35–75.

———. 1997. "Meta-power, Social Organization, and the Shaping of Social Action." *Symbolic Interaction* 20 (4): 397–418.

———. 2003. "Interactionism, Social Organization, and Social Processes: Looking Back and Moving Ahead." *Symbolic Interaction* 26 (1): 33–55.

Hall, Peter M., and Patrick J. W. McGinty. 1997. "Policy as the Transformation of Intentions: Producing Program from Statute." *Sociological Quarterly* 38 (3): 439–467.

Hallet, Tim, and Emily Meanwell. 2016. "Accountability as an Inhabited Institution: Contested Meanings and the Symbolic Politics of Reform." *Symbolic Interaction* 39 (3): 374–396.

Hallet, Tim, and Marc J. Ventresca. 2006. "Inhabited Institutions: Social Interactions and Organizational Forms in Gouldner's *Patterns of Industrial Bureaucracy*." *Theory and Society* 35:213–236.

Hamilton, Lawrence C. 2010. "Education, Politics and Opinions about Climate Change Evidence for Interaction Effects." *Climatic Change* 104:231–242.

Hamilton, Lawrence C., and Barry D. Keim. 2009. "Regional Variation in Perceptions about Climate Change." *International Journal of Climatology* 29 (15): 2348–2352.

Hansen, Henry A., and Harvey K. Nelson. 1964. "Honkers Large and Small." In *Waterfowl Tomorrow*, edited by Joseph P. Linduska, Arnold L. Nelson, and Bob Hines, 109–124. Washington, DC: Government Printing Office.

Haraway, Donna. 1985. "Manifesto for Cyborgs: Science, Technology, and Socialist Feminism in the 1980s." *Socialist Review* 80:65–108.

———. 1988. "Situated Knowledges: The Science Question in Feminism and the Privilege of Partial Perspective." *Feminist Studies* 14 (3): 575–599.

———. 2008. *When Species Meet*. Minneapolis: University of Minnesota Press.

Harding, Sandra. 2004. "Rethinking Standpoint Epistemology: What Is 'Strong Objectivity'?" In *The Feminist Standpoint Theory Reader: Intellectual and Political Controversies*, edited by Sandra Harding, 127–140. New York: Routledge.

Hartigan, John Jr. 2003. "Who Are These White People? 'Rednecks,' 'Hillbillies,' and 'White Trash' as Marked Racial Subjects." In *White Out: The Continuing Significance of Racism*, edited by Ashley W. Doane and Eduardo Bonilla-Silva, 95–111. New York: Routledge.

Hartmann, Heidi I. 1979. "The Unhappy Marriage of Marxism and Feminism: Towards a More Progressive Union." *Capital and Class* 3 (2): 1–33.

Harvey, Daina Cheyenne. 2015. "Waiting in the Lower Ninth Ward in New Orleans: A Case Study of the Tempography of Hyper-marginalization." *Symbolic Interaction* 38 (4): 539–556.

Harvey, David. 2007. "Neoliberalism as Creative Destruction." *Annals of the American Academy of Political and Social Science* 610:22–44.

Hays, Sharon. 2000. "Constructing the Centrality of Culture—and Deconstructing Sociology?" *Contemporary Sociology* 29 (4): 594–602.

Heather, Barbara, Lynn Skillen, Jennifer Young, and Theresa Vladicka. 2005. "Women's Gendered Identities and the Restructuring of Rural Alberta." *Sociologia Ruralis* 45 (1–2): 86–97.

Heitmeyer, Mickey E., Timothy A. Nigh, Doreen C. Mengel, Paul. E. Blanchard, and Frank A. Nelson. 2011. "An Evaluation of Ecosystem Restoration and Management Options for Floodplains in the Lower Grand River Region, Missouri." Greenbrier Wetlands Services Report 11-01. Available at https://ecos.fws.gov/ServCat/DownloadFile/101838?Reference=61366.

Henderson, Jason, and Sean Moore. 2005. "The Impact of Wildlife Recreation on Farmland Values." Federal Reserve Bank of Kansas City Economic Research Department Research Working Paper 05-10. Available at https://www.kansascityfed.org/PUBLICAT/RESWKPAP/pdf/rwp05-10.pdf.

Henderson, Upton Bruce. 1965. "An Economic Analysis of the Waterfowl Resource of the Swan Lake National Wildlife Refuge and the Impact upon the Rural Community." Ph.D. diss., University of Missouri, Columbia.

Herda-Rapp, Ann, and Theresa L. Goedeke. 2005. *Mad about Wildlife: Looking at Social Conflict over Wildlife*. Boston: Brill.

Hernandez, Bernardo, M. Carmen Hidalgo, M. Esther Salazar-Laplace, and Stephany Hess. 2007. "Place Attachment and Place Identity in Natives and Non-natives." *Journal of Environmental Psychology* 27 (4): 310–319.

Hernandez, Leandra H. 2014. "'I Was Born This Way': The Performance and Production of Southern Masculinity in A&E's *Duck Dynasty.*" In *Reality Television: Oddities of Culture,* edited by Alison F. Slade, Amber J. Narro, and Burton P. Buchanan, 21–38. Lanham, MD: Lexington Books.

Hidalgo, M. Carmen, and Bernardo Hernandez. 2001. "Place Attachment: Conceptual and Empirical Questions." *Journal of Environmental Psychology* 21 (3): 273–281.

Hobsbawm, Eric, and Terence Ranger. 1983. *The Invention of Tradition.* New York: Cambridge University Press.

Hochschild, Arlie Russell. 2016. *Strangers in Their Own Land: Anger and Mourning on the American Right.* New York: New Press.

Hochschild, Arlie, and Anne Machung. 1989. *The Second Shift: Working Families and the Revolution at Home.* New York: Penguin Books.

Hoffman, David M. 2009. "Institutional Legitimacy and Co-management of a Marine Protected Area: Implementation Lessons from the Case of Xcalak Reefs National Park, Mexico." *Human Organization* 68 (1): 39–54.

Hoffman, Jessica. 2009. "Farm Subsidies Overwhelmingly Support White Farmers." *Colorlines,* January 29. Available at http://www.colorlines.com/articles/farm -subsidies-overwhelmingly-support-white-farmers.

Hogan, Maureen P., and Timothy Pursell. 2008. "Nostalgia and Rural Masculinity in the 'Last Frontier.'" *Men and Masculinities* 11 (1): 63–85.

Holstein, James A., and Jaber F. Gubrium. 2000. *The Self We Live By: Narrative Identity in a Postmodern World.* New York: Oxford University Press.

Hornborg, Alf. 2009. "Zero-Sum World: Challenges in Conceptualizing Environmental Load Displacement and Ecologically Unequal Exchange in the World-System." *International Journal of Comparative Sociology* 50 (3–4): 237–262.

Hubbs, Nadine. 2014. *Rednecks, Queers, and Country Music.* Berkeley: University of California Press.

Hughes, Annie. 1997. "Rurality and 'Cultures of Womanhood.'" In *Contested Countryside Cultures: Otherness, Marginalisation, and Rurality,* edited by Paul Cloke and Jo Little, 123–137. New York: Routledge.

Hughey, Matthew W. 2010. "The (Dis)Similarities of White Racial Identities: The Conceptual Framework of 'Hegemonic Whiteness.'" *Ethnic and Racial Studies* 33 (8): 1289–1309.

———. 2011. "Backstage Discourse and the Reproduction of White Masculinities." *Sociological Quarterly* 52:132–153.

———. 2012. *Whitebound: Nationalists, Antiracists, and the Shared Meanings of Race.* Stanford, CA: Stanford University Press.

Hulme, Mike. 2008. "Geographical Work at the Boundaries of Climate Change." *Transactions of the Institute of British Geographers* 33:5–11.

Igoe, Jim. 2004. *Conservation and Globalization: A Study of National Parks and Indigenous Communities from East Africa to South Dakota.* Belmont, CA: Wadsworth.

Ingalls, Micah L., and Richard C. Stedman. 2016. "The Power Problematic: Exploring the Uncertain Terrains of Political Ecology and the Resilience Framework." *Ecology and Society* 21 (1): 6.

Ingold, Tim. 2008. "Bindings against Boundaries: Entanglements of Life in an Open World." *Environment and Planning A* 40 (8): 1796–1810.

IPCC (Intergovernmental Panel on Climate Change). 2007. *Climate Change 2007: Synthesis Report; Contribution of Working Groups I, II and III to the Fourth Assessment*

Report of the Intergovernmental Panel on Climate Change. Geneva, Switzerland: IPCC.

———. 2013. *Climate Change 2013: The Physical Science Basis; Contribution of Working Group I to the Fifth Assessment Report of the Intergovernmental Panel on Climate Change.* Geneva, Switzerland: IPCC.

Irvine, Leslie. 2004. *If You Tame Me: Understanding Our Connection with Animals.* Philadelphia: Temple University Press.

Irwin, M., C. Tolbert, and T. Lyson. 1999. "There's No Place like Home: Nonmigration and Civic Engagement." *Environment and Planning A* 31:2223–2238.

Jacoby, Karl. 2001. *Crimes against Nature: Squatters, Poachers, Thieves, and the Hidden History of American Conservation.* Berkeley: University of California Press.

Jacques, Peter J., Riley E. Dunlap, and Mark Freeman. 2008. "The Organisation of Denial: Conservative Think Tanks and Environmental Scepticism." *Environmental Politics* 17 (3): 349–385.

Jang, S. Mo, and P. Sol Hart. 2015. "Polarized Frames on 'Climate Change' and 'Global Warming' across Countries and States: Evidence from Twitter Big Data." *Global Environmental Change* 32:11–17.

Jantarasami, Lesley C., Joshua J. Lawler, and Craig W. Thomas. 2010. "Institutional Barriers to Climate Change Adaptation in U.S. National Parks and Forests." *Ecology and Society* 15 (4). Available at http://www.ecologyandsociety.org/vol15/iss4/art33.

Jarosz, Lucy, and Victoria Lawson. 2002. "'Sophisticated People versus Rednecks': Economic Restructuring and Class Difference in America's West." *Antipode* 34:8–27.

Jarvis, Robert L. 1976. "Soybean Impaction in Canada Geese." *Wildlife Society Bulletin* 4 (4): 175–179.

Jasanoff, Sheila. 2010. "A New Climate for Society." *Theory, Culture and Society* 27:233–253.

Jefferies, R. L., R. F. Rockwell, and K. F. Abraham. 2003. "The Embarrassment of Riches: Agricultural Food Subsidies, High Goose Numbers, and Loss of Arctic Wetlands—a Continuing Saga." *Environmental Reviews* 11:193–232.

Jerolmack, Colin. 2007. "Animal Practices, Ethnicity and Community: The Turkish Pigeon Handlers of Berlin." *American Sociological Review* 72 (6): 874–894.

———. 2008. "How Pigeons Became Rats: The Cultural-Spatial Logic of Problem Animals." *Social Problems* 55 (1): 72–94.

———. 2013. *The Global Pigeon.* Chicago: University of Chicago Press.

Jerolmack, Colin, and Shamus Khan. 2014. "Talk Is Cheap: Ethnography and the Attitudinal Fallacy." *Sociological Methods and Research* 43 (2): 178–209.

Jerolmack, Colin, and Iddo Tavory. 2014. "Molds and Totems: Nonhumans and the Constitution of the Social Self." *Sociological Theory* 32 (1): 64–77.

Johnson, Cathryn. 1994. "Gender, Legitimate Authority, and Leader-Subordinate Conversations." *American Sociological Review* 59 (1): 122–135.

Johnston, Hank, and John A. Noakes. 2005. *Frames of Protest: Social Movements and the Framing Perspective.* Lanham, MD: Rowman and Littlefield.

Jones, Hezekiah S. 1994. "Federal Agricultural Policies: Do Black Farm Operators Benefit?" *Review of Black Political Economy* 22 (4): 25–50.

Jordan, Jennifer A. 2015. *Edible Memory: The Lure of Heirloom Tomatoes and Other Forgotten Foods.* Chicago: University of Chicago Press.

Jorgenson, Andrew K. 2006. "Global Warming and the Neglected Greenhouse Gas: A Cross-National Study of the Social Causes of Methane Emissions Intensity, 1995." *Social Forces* 84 (3): 1779–1798.

Jorgenson, Andrew K., James Rice, and Brett Clark. 2010. "Cities, Slums, and Energy Consumption in Less Developed Countries, 1990 to 2005." *Organization and Environment* 23 (2): 189–204.

Kahl, Richard B., and Fred B. Samson. 1984. "Factors Affecting Yield of Winter Wheat Grazed by Geese." *Wildlife Society Bulletin* 12 (3): 256–262.

Kaijser, Anna, and Annica Kronsell. 2014. "Climate Change through the Lens of Intersectionality." *Environmental Politics* 23 (3): 417–433.

Kaplan, Danny. 2005. "Public Intimacy: Dynamics of Seduction in Male Homosocial Interactions." *Symbolic Interaction* 28 (4): 571–595.

Katz, Cindi. 2008. "Bad Elements: Katrina and the Scoured Landscape of Social Reproduction." *Gender, Place and Culture* 15 (1): 15–29.

Kefalas, Maria. 2003. *Working-Class Heroes: Protecting Home, Community, and Nation in a Chicago Neighborhood*. Berkeley: University of California Press.

Kendrick, Anne. 2003. "Caribou Co-management in Northern Canada: Fostering Multiple Ways of Knowing." In *Navigating Social-Ecological Systems: Building Resilience for Complexity and Change*, edited by Fikret Burkes, Johan Colding, and Carl Folke, 123–137. New York: Cambridge University Press.

Kenney, Martin, Linda M. Lobao, James Curry, and W. Richard Goe. 1989. "Midwestern Agriculture in US Fordism." *Sociologia Ruralis* 29 (2): 130–148.

Khan, Shamus, and Colin Jerolmack. 2013. "Saying Meritocracy and Doing Privilege." *Sociological Quarterly* 54 (1): 9–19.

Kheel, Marti. 2008. *Nature Ethics: An Ecofeminist Perspective*. Lanham, MD: Rowman and Littlefield.

Kim, Claire Jean. 2015. *Dangerous Crossings: Race, Species, and Nature in a Multicultural Age*. New York: Cambridge University Press.

Kimmel, Michael. 2017. *Angry White Men: American Masculinity at the End of an Era*. New York: Nation Books.

Kimmel, Michael, and Abby L. Ferber. 2000. "'White Men Are This Nation': Right-Wing Militias and the Restoration of Rural American Masculinity." *Rural Sociology* 65 (4): 582–604.

Klein, Naomi. 2014. *This Changes Everything: Capitalism vs. the Climate*. New York: Simon and Schuster.

Klineberg, Stephen L., Matthew McKeever, and Bert Rothenback. 1998. "Demographic Predictors of Environmental Concern: It Does Make a Difference How It's Measured." *Social Science Quarterly* 79 (4): 734–753.

Kohn, Eduardo. 2013. *How Forests Think: Toward an Anthropology beyond the Human*. Berkeley: University of California Press.

Kojola, Erik. 2018. "Indigeneity, Gender and Class in Decision-Making about Risks from Resource Extraction." *Environmental Sociology*, January 16. Available at https://doi.org/10.1080/23251042.2018.1426090.

Kollock, Peter, Philip Blumstein, and Pepper Schwartz. 1985. "Sex and Power in Interaction: Conversational Privileges and Duties." *American Sociological Review* 50 (1): 34–46.

Konisky, David M., Jeffrey Milyo, and Lilliard E. Richardson Jr. 2008. "Environmental Policy Attitudes: Issues, Geographical Scale, and Political Trust." *Social Science Quarterly* 89 (5): 1066–1085.

Kosek, Jake. 2006. *Understories: The Political Life of Forests in Northern New Mexico*. Durham, NC: Duke University Press.

Krauss, Celene. 1993. "Women and Toxic Waste Protests: Race, Class and Gender as Resources of Resistance." *Qualitative Sociology* 16 (3): 247–262.

Krogman, Naomi T. 1996. "Frame Disputes in Environmental Controversies: The Case of Wetland Regulations in Louisiana." *Sociological Spectrum* 16 (4): 371–400.

Krumm, Kenneth. 1938. *Development Plan for the Swan Lake Migratory Waterfowl Refuge*. Sumner, MO: U.S. Bureau of Biological Survey.

———. 1939. *Annual Report: Swan Lake Migratory Waterfowl Refuge, July 1, 1938–June 30, 1939*. Sumner, MO: U.S. Bureau of Biological Survey.

———. 1940. *Annual Report: Swan Lake Migratory Waterfowl Refuge, July 1, 1939–June 30, 1940*. Sumner, MO: U.S. Fish and Wildlife Service.

———. 1941. *Annual Report: Swan Lake National Wildlife Refuge, July 1, 1940–June 30, 1941*. Sumner, MO: U.S. Fish and Wildlife Service.

———. 1942. *Annual Report: Swan Lake National Wildlife Refuge, July 1, 1941–June 30, 1942*. Sumner, MO: U.S. Fish and Wildlife Service.

Kruse, Jack, Dave Klein, Steve Braund, Lisa Moorehead, and Bill Simeone. 1998. "Co-management of Natural Resources: A Comparison of Two Caribou Management Systems." *Human Organization* 57 (4): 447–458.

Kuletz, Valerie L. 1998. *The Tainted Desert: Environmental Ruin in the American West.* New York: Routledge.

LaDuke, Winona. 1999. *All Our Relations: Native Struggles for Land and Life.* Cambridge, MA: South End Press.

Lamont, Michelle. 2000. *The Dignity of Working Men: Morality and Boundaries of Race, Class, and Immigration.* Cambridge, MA: Harvard University Press.

Lapegna, Pablo. 2016. *Soybeans and Power: Genetically Modified Crops, Environmental Politics, and Social Movements in Argentina.* New York: Oxford University Press.

Larkins, Michelle L. 2018. "Complicating Communities: An Intersectional Approach to Women's Environmental Justice Narratives in the Rocky Mountain West." *Environmental Sociology* 4 (1): 67–78.

Latour, Bruno. 1993. *We Have Never Been Modern.* Translated by Catherine Porter. Cambridge, MA: Harvard University Press.

———. 2005. *Reassembling the Social: An Introduction to Actor-Network Theory.* New York: Oxford University Press.

Lauer, Sean R. 2005. "Entrepreneurial Processes in an Emergent Resource Industry: Community Embeddedness in Main's Sea Urchin Industry." *Rural Sociology* 70 (2): 145–166.

Leap, Braden. 2014. "Collective Troubles: Transforming Neoliberalism through Interactions with Nonhumans." *Geoforum* 56:182–191.

———. 2015. "Redefining the Refuge: Symbolic Interactionism and the Emergent Meanings of Environmentally Variable Spaces." *Symbolic Interaction* 38 (4): 521–538.

———. 2017. "Survival Narratives: Constructing an Intersectional Masculinity through Stories of the Rural/Urban Divide." *Journal of Rural Studies* 55:12–21.

———. 2018a. "Not a Zero-Sum Game: Inequalities and Resilience in Sumner, Missouri, the Gooseless Goose Capital of the World." *Gender, Place and Culture* 25 (2): 288–308.

———. 2018b. "Seasonal Masculinities: The Seasonal Contingencies of Doing Gender." *Men and Masculinities*, February 12. Available at http://journals.sagepub.com/doi/abs/10.1177/1097184X18756710.

Leonard, Sonia, Meg Parsons, Knut Olawsky, and Frances Kofod. 2013. "The Role of Culture and Traditional Knowledge in Climate Change Adaptation: Insights from East Kimberley, Australia." *Global Environmental Change* 23:623–632.

Lewandowsky, Stephan, Naomi Oreskes, James S. Risbey, Ben R. Newell, and Michael Smithson. 2015. "Seepage: Climate Change Denial and Its Effect on the Scientific Community." *Global Environmental Change* 33:1–13.

Lewin, Philip G. 2017. "'Coal Is Not Just a Job, It's a Way of Life': The Cultural Politics of Coal Production in Central Appalachia." *Social Problems*, October 19. Available at https://doi.org/10.1093/socpro/spx030.

Lewis, Amanda E. 2004. "'What Group?' Studying Whites and Whiteness in the Era of 'Color-Blindness.'" *Sociological Theory* 22 (4): 623–646.

Liddle, Brantley. 2015. "What Are the Carbon Emissions for Income and Population? Bridging STIRPAT and EKC via Robust Heterogeneous Panel Estimates." *Global Environmental Change* 31:62–73.

Lipsitz, George. 1998. *The Possessive Investment in Whiteness: How White People Profit from Identity Politics*. Philadelphia: Temple University Press.

———. 2007. "The Racialization of Space and the Spatialization of Race: Theorizing the Hidden Architecture of Landscape." *Landscape Journal* 26 (1): 10–23.

Little, Jo. 1997a. "Constructions of Rural Women's Voluntary Work." *Gender, Place and Culture* 4 (2): 197–210.

———. 1997b. "Employment Marginality and Women's Self-Identity." In *Contested Countryside Cultures: Otherness, Marginalisation, and Rurality*, edited by Paul Cloke and Jo Little, 138–157. New York: Routledge.

———. 2002. "Rural Geography: Rural Gender Identity and the Performance of Masculinity and Femininity in the Countryside." *Progress in Human Geography* 26 (5): 665–670.

———. 2003. "'Riding the Rural Love Train': Heterosexuality and the Rural Community." *Sociologia Ruralis* 43 (4): 401–417.

Little, Jo, and Patricia Austin. 1996. "Women and the Rural Idyll." *Journal of Rural Studies* 12 (2): 101–111.

Lobao, Linda, and Katherine Meyer. 2001. "The Agricultural Transition: Crisis, Change, and Social Consequences of the Twentieth Century US Farming." *Annual Review of Sociology* 27:103–124.

Lobao, Linda, and Curtis W. Stofferahn. 2008. "The Community Effects of Industrialized Farming: Social Science Research and Challenges to Corporate Farming Laws." *Agriculture and Human Values* 25 (2): 219–240.

Lobell, David B., Wolfram Schlenker, and Justin Costa-Roberts. 2011. "Climate Trends and Global Crop Production since 1980." *Science* 333:616–620.

Loperena, Christopher Anthony. 2016. "Conservation by Racialized Dispossession: The Making of an Eco-Destination on Honduras's North Coast." *Geoforum* 69:184–193.

Lorenzoni, Irene, and Nick F. Pidgeon. 2006. "Public Views on Climate Change: European and USA Perspectives." *Climatic Change* 77:73–95.

Lorimer, Jamie. 2015. *Wildlife in the Anthropocene: Conservation after Nature*. Minneapolis: University of Minnesota Press.

Low, Bobbi, Elinor Ostrom, Carl Simon, and James Wilson. 2003. "Redundancy and Diversity: Do They Influence Optimal Management?" In *Navigating Social-Ecological Systems*, edited by Fikret Berkes, Johan Colding, and Carl Folke, 83–114. New York: Cambridge University Press.

Low, Setha M. 2000. *On the Plaza: The Politics of Public Space and Culture*. Austin: University of Texas Press.

Luke, Brian. 2004. "Animal Sacrifice: A Model of Paternal Exploitation." *International Journal of Sociology and Social Policy* 24 (9): 18–44.

Lynch, Michael. 2009. "Ethnomethodology and History: Documents and the Production of History." *Ethnographic Studies* 11:87–106.

Lynd, Robert S., and Helen Merrell Lynd. 1929. *Middletown*. New York: Harcourt Brace and World.

Lyson, Thomas A., Robert J. Torres, and Rick Welsh. 2001. "Scale of Agricultural Production, Civic Engagement, and Community Welfare." *Social Forces* 80 (1): 311–327.

Macgregor, Lyn C. 2010. *Habits of the Heartland: Small-Town Life in Modern America*. Ithaca, NY: Cornell University Press.

MacKinnon, Danny, and Kate Driscoll Derickson. 2012. "From Resilience to Resourcefulness: A Critique of Resilience Policy and Activism." *Progress in Human Geography* 37 (2): 253–270.

Manke, Alfred O. 1976. "Maxie: Bi-centennial Project of Sumner, Mo." Marceline, MO: Walsworth.

Manuel-Navarrete, David, Mark Pelling, and Michael Redclift. 2011. "Critical Adaptation to Hurricanes in the Mexican Caribbean: Development Visions, Governance Structure, and Coping Strategies." *Global Environmental Change* 21:249–258.

Manzo, Lynne C., and Patrick Devine-Wright. 2014. *Place Attachment: Advances in Theory, Methods and Applications*. New York: Routledge.

Marks, Stuart A. 1991. *Southern Hunting in Black and White: Nature, History, and Ritual in a Carolina Community*. Princeton, NJ: Princeton University Press.

Marquart-Pyatt, Sandra T., Aaron M. McCright, Thomas Dietz, and Riley E. Dunlap. 2014. "Politics Eclipses Climate Extremes for Climate Change Perceptions." *Global Environmental Change* 29:246–247.

Marshall, Brent K. 2004. "Gender, Race, and Perceived Environmental Risk: The 'White Male' Effect in Cancer Alley, LA." *Sociological Spectrum* 24:453–478.

Marshall, N. A., S. E. Park, W. N. Adger, K. Brown, and S. M. Howden. 2012. "Transformational Capacity and the Influence of Place and Identity." *Environmental Research Letters* 7:1–9.

Martyris, Nina. 2015. "How Suffragists Used Cookbooks as a Recipe for Subversion." *National Public Radio*, November 5. Available at http://www.npr.org/sections/thesalt/2015/11/05/454246666/how-suffragists-used-cookbooks-as-a-recipe-for-subversion.

Marx, Karl. 1983. "The Communist Manifesto." In *The Portable Karl Marx*, translated by Eugene Kamenka, 203–241. New York: Penguin Books.

McCall, Leslie. 2005. "The Complexity of Intersectionality." *Signs* 30 (3): 1771–1800.

McCarthy, James, and Scott Prudham. 2004. "Neoliberal Nature and the Nature of Neoliberalism." *Geoforum* 35 (3): 275–283.

McCright, Aaron M., and Riley E. Dunlap. 2011a. "Cool Dudes: The Denial of Climate Change among Conservative White Males in the United States." *Global Environmental Change* 21:1163–1172.

———. 2011b. "The Politicization of Climate Change and Polarization in the American Public's Views of Global Warming, 2001–2010." *Sociological Quarterly* 52:155–194.

McCright, Aaron M., Riley E. Dunlap, and Chenyang Xiao. 2013. "Perceived Scientific Agreement and Support for Government Action on Climate Change in the USA." *Climatic Change* 119:511–518.

McDonnell, Terence E. 2010. "Cultural Objects as Objects: Materiality, Urban Space, and the Interpretation of AIDS Campaigns in Accra, Ghana." *American Journal of Sociology* 115 (6): 1800–1852.

McDougle, Harold C., and Richard W. Vaught. 1968. "An Epizootic of Aspergillosis in Canada Geese." *Journal of Wildlife Management* 32 (2): 415–417.

McLaughlin, Diane K. 2002. "Changing Income Inequality in Nonmetropolitan Counties, 1980 to 1990." *Rural Sociology* 67 (4): 512–533.

McLaughlin, Paul. 2011. "Climate Change, Adaptation, and Vulnerability: Reconceptualizing Societal-Environment Interaction within a Socially Constructed Adaptive Landscape." *Organization and Environment* 24 (3): 269–291.

McNeeley, Shannon M. 2012. "Examining Barriers and Opportunities for Sustainable Adaptation to Climate Change in Interior Alaska." *Climatic Change* 111:835–857.

Mead, George Herbert. 1934. *Mind, Self, and Society: From the Standpoint of a Social Behaviorist*, edited by Charles W. Morris. Chicago: University of Chicago Press.

Melillo, Jerry M., Terese Richmond, and Gary W. Yohe, eds. 2014. *Climate Change Impacts in the United States: The Third National Climate Assessment*. Washington, DC: Government Printing Office.

Messer, Chris M., Thomas E. Shriver, and Alison E. Adams. 2015. "Collective Identity and Memory: A Comparative Analysis of Community Response to Environmental Hazards." *Rural Sociology* 80 (3): 314–339.

Messner, Michael. 1992. *Power at Play: Sports and the Problem of Masculinity*. Boston: Beacon.

Meyer, John W., and Brian Rowan. 1977. "Institutionalized Organizations: Formal Structure as Myth and Ceremony." *American Journal of Sociology* 83 (2): 340–363.

Midgley, Jane. 2006. "Gendered Economies: Transferring Private Gender Roles into the Public Realm through Rural Community Development." *Journal of Rural Studies* 22 (2): 217–231.

Mills, C. Wright. 1959. *The Sociological Imagination*. New York: Oxford University Press.

Milroy, Beth Moore, and Susan Wismer. 1994. "Communities, Work and Public/Private Sphere Models." *Gender, Place and Culture* 1 (1): 71–90.

Mintz, Sidney. 1986. *Sweetness and Power: The Place of Sugar in Modern History*. New York: Penguin.

Mishra, Sasmita, Sanjoy Mazumdar, and Damodar Suar. 2010. "Place Attachment and Flood Preparedness." *Journal of Environmental Psychology* 30 (2): 187–197.

Missouri Census Data Center. 2014. "Missouri Population, 1900–1990 (All Incorporated Places)." Available at http://mcdc.missouri.edu/trends/historical/cities1900-1990.pdf.

Missouri Department of Labor and Industrial Relations. n.d. "Unemployment Benefits by County." Available at http://apps.labor.mo.gov/des/tool/ui_ben_stats.asp?Submit=Yes (accessed December 9, 2015).

Mizelle, Richard M. 2014. *Backwater Blues: The Mississippi Flood of 1927 in the African American Imagination*. Minneapolis: University of Minnesota Press.

Mohanty, Chandra Talpade. 1988. "Under Western Eyes: Feminist Scholarship and Colonial Discourses." *Feminist Review* 30:61–88.

———. 2003. *Feminism without Borders: Decolonizing Theory, Practicing Solidarity*. Durham, NC: Duke University Press.

Moore, Lisa Jean, and Mary Kosut. 2013. *Buzz: Urban Beekeeping and the Power of the Bee.* New York: New York University Press.

Morris, Edward W. 2007. "'Ladies' or 'Loudies'? Perceptions and Experiences of Black Girls in Classrooms." *Youth and Society* 38 (4): 490–515.

———. 2008. "'Rednecks,' 'Rutters,' and 'Rithmetic: Social Class, Masculinity, and Schooling in a Rural Context." *Gender and Society* 22 (6): 728–751.

Mueller, Jennifer C. 2017. "Producing Colorblindness: Everyday Mechanisms of White Ignorance." *Social Problems* 64:219–238.

Mulligan, Martin John. 2014. "Towards a More Grounded and Dynamic Sociology of Climate-Change Adaptation." *Environmental Values* 23:165–180.

Munster, Daniel, and Ursula Munster. 2012. "Consuming the Forest in an Environment of Crisis: Nature Tourism, Forest Conservation and Neoliberal Agriculture in South India." *Development and Change* 43 (1): 205–227.

Murdoch, Jonathan, and Andy C. Pratt. 1993. "Rural Studies: Modernism, Postmodernism and the 'Post-rural.'" *Journal of Rural Studies* 9 (4): 411–427.

Nading, Alex M. 2014. *Mosquito Trails: Ecology, Health, and the Politics of Entanglement.* Berkeley: University of California Press.

Naples, Nancy A., ed. 1998a. *Community Activism and Feminist Politics: Organizing across Race, Class, and Gender.* New York: Routledge.

———, ed. 1998b. *Grassroots Warriors: Activist Mothering, Community Work, and the War on Poverty.* New York: Routledge.

Nash, Roderick Frazier. 1967. *Wilderness and the American Mind.* New Haven, CT: Yale University Press.

Nass, Roger D. 1964. "Sex- and Age-Ration Bias of Cannon-Netted Geese." *Journal of Wildlife Management* 28 (3): 522–527.

National Black Farmers Association and Environmental Working Group. 2007. "Short Crop: How a Widening Farm Subsidy Gap Is Leaving Black Farmers Further Behind." July 25. Available at http://static.ewg.org/pdf/ShortCrop.pdf.

Nelson, Donald R., Colin Thor West, and Timothy J. Finan. 2009. "Introduction to 'In Focus: Global Change and Adaptation in Local Places.'" *American Anthropologist* 111 (3): 271–274.

Neo, Harvey. 2012. "'They Hate Pigs, Chinese Farmers . . . Everything!' Beastly Racialization in Multiethnic Malaysia." *Antipode* 44 (3): 950–970.

Neumann, Roderick P. 1998. *Imposing Wilderness: Struggles over Livelihood and Nature Preservation in Africa.* Berkeley: University of California Press.

Nielsen, Jonas Ostergaard, and Anette Reenberg. 2010. "Cultural Barriers to Climate Change Adaptation: A Case Study from Northern Burkina Faso." *Global Environmental Change* 20:142–152.

NOAA (National Oceanic and Atmospheric Administration). 2018. "Climate at a Glance: Statewide Time Series." Available at https://www.ncdc.noaa.gov/cag.

Norgaard, Kari Marie. 2011. *Living in Denial: Climate Change, Emotions, and Everyday Life.* Cambridge, MA: MIT Press.

Ogden, Laura A. 2011. *Swamplife: People, Gators, and Mangroves Entangled in the Everglades.* Minneapolis: University of Minnesota Press.

Oliver, Melvin L., and Thomas M. Shapiro. 2006. *Black Wealth/White Wealth: A New Perspective on Racial Inequality.* New York: Routledge.

Omi, Michael, and Howard Winant. 1994. *Racial Formation in the United States.* New York: Routledge.

Oreskes, Naomi, and Erik M. Conway. 2011. *Merchants of Doubt: How a Handful of Scientists Obscured the Truth on Issues from Tobacco Smoke to Global Warming.* New York: Bloomsbury Press.

Ostrom, Elinor. 1992. "Community and the Endogenous Solutions of Commons Problems." *Journal of Theoretical Politics* 4 (3): 343–351.

Outka, Paul. 2008. *Race and Nature: From Transcendentalism to the Harlem Renaissance.* New York: Palgrave Macmillan.

Park, Lisa Sun-Hee, and David Naguib Pellow. 2011. *Slums of Aspen: Immigrants versus the Environment in America's Eden.* New York: New York University Press.

Park, S. E., N. A. Marshall, E. Jakku, A. M. Down, S. M. Howden, E. Mendham, and A. Fleming. 2012. "Informing Adaptation Responses to Climate Change through Theories of Transformation." *Global Environmental Change* 22:115–126.

Parmesan, Camille, and Gary Yohe. 2003. "A Globally Coherent Fingerprint of Climate Change Impacts across Natural Systems." *Nature* 42 (1): 37–42.

Pascoe, C. J. 2007. *Dude, You're a Fag: Masculinity and Sexuality in High School.* Berkeley: University of California Press.

Peck, Jamie, and Adam Tickell. 2002. "Neoliberalizing Space." *Antipode* 34 (3): 380–404.

Peluso, Nancy. 1993. "Coercing Conservation? The Politics of State Resource Control." *Global Environmental Change* 3 (2): 199–217.

Perez, C., E. M. Jones, P. Kristjanson, L. Cramer, P. K. Thornton, W. Forch, and C. Barahona. 2015. "How Resilient Are Farming Households and Community to a Changing Climate in Africa? A Gender-Based Perspective." *Global Environmental Change* 34:95–107.

Perkins, Tracy E. 2012. "Women's Pathways into Activism: Rethinking the Women's Environmental Justice Narrative in California's San Joaquin Valley." *Organization and Environment* 25 (1): 76–94.

Peter, Gregory, Michael Mayerfeld Bell, Susan Jarnagin, and Donna Bauer. 2000. "Coming Back across the Fence: Masculinity and the Transition to Sustainable Agriculture." *Rural Sociology* 65 (2): 215–233.

Petheram, L., K. K. Zander, B. M. Campbell, C. High, and N. Stacey. 2010. "'Strong Changes': Indigenous Perspectives of Climate Change and Adaptation in NE Arnhem Land (Australia)." *Global Environmental Change* 20:681–692.

Pickering, Andrew. 2005. "Asian Eels and Global Warming: Posthumanist Perspective on Society and the Environment." *Ethics and the Environment* 12 (2): 29–43.

Pidgeon, Nick. 2012. "Public Understanding of, and Attitudes to, Climate Change: UK and International Perspectives and Policy." *Climate Policy* 12:85–106.

Pigford v. Glickman. 1999. 185 F.R.D. 82.

Pini, Barbara. 2004. "Gender and Farming in the Information Economy." *Australian Journal of Communication* 31 (2): 135–148.

Plumwood, Val. 1993. *Feminism and the Master of Nature.* New York: Routledge.

Polanyi, Karl. 1944. *The Great Transformation: The Political and Economic Origins of Our Time.* Boston: Beacon Press.

Pope, C. Arden, III, Clark E. Adams, and John K. Thomas. 1984. "The Recreational and Aesthetic Value of Wildlife in Texas." *Journal of Leisure Research* 16 (1): 51–60.

Powell, Walter W., and Paul J. DiMaggio. 1991. *The New Institutionalism in Organizational Analysis.* Chicago: University of Chicago Press.

Pretty, Jules. 2003. "Social Capital and the Collective Management of Resources." *Science* 302:1912–1914.

Pretty, Jules, and Hugh Ward. 2001. "Social Capital and the Environment." *World Development* 29 (2): 209–227.

Prew, Paul. 2010. "World-Economy Centrality and Carbon Dioxide Emissions: A New Look at the Position in the Capitalist World-System and Environmental Pollution." *Journal of World-Systems Research* 16 (2): 162–191.

Price, Anne M., and Lindsey Peterson. 2016. "Scientific Progress, Risk, and Development: Explaining Attitudes toward Science Cross-nationally." *International Sociology* 31 (1): 57–80.

Price, Linda, and Nick Evans. 2006. "From 'as Good as Gold' to 'Gold Diggers': Farming Women and the Survival of British Family Farming." *Sociologia Ruralis* 46 (4): 280–298.

Pronger, Brian. 1990. *The Arena of Masculinity: Sports, Homosexuality, and the Meaning of Sex*. New York: St. Martin's.

Prudham, Scott. 2004. "Poisoning the Well: Neoliberalism and the Contamination of Municipal Water in Walkerton, Ontario." *Geoforum* 35 (3): 343–359.

Pryor, Sara C., Donald Scavia, Charles Downer, Marc Gaden, Louis Iverson, Rolf Nordstrom, Jonathan Patz, and G. Phillip Robertson. 2014. "Midwest." In *Climate Change Impacts in the United States: The Third National Climate Assessment*, edited by J. M. Melillo, Terese Richmond, and G. W. Yohe, 418–440. Available at http://nca2014.globalchange.gov/report/regions/midwest.

Pugh, Allison J. 2009. *Longing and Belonging: Parents, Children, and Consumer Culture*. Berkeley: University of California Press.

Raedeke, Andrew, David Andersen, Dale Caswell, Steve Cordts, Murray Gillespie, Jim Leafloor, Steve Maxson, Luke Naylor, Steve Wilds, and Guy Zenner. 2006. "A Management Plan for the Eastern Prairie Population of Canada Geese: 2006 Update." Report prepared by the Mississippi Flyway Council Technical Section, EPP Canada Goose Committee. In the author's possession.

Raleigh, Clionadh, Hyun Jin Choi, and Dominic Kniveton. 2015. "The Devil Is in the Details: An Investigation of the Relationships between Conflict, Food Price, and Climate across Africa." *Global Environmental Change* 32:187–199.

Rawls, Anne Warfield. 1987. "The Interaction Order Sui Generis: Goffman's Contribution to Social Theory." *Sociological Theory* 5 (2): 136–149.

Rebotier, Julien. 2012. "Vulnerability Conditions and Risk Representations in Latin-America: Framing the Territorializing Urban Risk." *Global Environmental Change* 22:391–398.

Ribot, Jesse C., and Nancy Lee Peluso. 2003. "A Theory of Access." *Rural Sociology* 68 (2): 153–181.

Risman, Barbara J. 2009. "From Doing to Undoing: Gender as We Known It." *Gender and Society* 23 (1): 81–84.

Robbins, Paul. 2007. *Lawn People: How Grasses, Weeds, and Chemicals Make Us Who We Are*. Philadelphia: Temple University Press.

Robertson, Morgan M. 2004. "The Neoliberalization of Ecosystem Services: Wetland Mitigation Banking and Problems in Environmental Governance." *Geoforum* 35:361–373.

Robinson, Dawn T., and Lynn Smith-Lovin. 2001. "Getting a Laugh: Gender, Status, and Humor in Task Discussions." *Social Forces* 80 (1): 123–158.

Robinson, L. M., D. C. Gledhill, N. A. Moltschaniwskyj, A. J. Hobday, S. Frusher, N. Barrett, J. Stuart-Smith, and G. T. Pecl. 2015. "Rapid Assessment of an Ocean

Warming Hotspot Reveals 'High' Confidence in Potential Species' Range Extensions." *Global Environmental Change* 31:28–37.

Rose, Gillian. 1993. *Feminism and Geography: The Limits of Geographical Knowledge*. Minneapolis: University of Minnesota Press.

Rubin, Herbert J., and Irene S. Rubin. 2012. *Qualitative Interviewing: The Art of Hearing Data*. 3rd ed. Thousand Oaks, CA: Sage.

Russell, Robert F. 1952. *Annual Report: Swan Lake National Wildlife Refuge, September 1, 1951–December 31, 1951*. Sumner, MO: U.S. Fish and Wildlife Service.

———. 1953. *Annual Report: Swan Lake National Wildlife Refuge, September 1, 1952–December 31, 1952*. Sumner, MO: U.S. Fish and Wildlife Service.

———. 1955. *Annual Report: Swan Lake National Wildlife Refuge, September 1, 1954–December 31, 1954*. Sumner, MO: U.S. Fish and Wildlife Service.

———. 1956. *Annual Report: Swan Lake National Wildlife Refuge, September 1, 1955–December 31, 1955*. Sumner, MO: U.S. Fish and Wildlife Service.

Rutherford, Stephanie. 2011. *Governing the Wild: Ecotours of Power*. Minneapolis: University of Minnesota Press.

Sacks, Harvey, Emanuel A. Schegloff, and Gail Jefferson. 1974. "A Simplest Systematics for the Organization of Turn-Taking for Conversation." *Language* 50 (4): 696–735.

Sacks, William J., and Christopher J. Kucharik. 2011. "Crop Management and the Phenology Trends in the U.S. Corn Belt: Impacts on Yields, Evapotranspiration and Energy Balance." *Agricultural and Forest Meteorology* 151 (7): 882–894.

Said, Edward W. 1978. *Orientalism*. New York: Vintage Books.

Sakurai, Ryo, Susan K. Jacobson, Hiromi Kobori, Richard Primack, Kohei Oka, Naoya Komatsu, and Ryo Machida. 2011. "Culture and Climate Change: Japanese Cherry Blossom Festivals and Stakeholders' Knowledge and Attitudes about Global Climate Change." *Biological Conservation* 144:654–658.

Samenow, Jason. 2016. "America's Year without a Winter: The 2015–2016 Season Was the Warmest on Record." *Washington Post*, March 8. Available at https://www .washingtonpost.com/news/capital-weather-gang/wp/2016/03/08/americas-year -without-a-winter-the-2015-2016-season-was-the-warmest-on-record.

Sanders, Clinton R. 2003. "Actions Speak Louder than Words: Close Relationships between Humans and Nonhuman Animals." *Symbolic Interaction* 26 (3): 405–426.

Santiago, Anna Maria. 2015. "Fifty Years Later: From the War on Poverty to a War on the Poor." *Social Problems* 62:2–14.

Schegloff, Emanuel A. 1988. "Goffman and the Analysis of Conversation." In *Erving Goffman: Exploring the Interaction Order*, edited by Paul Drew and Anthony Wootton, 89–135. Oxford: Polity Press.

———. 1992. "Repair after Next Turn: The Last Structurally Provided Defense of Intersubjectivity in Conversation." *American Journal of Sociology* 97 (5): 1295–1345.

Schnaiberg, Allan. 1980. *The Environment: From Surplus to Scarcity*. New York: Oxford University Press.

Schneider, Susan A. 2013. "Discrimination at USDA: Response to New York Times." *Agricultural Law*, May 1. Available at http://aglaw.blogspot.com/2013/05/ discrimination-at-usda-response-to-new.html.

Schwartz, Katrina Z. S. 2013. "Panther Politics: Neoliberalizing Nature in Southwest Florida." *Environment and Planning A* 45 (10): 2324–2343.

Scott, James C., 1998. *Seeing like a State: How Certain Schemes to Improve the Human Condition Have Failed.* New Haven, CT: Yale University Press.

Scott, Rebecca. 2010. *Removing Mountains: Extracting Nature and Identity in the Appalachia Coalfields.* Minneapolis: University of Minnesota Press.

———. 2017. "Love." In *Veer Ecology: A Companion for Environmental Thinking,* edited by Jeffrey Jerome Cohen and Lowell Duckert, 377–391. Minneapolis: University of Minnesota Press.

Seek, George. 1980. *Report of Operations: Swan Lake Wildlife Management Area.* Sumner, MO: Missouri Department of Conservation.

Selfa, Theresa, Albert Iaroi, and Morey Burnham. 2015. "Promoting Ethanol in Rural Kansas: Local Framing and Cultural Politics." *Journal of Rural Studies* 39:63–73.

Shandra, John M., Bruce London, Owen P. Whooley, and John B. Williamson. 2004. "International Nongovernmental Organizations and Carbon Dioxide Emissions in the Developing World: A Quantitative, Cross-national Analysis." *Sociological Inquiry* 74 (4): 520–545.

Sheaffer, Susan E., Donald H. Rusch, Dale D. Humburg, Jeffery S. Lawrence, Guy G. Zenner, Murray M. Gillespie, F. Dale Caswell, Steve Wilds, and Scott C. Yaich. 2004. "Survival, Movements, and Harvest of Eastern Prairie Population Canada Geese." *Wildlife Monographs* 156:1–54.

Sherman, Jennifer. 2009. *Those Who Work, Those Who Don't: Poverty, Morality, and Family in Rural America.* Minneapolis: University of Minnesota Press.

Shiva, Vandana. 1997. *Biopiracy: The Plunder of Nature and Knowledge.* New York: South End Press.

Shortall, Sally. 2002. "Gendered Agricultural and Rural Restructuring: A Case Study of Northern Ireland." *Sociologia Ruralis* 42 (2): 160–175.

Shriver, Thomas E., Sherry Cable, Lachelle Norris, and Donald W. Hastings. 2000. "The Role of Collective Identity in Inhibiting Mobilization: Solidarity and Suppression in Oak Ridge." *Sociological Spectrum* 20 (1): 41–64.

Shriver, Thomas E., and Charles Peaden. 2009. "Frame Disputes in a Natural Resource Controversy: The Case of the Arbuckle Simpson Aquifer in South-Central Oklahoma." *Society and Natural Resources* 22:143–157.

Shwom, Rachel L, Aaron M. McCright, Steven R. Brechin, Riley E. Dunlap, Sandra T. Marquart-Pyatt, and Lawrence C. Hamilton. 2015. "Public Opinion on Climate Change." In *Climate Change and Society: Sociological Perspective,* edited by Riley E. Dunlap and Robert J. Brulle, 269–299. New York: Oxford University Press.

Silva, Tony. 2017. "Bud-Sex: Constructing Normative Masculinity among Rural Straight Men That Have Sex with Men." *Gender and Society* 31 (1): 51–73.

Simmel, Georg. 1957. "The Metropolis and Mental Life." In *Cities and Society,* edited by P. K. Hatt and A. J. Reiss Jr., 635–646. New York: Free Press.

Singleton, Sara, and Michael Taylor. 1992. "Common Property, Collective Action and Community." *Journal of Theoretical Politics* 4 (3): 309–324.

Slater, Candace. 2002. *Entangled Edens: Visions of the Amazon.* Berkeley: University of California Press.

Smit, Barry, and Johanna Wandel. 2006. "Adaptation, Adaptive Capacity and Vulnerability." *Global Environmental Change* 16:282–292.

Smith, Dorothy E. 2005. *Institutional Ethnography: A Sociology for People.* New York: Altamira Press.

Smith, Ronald W., and Valerie Bugni. 2006. "Symbolic Interaction Theory and Architecture." *Symbolic Interaction* 29 (2): 123–155.

Smithers, John, and Barry Smit. 1997. "Human Adaptation to Climate Variability and Change." *Global Environmental Change* 7 (2): 129–146.

Snorek, Julie, Fabrice G. Renaud, and Julia Kloos. 2014. "Divergent Adaptation to Climate Variability: A Case Study of Pastoral and Agricultural Societies in Niger." *Global Environmental Change* 29:371–386.

Snow, David A., and Robert D. Benford. 1988. "Ideology, Frame Resonance, and Participant Mobilization." In *From Structure to Action: Comparing Social Movement Research*, edited by Bert Klandermans, Hanspeter Kriesi, and Sidney Tarrow, 197–217. Greenwich, CT: JAI Press.

———. 1992. "Master Frames and Cycles of Protest." In *Frontiers in Social Movement Theory*, edited by Aldon D. Morris and Carl McClurg Mueller, 135–155. New Haven, CT: Yale University Press.

Sobel, Russell S., and Peter L. Leeson. 2006. "Government's Response to Hurricane Katrina: A Public Choice Analysis." *Public Choice* 127:55–73.

Somers, Margaret. 2008. *Genealogies of Citizenship: Markets, Statelessness, and the Right to Have Rights*. Cambridge: Cambridge University Press.

Spence, A., W. Poortinga, C. Butler, and N. F. Pidgeon. 2011. "Perceptions of Climate Change and Willingness to Save Energy Related to Flood Experience." *Nature Climate Change* 1:46–49.

Spence, Mark David. 1999. *Dispossessing the Wilderness: Indian Removal and the Making of the National Parks*. New York: Oxford University Press.

Stange, Mary Zeiss. 1997. *Woman the Hunter*. Boston: Beacon Press.

Stedman, Richard C. 2003. "Is It Really Just a Social Construction? The Contribution of the Physical Environment to Sense of Place." *Society and Natural Resources* 16:671–685.

Stevens, Stan. 1997. *Conservation through Cultural Survival: Indigenous Peoples and Protected Areas*. Washington, DC: Island Press.

Stuart, Diana, Rebecca L. Schewe, and Ryan Gunderson. 2013. "Extending Social Theory to Farm Animals: Addressing Alienation in the Dairy Sector." *Sociologia Ruralis* 53 (2): 201–222.

Sugden, Fraser, Niki Maskey, Floraine Clement, Vidya Ramesh, Anil Phillip, and Ashok Rai. 2014. "Agrarian Stress and Climate Change in the Eastern Gangetic Plains: Gendered Vulnerability in a Stratified Social Formation." *Global Environmental Change* 29:258–269.

Swidler, Ann. 1986. "Culture in Action: Symbols and Strategies." *American Sociological Review* 51 (2): 273–286.

Taussig, Michael. 1987. *Shamanism, Colonialism, and the Wild Man: A Study in Terror and Healing*. Chicago: University of Chicago Press.

Tavory, Iddo, and Nina Eliasoph. 2013. "Coordinating Futures: Toward a Theory of Anticipation." *American Journal of Sociology* 118 (4): 908–942.

Taylor, Dorceta E. 2016. *The Rise of the American Conservation Movement: Power, Privilege, and Environmental Protection*. Durham, NC: Duke University Press.

Theophano, Janet. 2002. *Eat My Words: Reading Women's Lives through the Cookbooks They Wrote*. New York: Palgrave Macmillan.

Thody, Louise. 2014. "From Working Class to Hipster Flash: Locating Newcastle City in Newcastle Brown Ale." *Visual Culture in Britain* 15 (2): 173–191.

Thomas, David S. G., and Chasca Twyman. 2005. "Equity and Justice in Climate Change Adaptation amongst Natural-Resource-Dependent Societies." *Global Environmental Change* 15:115–124.

Thompson, Diego. 2016. "Community Adaptations to Environmental Challenges under Decentralized Governance in Southwestern Uruguay." *Journal of Rural Studies* 43:71–83.

Thompson, E. P. 1966. *The Making of the English Working Class.* New York: Vintage Books.

———. 2013. *Whigs and Hunters: The Origin of the Black Act.* London: Breviary Stuff.

Thorn, Jessica, Thomas F. Thornton, and Ariella Helfgott. 2015. "Autonomous Adaptation to Global Environmental Change in Peri-urban Settlements: Evidence of a Growing Culture of Innovation and Revitalization in Mathare Valley Slums, Nairobi." *Global Environmental Change* 31:121–131.

Thornsberry, William H. 1969. "A Compound Leverage Banding Pliers." *Bird-Banding* 40 (2): 130–132.

Tierney, Kathleen. 2014. *The Social Roots of Risk: Producing Disasters, Promoting Resilience.* Stanford, CA: Stanford University Press.

Tipton-Martin, Toni. 2015. *The Jemima Code: Two Centuries of African American Cookbooks.* Austin: University of Texas Press.

Tolbert, Charles M., Thomas A. Lyson, and Michael D. Irwin. 1998. "Local Capitalism, Civic Engagement, and Socioeconomic Well-Being." *Social Forces* 77 (2): 401–427.

Tompkins, Emma L., and W. Neil Adger. 2004. "Does Adaptive Management of National Resources Enhance Resilience to Climate Change?" *Ecology and Society* 9 (2): 10.

Tompkins, Emma L., W. Neil Adger, Emily Boyd, Sophie Nicholson-Cole, Keith Weatherhead, and Nigel Arnell. 2010. "Observed Adaptation to Climate Change: UK Evidence of Transition to a Well-Adapting Society." *Global Environmental Change* 20:627–635.

Tompkins, Emma L., Roger Few, and Katrina Brown. 2008. "Scenario-Based Stakeholder Engagement: Incorporating Stakeholders Preferences into Coastal Planning for Climate Change." *Journal of Environmental Management* 88:1580–1592.

Tracy, Sarah J. 2010. "Qualitative Quality: Eight 'Big-Tent' Criteria for Excellent Qualitative Research." *Qualitative Inquiry* 16 (10): 837–851.

Tranter, Bruce, and Kate Booth. 2015. "Skepticism in a Changing Climate: A Cross-national Study." *Global Environmental Change* 33:154–164.

Trudeau, Daniel. 2006. "Politics of Belonging in the Construction of Landscapes: Place-Making, Boundary Drawing, and Exclusion." *Cultural Geographies* 13 (3): 421–443.

Truelove, Heather Barnes, Amanda R. Carrico, and Lanka Thabrew. 2015. "A Sociopsychological Model for Analyzing Climate Change Adaptation: A Case Study in Sri Lankan Paddy Farmers." *Global Environmental Change* 31:85–97.

Tsing, Anna Lowenhaupt. 2005. *Friction: An Ethnography of Global Connection.* Princeton, NJ: Princeton University Press.

———. 2015. *The Mushroom at the End of the World: On the Possibility of Life in Capitalist Ruins.* Princeton, NJ: Princeton University Press.

Turhan, Ethemcan, Christos Zografos, and Giorgos Kallis. 2015. "Adaptation as Biopolitics: Why State Policies in Turkey Do Not Reduce the Vulnerability of Seasonal Agricultural Workers to Climate Change." *Global Environmental Change* 31:296–306.

Turner, Matthew D. 2013. "Political Ecology I: An Alliance with Resilience?" *Progress in Human Geography* 38 (4): 1–8.

Twine, Tracy E., and Christopher J. Kucharik. 2009. "Climate Impacts on Net Primary Productivity Trends in the Natural and Managed Ecosystems of the Central and Eastern United States." *Agricultural and Forest Meteorology* 149 (12): 2143–2161.

Urry, John. 2011. *Climate Change and Society.* Malden, MA: Polity.

U.S. Bureau of Labor Statistics. 2015. "CPI Inflation Calculator." Available at http://data .bls.gov/cgi-bin/cpicalc.pl.

U.S. Census Bureau. 2014a. "All Ages in Poverty." Available at https://www.census.gov/ data-tools/demo/saipe/saipe.html?s_appName=saipe&map_yearSelector=2014& map_geoSelector=aa_c&s_state=29&s_county=&s_year=2014&menu=grid_proxy.

———. 2014b. "Median Income in the Past 12 Months: 2010–2014 American Community Survey 5-Year Estimates, Sumner Town, Missouri, 2014." Available at https:// factfinder.census.gov/faces/tableservices/jsf/pages/productview.xhtml?pid=ACS_14 _5YR_S1903&prodType=table.

U.S. Department of Agriculture. 2012. "Climate Change and Agriculture in the United States: Effects and Adaptation." Available at https://www.usda.gov/oce/climate _change/effects_2012/CC%20and%20Agriculture%20Report%20(02-04-2013)b .pdf.

———. 2014. "Quick Stats." Available at https://quickstats.nass.usda.gov.

U.S. Department of Housing and Urban Development. 2016. "HUD Awards $1 Billion through National Disaster Resilience Competition." January 29. Available at https:// www.hudexchange.info/news/hud-awards-1-billion-through-national-disaster -resilience-competition.

U.S. Fish and Wildlife Service. 2014. "2011 National Survey of Fishing, Hunting, and Wildlife-Associated Recreation." Available at http://www.census.gov/prod/2012 pubs/fhw11-nat.pdf.

Van Liere, Kent D., and Riley E. Dunlap. 1981. "Environmental Concern: Does It Make a Difference How It's Measured?" *Environment and Behavior* 13 (6): 651–676.

Vaught, Richard W., and Leo M. Kirsch. 1966. *Canada Geese of the Eastern Prairie Population, with Special Reference to the Swan Lake Flock.* Jefferson City: Missouri Department of Conservation.

Voß, Jan-Peter, and Basil Bornemann. 2011. "The Politics of Reflexive Governance: Challenges for Designing Adaptive Management and Transition Management." *Ecology and Society* 16 (2). Available at https://www.ecologyandsociety.org/vol16/iss2/art9.

Voyles, Traci Brynne. 2015. *Wastelanding: Legacies of Uranium Mining in Navajo Country.* Minneapolis: University of Minnesota Press.

Walton, John. 2001. *Storied Land: Community and Memory in Monterey.* Berkeley: University of California Press.

Weber, Max. 1946a. "Bureaucracy." In *From Max Weber: Essays in Sociology,* translated and edited by H. H. Gerth and C. Wright Mills, 196–244. New York: Oxford University Press.

———. 1946b. "Class, Status, Party." In *From Max Weber: Essays in Sociology,* translated and edited by H. H. Gerth and C. Wright Mills, 180–195. New York: Oxford University Press.

Weise, Elizabeth. 2013. "Some Crops Migrate North with Warmer Temperatures." *USA Today,* September 17. Available at https://www.usatoday.com/story/news/nation/ 2013/09/17/climate-change-agriculture-crops/2784561.

West, Candace, and Don H. Zimmerman. 1977. "Women's Place in Everyday Talk: Reflections on Parent-Child Interactions." *Social Problems* 24:521–528.

———. 1987. "Doing Gender." *Gender and Society* 1 (2): 125–251.

West, Paige. 2006. *Conservation Is Our Government Now: The Politics of Ecology in Papua New Guinea.* Durham, NC: Duke University Press.

Weszkalnys, Gisa. 2014. "Anticipating Oil: The Temporal Politics of a Disaster Yet to Come." *Sociological Review* 62 (S1): 211–235.

Williams, Raymond. 1973. *The Country and the City*. New York: Oxford University Press.

Willits, Fern K., Robert C. Bealer, and Vincent L. Timbers. 1990. "Popular Images of 'Rurality': Data from the Pennsylvania Survey." *Rural Sociology* 55 (4): 559–578.

Wirth, Louis. 1938. "Urbanism as a Way of Life." *American Journal of Sociology* 44:1–24.

Wolcott, Harry F. 1994. *Transforming Qualitative Data: Description, Analysis and Interpretation*. Thousand Oaks, CA: Sage.

Wolf, Johanna, and Susanne C. Moser. 2011. "Individual Understandings, Perceptions, and Engagement with Climate Change: Insights from In-Depth Studies across the World." *WIREs Climate Change* 2:547–569.

Wright, Christopher K., and Michael C. Wimberly. 2013. "Recent Land Use Change in the Western Corn Belt Threatens Grasslands and Wetlands." *Proceedings of the National Academy of Sciences* 110 (10): 4134–4139.

Wright, Sarah. 2014. "More-than-Human, Emergent Belongings: A Weak Theory Approach." *Progress in Human Geography* 38:1–21.

Wright, Wynne, and Alexis Annes. 2014. "Farm Women and Agritourism: Representing a New Rurality." *Sociologia Ruralis* 54 (4): 477–499.

Wulfhorst, J. D. 2000. "Collective Identity and Hazardous Waste Management." *Rural Sociology* 65 (2): 275–294.

Wuthnow, Robert. 2011. *Remaking the Heartland: Middle America since the 1950s*. Princeton, NJ: Princeton University Press.

York, Richard. 2010. "The Paradox at the Heart of Modernity: The Carbon Efficiency of the Global Economy." *International Journal of Sociology* 40 (2): 6–22.

York, Richard, and Philip Mancus. 2013. "The Invisible Animal: Anthrozoology and Macrosociology." *Sociological Theory* 31 (1): 75–91.

York, Richard, Eugene A. Rosa, and Thomas Dietz. 2003. "A Rift in Modernity? Assessing the Anthropogenic Sources of Global Climate Change with the STIRPAT Model." *International Journal of Sociology and Social Policy* 23 (10): 31–51.

Young, Kenneth R., and Jennifer K. Lipton. 2006. "Adaptive Governance and Climate Change in the Tropical Highlands of Western South America." *Climatic Change* 78:63–102.

Yuval-Davis, Nira. 2006. "Intersectionality and Feminist Politics." *European Journal of Women's Studies* 13 (3): 193–209.

Zehr, Stephen. 2015. "The Sociology of Global Climate Change." *WIREs Climate Change* 6:129–150.

Zerubavel, Eviatar. 1991. *The Fine Line: Making Distinctions in Everyday Life*. Chicago: University of Chicago Press.

Zimmerer, Karl S. 2006. "Cultural Ecology: At the Interface with Political Ecology—the New Geographies of Environmental Conservation and Globalization." *Progress in Human Geography* 30 (1): 63–78.

Index

Page numbers italics indicate material in figures or tables.

Braden T. Leap is an Assistant Professor of Sociology at Mississippi State University.

DISCARD